The Long 19th Century: European History from 1789–1917

Part I

Professor Robert I. Weiner

THE TEACHING COMPANY ®

PUBLISHED BY:

THE TEACHING COMPANY
4840 Westfields Boulevard, Suite 500
Chantilly, Virginia 20151-2299
1-800-TEACH-12
Fax—703-378-3819
www.teach12.com

ISBN 1-56585-997-9

Robert I. Weiner, Ph.D.

Professor of History, Lafayette College

Having taught at Lafayette College since 1969, Robert Weiner is currently Thomas Roy and Lura Forrest Jones Professor of History; he is also a Jewish chaplain. Receiving his B.A. from Temple University and a Hebrew teaching certificate from Gratz Hebrew College, Dr. Weiner received his M.A. and Ph.D. degrees from Rutgers University. He has taught a wide range of courses in the fields of modern European history and modern Jewish history and has published a number of articles and commentaries in both of these fields. While teaching at Lafayette, Dr. Weiner also served for eight years as Director of Contemporary Civilization at the Reconstructionist Rabbinical College. At Lafayette College, he has been awarded five Student Government Awards for Superior Teaching and an equal number of other institutional awards for teaching, service, and leadership.

Dr. Weiner and his wife of 40 years, Sanda Weiner, have three sons, Mark (and wife, Ruth), David, and Craig, and one grandson, Alexander Abraham Weiner-Goldsmith.

Dr. Weiner wishes to give a special thanks to EXCEL Scholar Justin Kruger, EXCEL Scholar Emily Gould, and secretary Kathleen Anckaitis for their essential help in preparing the study guides for this course.

Table of Contents
The Long 19th Century:
European History from 1789 to 1917
Part I

The Long 19th Century:
European History from 1789 to 1917

Scope:

How, when, and where did the modern world take form? What did this mean for peasants, workers, the middle class, aristocrats, women, and minorities? Why did an era that began with the idealism of the French Revolution and the power of the Industrial Revolution reach closure during World War I—the greatest tragedy of modern European history? Did nationalism and imperialism inevitably lead in such a direction?

These are some of the issues we will encounter, as we move from the impact of the French and Industrial Revolutions, 1789–1848, into the "unifications" of Italy and Germany in the 1850s and 1860s, followed by the spread of industrialism and nationalism into the furthest reaches of Europe toward the end of the century. By that time, British and French predominance was eclipsed by a rapidly modernizing Germany, Austria-Hungary was struggling to survive as a multinational empire, Russia was facing the stresses of inadequate modernization, the United States and Japan were beginning to play roles in an emerging world balance of power, and almost all of Africa and much of Asia had been gobbled up in a final spasm of imperial expansion. Moreover, the European great powers, organized in alliances and enmeshed in an arms race, confronted increasingly dangerous international crises. Although more people in Europe lived better than ever before, Europe had become a dangerous place.

During these lectures, I will concentrate on the political and diplomatic history of the great powers—Great Britain, France, Germany, Austria-Hungary, Russia, and Italy—but always in the context of deeper economic, social, and cultural forces. Each segment of the course will begin with general overviews, as needed, then proceed to national histories. The course will conclude with the events that led to World War I and the devastating impact the Great War had on contemporaries and the following generation. Although Lenin, Stalin, Mussolini, and Hitler were neither inevitable nor likely candidates for national leadership in prewar Europe, they were rooted in their national cultures, children of their age. What had gone wrong?

This course can be experienced on many levels. I assume no prior knowledge, no professional vocabulary—just interest, curiosity, and, one hopes, passion. The more you give, the more you will get. Course readings have been selected carefully and tested on generations of students. This course is dedicated to my family, friends, teachers, former students—and to you. I hope you enjoy it!

Lecture One
The Long 19th Century

Scope:

What's in a number? Although historians would give different answers as to how to define the 19th century (1789–1917, 1815–1914, 1789–1919), I have chosen 1789–1917, because 1789 was the point at which the masses and modern nationalism first presented themselves, in Europe's most powerful country—France—while 1917 was the point at which the 19th-century Eurocentric world order collapsed, with the Bolshevik victory in Russia and American entry in World War I.

Moreover, the 19th century can be divided into segments, although historians differ somewhat as to the exact dates, based on different understandings of which movements or events were most significant. Besides explaining my choice of macro and micro dates, I will explain some of the possible alternative claims and further present some of the challenges we will encounter during our "dialogue" concerning this crucial era.

Outline

I. The 19th century was a time of European modernization and change.

 A. The most important factors instigating change were the French and Industrial Revolutions.

 B. Given that these historical processes began in France and Great Britain, respectively, the process of modernization generally proceeded from western to eastern Europe and from northern to southern Europe. *West > East* *No?South?*

 C. Change occurred (unevenly) within countries and between countries, with the most radical gaps existing between Great Britain in the west and Russia in the east and between urban and rural areas.

 D. The process of change itself was inherently destabilizing.

 E. Because modernization itself changed power relationships between classes and states, it took on a momentum of its own. Those who adapted best were more successful; others were often humiliated.

II. The 19th century was the zenith of modern European history.

  A. Although the concept of modernity is subjective, causing leading scholars to disagree on its components and when they came to predominate, most agree that Europe modernized during this era.

Industrial Revolution late 18th c Britain

  1. Economic modernization was spurred by the Industrial Revolution, which began in late 18th-century Great Britain and reached Russia toward the end of the next century.

change

  2. Among the effects of the Industrial Revolution were increased productivity; new technologies; urbanization; new forms of enterprise; new relationships among classes, genders, and states; expanded education, transportation, and communications; secularization; nationalism; the expansion of a world economic structure; and the zenith of European power worldwide.

  B. Political modernization was first spurred most radically by the French Revolution and Napoleonic era.

1789 - 1815

Spread - ideologies - liberal - democracy socialist conservatism nationalism

  1. Among the most important results of the 1789–1815 era were the further definition and spread of modern political ideologies, such as liberalism, democracy, socialism, and modern conservatism, as well as nationalism itself.

Revolution as legitimate

  2. Revolution itself gained legitimacy as a means to achieve change.

  3. Not only did the masses first enter "history" in a self-conscious manner, but so did women and previously excluded minorities.

woman minorities

centralized states

  4. More highly centralized state structures were spurred on by the French Revolution and made possible by the Industrial Revolution.

mass culture

  C. Mass culture and mass society are implications of the French and Industrial Revolutions and are central to modernity.

III. Europeans initially predominated in modernization, but European outposts, such as the United States, and non-European states, such as Japan, underwent many of the same changes, as did areas that came in contact with Europe. Modernization was never a one-way street; cultural exchange was constant.

IV. This course can easily be divided into four teaching segments.

    A. This first segment runs from the French Revolution of 1789 through the revolutions of 1848.

        1. The most important forces during this period were derived from the French Revolution and the Napoleonic era.

        2. Although the Industrial Revolution, underway by 1780, did not spread to Belgium and France until about 1830, its impact became prominent in segments of western and central Europe in the 1840s.

        3. The post-Napoleonic era of Metternich came to a close with the revolutions of 1848–1849.

    B. The second era covered in our course runs from the repression of the 1848 revolutions until the unification of Germany in 1870–1871.

        1. This era saw the spread of the Industrial Revolution to expanded urban areas in western and central Europe.

        2. Its most profound political change was the creation of a "unified" Italian state, along with the emergence of Prussian/German dominance in central Europe, at the expense of Austria and France.

        3. The defeat of "backward" Russia by more "modernized" Great Britain and France, in the Crimean War (1854–1856), had made possible this radical change.

    C. The third section of our course will analyze the major domestic developments of the 1871–1914 era. This age saw the full impact of the Second Industrial Revolution, the spread of more exclusive nationalism—often tinged with racialism and social Darwinism—rapid urbanization, industrial capitalism and socialism, mass society, the decline of liberalism, expanded feminism, the cultural determinism of modern science, and the beginning of a leisure-oriented world.

    D. The final segment of our course will cover the developments in European diplomacy that led to World War I, as well as the war's dramatic impact.

1. The era from 1871–1890 was the age of Bismarck; he introduced a series of alliances that isolated France, preventing serious thought of revenge.
2. From the 1880s until 1905, an expanded age of imperialism ravaged most of Africa and much of Asia, also serving as a safety valve for the excess energy of European states, Japan, and the United States.
3. The collapse of the Bismarckian alliance system after 1890 and the emergence of Wilhelmenian *Weltpolitik* ("world politics") facilitated a diplomatic revolution that, by 1907, saw Germany and Austria facing a coalition of France, Russia, and Great Britain, with Italy on the fence.
4. The breakdown of Austro-Russian cooperation in the Balkans, as well as growing German support for Austria and Russian support for Serbia, made a European-wide war likely.
5. Militarism and violence-prone cultural assumptions—including a belief that war would be short and cost-effective—made the likelihood a reality in July–August 1914.
6. Instead of a brief war came industrial mass slaughter.
7. The Russian Revolution, the subsequent Bolshevik *coup d'état*, and the entry of the United States in World War I symbolized the collapse of the modern European state system, much as the French and Industrial Revolutions had put a finish to the pre-1789 Old Regime.

Essential Reading:

T. C. W. Blanning, ed., *Modern Europe*, pp. 1–165.

E. H. Carr, *What Is History?*

Supplementary Reading:

John Lukacs, *At the End of an Age*.

Barbara Tuchman, *Practicing History*.

Questions to Consider:

1. Why are you taking this particular course, and what do you hope to learn?
2. What is the best way for you to achieve these goals?

Lecture One—Transcript
The Long 19th Century

Good morning, ladies and gentlemen. My name is Robert Weiner, and I have been a professor of history at Lafayette College for longer than I would like to remember—in fact, just over 35 years.

Today we're going to begin a series of 36 brief encounters on behalf of The Teaching Company, dealing with the issue of "The Long 19th Century: 1789–1917." The question immediately arises, "Why 1789–1917?" Other scholars might choose 1815–1914. Or even 1780–1919. I've chosen these dates—not because they are absolute, but because to me they represent the best ways of encapsulating the long 19th century, which I think really begins with the outbreak of the French Revolution in 1789—the French Revolution being the most powerful political force of the first half of the long 19th century, and even beyond—and because 1917, during World War I, was the time period in which the Russian Revolution broke out—two Russian Revolutions, in fact, in 1917, leading to a Bolshevik victory. But at the same time, the United States entered World War I, on behalf of the Allies, tilting the balance overwhelmingly on behalf of the Allies and bringing the war to a final closure.

Some scholars—many scholars, in fact—believe that the dual revolutions of the Russian and the American entry involve what is known (in a book by a historian Hajo Holborn) as *The Political Collapse of Europe*—when modern Europe first lost complete control over its own destiny. In that sense, Bolshevik Russia and the United States are both viewed as somewhat extra-European mechanisms, as indeed they should be, given the nature of the history of most of Europe during the course of the long 19th century.

The long 19th century was, above all, a period of European modernization and change. European modernization and change always introduce the themes of continuity and change. Throughout the entire drama of this course, we will be following the themes of continuity and change, always in tension with one another.

Since both of these historical processes—the French Revolution in France and the Industrial Revolution in Great Britain, which was the parallel revolution with the French Revolution—occurred in the West, the process generally moved from western to eastern Europe and from northern to southern Europe. That is, political modernization in France and economic modernization and political modernization in Great Britain occur first, and then pass across central Europe as they spread, reaching Russia at the end of the 19th century. What that also generally means is that the nations that modernized earlier and more successfully had an enormous advantage over those nations that modernized later and less successfully, because modernization in the 19th century equaled power—political power and, above all, military power, as well. So there were radical gaps between those powers that modernized and those that did not, and there were equally gaps between areas within even modernizing societies, between urban areas and rural areas— between those that modernized quickly and successfully and those that did not. The modernization process was also inherently destabilizing. Modernization was an agent of change.

Since modernization itself changed power relationships between classes and states, not only did the process begin to take on a momentum of its own inherently once it began, but, because those who modernized successfully did best, and those who modernized less successfully were often humiliated and left behind, other societies were forced to enter the process of modernization whether they wished to or whether they did not wish to. That was true for Tsarist Russia at the end of the 19th century, just as it was true for Japan, which was "opened up" by the United States in the 1850s. Japan is an example (the best example) of non-European successful modernization leading to adaptation and change so that modernizing, non-European Japan is capable of defeating poorly- modernizing Russia in the Russo-Japanese War in the beginning of the 20th century, or at the end of the long 19th century, as we're calling it.

The long 19th century is also known as the heyday or the zenith of modern European history. While modernity itself is a subjective concept, leading scholars disagree both on its components and when they came to predominate, either separately or collectively. Most would agree that Europe became increasingly modern during this era and that modernization has a general series of overall components. In the long run, economic modernization, which was spurred most intensely by the Industrial Revolution, which began in late-18th-century Great Britain and finally reached Russia toward the end of the 19th century, economic modernization was the most powerful force because it got down most deeply to the average person when it occurred.

Among the major effects of the Industrial Revolution were increased *Industrial Revolution changes* productivity; new technologies; urbanization; new relationships between classes, genders, and states; increasing education; transportation and communications; revolutions; general secularization; modern nationalism of a mass kind, which requires a level of literacy that is only possible with some sort of industrial revolution; the expansion of a world economic structure and its integration, based more on the whims of Europe; and the zenith of European power worldwide. *French Revolution + Napoleon politics modernized*

Political modernization was at first spurred most radically by the French Revolution and the Napoleonic era. In some respects, the French Revolution and the Napoleonic era was the second half of the midwives of modern European history. The French Revolution and the Industrial Revolution were the major catalysts of modern European history. Among the most important results of the 1789–1815 era were the further definition and spread of modern political ideologies such as liberalism, democracy, socialism, a more modern conservatism, as well as the clearer and further definition and spread of nationalism itself. Nationalism became, during the course of the 19th century, actually the most powerful secular religion of the age, especially in the second half of the 19th century.

Moreover, revolution itself gained legitimacy as a means to achieve change, further threatening the status quo—the combined impact of what was viewed as the successful revolt of the American colonies without all the radicalism of the French Revolution; but, for others, the even more radical success of the French Revolution gave revolution a legitimacy of its own. In fact, it left a myth that cast a very, very large shadow over the whole first half of the 19th century, and even beyond. That shadow was a shadow of fear for conservatives and a shadow of hope frequently for democrats, radicals, and socialists—and in many cases, even for moderate liberals. Soon, in another commentary, we'll define 19th-century liberalism more carefully, because it is very different from the 20th-century variety—more a mixture of liberalism and conservatism. Nineteenth-century liberalism has a texture all its own.

During this process, not only did the masses first enter "history" in a self-conscious manner, but the process included women and previously excluded minorities, as well. The process included urban workers; the process included peasants. The integration of mass society and modern states through increasing state centralization and efficiency was spurred by the energy of the French Revolution and the passion and nationalism of the French Revolution, and even more so made possible by the new technology and power of the Industrial Revolution. In other words, Louis XIV in the 17th century had a very hard time knowing what was going on in most of France, because he couldn't get there quickly. But anyone in the late 19th century in a modernized society knew better what was going on in the societies in which they lived.

Mass culture and mass society are also implications of the French and Industrial Revolutions, and they are central to the concept of modernity itself. For example, if an 18th-century scholar thinks that modernity happened more directly during the course of the 18th century (and many do), most 19th-century scholars will not agree to that because the peasants are not included until the end of the 19th century, and the majority of the population is still composed of peasants who were illiterate in the 18th century, and they only began to become more literate in the most modernized states during the course of the second half of the 19th century.

Although Europeans originally predominated in this process of modernization, not only did European outposts such as the United States take part in it, but also non-European states, such as Japan, underwent some of the same basic kinds of changes in the context of modernization. Coming into contact with Europe willingly or by force inherently leads to cultural exchange, technological exchange, economic exchange, and modernization. Here, Europeanists and world historians sometimes have different emphases because Europeanists tend to see the process as being more Euro-dominant, or as many world historians emphasize even more so the flow and exchange of cultures between different peoples—even between the weaker non-European societies to the stronger European societies. One has to find a middle ground between these two overall ways of viewing reality. I think you've probably caught on by now that this material is complicated. This material is deeply complicated, and our understanding of it among historians is changing while I am standing in front of you. That's the way history works. It is constantly changing. Otherwise it wouldn't be an exciting enterprise. And what makes it exciting is having to continuously update, relearn, and rethink. That's what keeps us vital. Fortunately, however, the long 19th century can easily be divided into a series of components that make sense—and, importantly for us, will also make it much easier to convey, teach, analyze, and comprehend the material.

The first section, 1789–1848 or so, is usually known as the Age of Revolution. As already indicated, the most important immediate forces during this time period were derived from the French Revolution and the Napoleonic era and all of their manifestations, and from the Industrial Revolution already underway in Great Britain certainly by 1780 (and some would even say as early as 1760). However, the Industrial Revolution does not spread in any serious way to parts of western Europe and then to central Europe until 1830 or so in Belgium and France and the 1840s in some segments of central Europe and northern Italy. So, although the Industrial Revolution is already having a very significant material and political and social and cultural effect in Great Britain between 1760 and 1850, it is only beginning to have that effect on the continent in a more apparent way after 1830. Because of that, the most important emphasis in this 1789–1850 period is the impact of the French Revolution and the Napoleonic era.

The post-Napoleonic era, known as the era of Metternich, from 1815–1848, which brought the French Revolution and the reign of Napoleon to a close and attempted to re-establish the old order as much as it possibly could, always with difficulty, but with some success at first—this post-Napoleonic era came to an end with the revolutions of 1848 and 1849, which served as a very, very useful transition to the next historical era, and which really do represent a turning point in European history of some substance. Here we can see that change begins to become (at least between the post-1850 and pre-1850 era) change begins to become even more powerful than continuity. The reason for this, as we will talk about in more detail in another set of comments—the reason for this is that after 1850, above all, this era saw the spread of that Industrial Revolution, sometimes called the Second Industrial Revolution, in more dramatic ways—with more state intervention and guidance in western Europe and in central Europe and in northern Italy, leading to some dramatic change, to a radical increase in productivity, to the growth in cities, to the different cultural norms and all of the rest.

And, moreover, the failure or the incomplete success (predominantly failure) of the revolutions of 1848 and 1849, also combined with the power and obvious nature of the material forces in the Industrial

Revolution, led people to look elsewhere, and led many revolutionaries to call it quits, to go underground, to enter business, to change professions, to go live in England or to go live in the United States, where it was safer. So the 1850–1870 era has a different texture of its own. However, one of the other things that makes this the case is the increased spread of nationalism during this time period, in some cases even tinged with the beginnings of social Darwinism and racism, although more of that would come after 1870, in two extremely important historical processes that we call the "unification of Italy" and the "unification of Germany."

What they have in common is that they are not really total unifications. The unification of Italy between the late 1850s and 1870–1871 was far more the expansion of the most powerful sector of Italy, the Piedmont in the north, than it was the unification of the rest of the peninsula. You have the Piedmontization of Italy more than the unification of Italy. The same was even more true with respect to Germany, in which what occurred in the 1860s was the Prussian expansion over the rest of Germany and the exclusion of Austria, which had been a historic part of Germany from that domain—so that the expansion of Piedmont took place also against Austria in northern Italy—Prussia against Austria in Germany, and of Prussia also very much defeating France. North German confederation, Prussia writ large, defeats France in the Franco-Prussian War in 1870–1871, creating the most important new political reality in the entire 19th century, the creation of a German state. I want to say a "modern" German state, but it was modern in some ways and very un-modern in other ways, and that will be the subject also of an entire discussion.

These things were made possible—these changes—by the defeat of Russia in the Crimean War between 1853 and 1856, which is another representation of what importance modernization meant because Britain and France defeated Russia in Russia's own territory (in the tip of Russia's own territory) in the Crimea, in the Black Sea. Their technology allowed them to get their troops there more efficiently and to have their people more mobilized and self-conscious and aware than Tsarist Russia's capability would allow because of the poor development of its railroads, the extent of its space, and the fact that the people were not integrated into society in a deep way, as they already were becoming integrated into British and French society. Removing Russia from stabilizing central Europe and also somewhat England, because England or Great Britain also didn't do all that well in the Crimean War, and entered into a reformist time period. The liberal bookend in the West and the conservative bookend in the East were partly removed during that 1850–1870 era, but especially in the 1860s, when statesmen who were willing to take risks in Italy and in France and in Germany could make their mark without Russia behaving as a policeman, or without British political intervention, as well.

We proceed to the last phase of the long 19th century—the last segment, 1871–1914. It's a long period. It's a somewhat integrated period. But we're going to divide it in half for the purposes of teaching, even though that's partly artificial. We'll divide it in half and first offer several overview lectures and topical lectures, followed by a series of domestic lectures dealing with the internal development of all of the great powers. Thereafter we will enter into a detailed, intense discussion of the diplomacy from 1870–1914, including the new European imperialism leading toward the origins and then the impact of World War I, which almost all historians agree was the greatest tragedy in modern European history, putting an end to a period of general optimism and considerable progress through a process of industrial, mass military slaughter.

In this time period, there is a lot of carryover from the 1850–1870 era, and again, it's the same characters coming back to haunt us. This age saw an even further expansion and deepening and spreading of the Industrial Revolution and of all of its implications. It saw the expansion of a harsher, more exclusivist, social Darwinian form of nationalism, often tinged with racialism as well. It saw modern urbanization, with metropolises really developing. Industrial capitalism and socialism. Mass society. The decline of a more tolerant, liberal attitude that marked a lot of the 19th century. Expanded feminism. The cultural determination of modern science, a religion of its own, and a revolt against some of its extreme rational implications, and even the beginning of a more leisure-oriented society, with football teams (or soccer in Europe—football) and even basketball teams invented in the United States. We'll cover that in some detail, state by state.

Then we will proceed to the origins and impact of World War I, 1870–1914. The era from 1871–1890 is generally and justly called the age of Bismarck; he was the dominant force of that age, especially since he introduced a new means of diplomacy, alliances in time of peace—intended to be defensive (to isolate France and to prevent French revenge). The implications later, after Bismarck's death, unfortunately, were mainly negative. From the 1880s until about 1905 or so, we will cover the radically expanded age of the new European imperialism—questioning what was new about that imperialism as it ravaged most of Africa, and also many parts of Asia, as well—serving, some say, as a safety valve for European energy, and others say, as one of the primary causes of World War I.

The collapse of the Bismarckian alliance system after 1890 and the emergence of Wilhelmenian (Kaiser Wilhelm II's) *Weltpolitik* ("world politics") was a tragedy for Germany and for Europe. Bismarck understood that Germany was strong enough already, and more might become too much. By 1907, instead of Germany being part of an alliance with a series of states isolating France, fear of Germany had created a coalition of France, Britain, and Russia versus an Austro-German core alliance. Italy actually allied with Germany, but was actually already closer with France and England.

The breakdown of Austro-Russian cooperation in the Balkans, the parallel increased support of Germany for Austria, of Russia for Serbia (an enemy of Austria), of France for Russia, brought all of the powers to the possibility of ultimate conflict and crisis.

Growing militarism accompanied by a number of violence-prone cultural assumptions—including a belief that war would be short and, therefore, cost-effective—made the likelihood a reality in July–August of 1914. Instead of a brief war that many expected came industrial mass slaughter verging on genocide, the greatest tragedy in all of modern European history. This brought on the Russian Revolution by pushing the Russian people beyond what they could possibly bear. It brought the United States finally into World War I. These two events symbolize, really, the political collapse of modern Europe—the modern European state system—as it had existed, really, from the 18th century. It brought on the beginning of the world in which we have lived, collectively.

Some concluding comments: In all segments of this course, we will proceed from the general to the specific and from a series of overview lectures or topical lectures into a series of case study lectures, emphasizing the great powers. Although the material is inherently complicated, I assume no prior knowledge on your part—

so don't worry about it. Prepare to be somewhat confused, especially in the beginning, before you become comfortable, and then you'll become enlightened. The selected course materials and suggested additional readings have been chosen carefully. The more you engage them, the more you will get. And they are also very, very carefully layered—from an overview text, to primary source readings, to deeper documents, to further interpretations, and even to the material in your guidebooks. Use those guidebooks. I worked hard on them. Read them. Look at them carefully. Look at the maps. Think about it a bit, if you can, before you engage me in these conversations. You will understand our world and your place in it much better having stayed with this course.

One last additional series of comments. A final word about our common journey. I don't claim to fully comprehend the past or to describe it accurately. What I'm offering are approximations, best guess analyses, and models, rather than actual truth. We can't really know the past. We hardly know the present. And we only partly understand ourselves and our relationships with our surroundings. Still, the search for the actual past is a self-conscious search for truth. I view it as a secularized spiritual quest of the highest order since understanding the past on some meaningful level, recovering as much of our collective memory as is possible, can give additional meaning to our lives—a sense of balance and perspective that facilitates civilized behavior, the ability to empathize and not to take ourselves too seriously.

Lastly, unknowingly or knowingly, every historian wears colored glasses. Situations, contexts, prejudices, that sometimes cloud our vision and sometimes enable us to see more clearly. As far as I can tell, mine are male, Jewish, middle-class, liberal, and American, and even being an expert on modern European history—which makes me emphasize its importance even more so than the history of other areas. Since we will not see each other face-to-face and you will have an advantage over me in this context, it's only fair for me to let you know these things. I work hard to transcend my context and my limitations. I do not claim to always succeed. What is your context? What are your limitations? Beware, and let's grow and learn together.

Thank you.

Lecture Two
The Legacy of the Past—The Old Regime

Scope:

Although Europe, and especially western Europe, had experienced substantial changes from the Renaissance until the French Revolution, it was still a transformed medieval society, especially for the peasants, 75–90 percent of the population. Still, in terms of the structure of the state and the culture of aristocratic elites and newer middle-class elements, considerable changes had occurred and were accelerating during the 18th century. Moreover, on the eve of the French Revolution, most states were sovereign, territorial, and more centralized, if not yet "nationalist" units, in which considerable new wealth was being generated by expanding commerce, both within Europe and worldwide. Moreover, in the more powerful states that constituted the European balance of power—England, France, Prussia, Austria, and Russia—especially in England and France, corrosive Enlightenment ideas permeated literate society.

Almost inevitably, the structures of early-modern Europe were challenged by new economic, social, and cultural forces, although the mass of Europeans would not be radically affected until more profound agrarian and industrial "revolutions" spread. However, in the areas of state centralization and military modernization, Prussia developed more rapidly, presenting the possibility of changing the European balance of power. Meanwhile, France was still the most powerful European power, while England was a bonafide world power, despite the loss of the 13 colonies between 1776 and 1783. A "new" world was about to take form, though the legacy of the past was profound.

Outline

I. In many ways, 18th-century Europe was a transformed medieval society.

   A. Europe's economic structure was still overwhelmingly agrarian, and scarcity of food was common.
      1. Most farming was still subsistence in nature, based on a manorial or localized economy.

©2005 The Teaching Company.

2. The most serious problems were limited crop yields and natural disasters; hunger and even starvation were realities.
B. Europe's social structure was also traditional.
1. Most European societies were divided into legal classes, known as *estates*: the first estate was the clergy; the second was the aristocracy or nobility; the third comprised everyone else.
2. In larger societies, even those that were well developed, the overwhelming majority of people were peasants, and the majority of peasants in central and eastern Europe remained serfs.
3. The clergy and aristocracy made up small segments of the population (usually less than 5 percent each) and were bound by different obligations, laws, and privileges.
4. The middle classes, part of the third estate, were also a small group, although they were growing in western Europe.
5. Although wealth was important, greater status and access to wealth came from birth rather than from accomplishment.
C. Europe's political structure was also traditional in nature.
1. Most states were sovereign and territorial but not truly national.
2. Most states were dominated by "divine-right" monarchs, usually supported by aristocrats and the middle classes.
3. The overwhelming majority of Europeans were, therefore, subjects rather than citizens.
4. By the 18th century, several important states were more constitutional in nature, such as Great Britain and Holland.
D. Most Europeans were enmeshed in a traditional culture or civilization.
1. Most people were religious, superstitious, and illiterate.
2. Even most clergy were barely literate.
3. The overwhelming majority lived in a narrow cultural environment, based on family, clan, village, and face-to-face relationships.

II. The 18th century was the last era in what is called early-modern European history; it was a time of accelerating change, which began during the Italian Renaissance and ended with the French and Industrial Revolutions.

A. The Renaissance, lasting from the mid-14th to the mid-16th centuries, placed emphasis on classical learning, textual criticism, secularism, individualism, and humanism.

B. The Reformation, or Protestant Revolt, from the early 16th century to the mid-17th century, destroyed the unity of medieval Catholic civilization and enhanced the power of "secular" princes.

C. The Scientific Revolution, or the Age of Reason, by which the 17th century is often known, led to a feeling of empowerment for educated elites, stemming from a greater understanding of the universe and a more modern scientific methodology; progress was possible and the future was more relevant than the past.

D. By the 18th century, the forces of change were numerous and important. This was clearly evident in the area of economic change.

    1. Especially in western and central Europe, and more so in states that had international empires, such as Great Britain, Holland, and France, commerce was expanding and created fluid wealth.

    2. Where commercial capitalism was most developed, handicraft industries, dominated by merchant capitalists, expanded.

    3. During the second half of the 18th century, mainly in the Low Countries and Great Britain, an agrarian revolution began to yield surplus food supplies, making urban growth possible.

    4. Around 1760–1780 in Great Britain, a process later known as the First Industrial Revolution was underway.

    5. Economic change brought increasing social change, especially growth in the highly variegated middle class or the middle classes; generally, the more economic development, the larger the middle class.

    6. With increased economic dynamism and competition within and between states, states became more centralized and efficient; a number of 18th-century rulers, known as *enlightened despots*, realized that the state was more than the expanded "person" of the monarch.

7. The cumulative impact of cultural and other changes produced a rich and variegated 18th-century cultural synthesis known as the *Enlightenment*.

8. Most "enlightened" thinkers, whether aristocrats, clergy, or members of the middle class, believed that governments existed for the purposes of the governed; they should be efficient and tolerant.

9. Most "enlightened" thinkers believed that progress was possible, that institutions were subject to rational scrutiny, and that education could bring greater happiness.

III. As a rule of thumb, states and societies of western Europe had changed more than those of central Europe and still more than those of eastern Europe; the same was generally true from northern to southern Europe.

IV. The highly competitive and often warring states were aware that they existed in a European state system with a balance of power whose main purpose was to prevent "universal monarchy," or hegemony.

A. By the second half of the 18th century, there were five recognized great powers: Great Britain, France, Prussia, Austria, and Russia.

B. On the eve of the French Revolution, Britain was the most dynamic European power, the first world power.

C. France, often known as the "great nation," was the strongest continental power.

D. The Austrian Empire, whose Habsburg ruler was still the head of a nearly meaningless structure of more than 330 Germanic states known as the *Holy Roman Empire*, was the historic counterweight to France in the west and the Ottoman Empire in the east.

E. Prussia became more powerful, especially under Frederic the Great, the Hohenzollern monarch who ruled from 1740–1786.

F. Russia first joined the European great power club upon entering the War of Austrian Succession, 1740–1748.

V. If most Europeans still had a profoundly traditional worldview and way of life, some were already living in a far more modern and dynamic universe; at that point, greater change was virtually inevitable.

Essential Reading:

John Carey, *Eyewitness to History*, pp. 174–245.

Isaac Kramnick, ed., *The Portable Enlightenment Reader*, pp. 1–7 (Kant), pp. 17–21 (Diderot), pp. 26–38 (Condorcet), pp. 51–60 (Voltaire), pp. 75–90 (Bayle, Locke), pp. 96–100 (Newton), pp. 109–133 (Hume, Voltaire), pp. 174–180 (Paine), pp. 222–235 (Locke, Rousseau), pp. 351–356 (Vico), pp. 395–441 (Locke, Montesquieu, Voltaire, Rousseau).

Robin Winks and Thomas Kaiser, *Europe, 1648–1815*, pp. 56–137.

Supplementary Reading:

John Merriman, *A History of Modern Europe*, volume I, pp. 177–465 (from the Renaissance to the age of Napoleon).

Read further selections from *The Portable Enlightenment Reader*.

Questions to Consider:

1. Why is this era referred to as *early-modern Europe*?
2. What seem to be the major forces of change and the greatest areas of continuity?

Lecture Two—Transcript
The Legacy of the Past—The Old Regime

Good afternoon, ladies and gentlemen. In our first encounter, we talked about the whole nature of the long 19th century, from 1789–1917, and why it's treated as such. We emphasized, above all, the themes of continuity and change and modernization. Today we're going to be speaking about the Old Regime or the *Ancien Regime,* as it was known in that time. The purpose of these comments is to give us an even greater appreciation of what life was like before the French and Industrial Revolutions, as a point of comparison between the early modern period even at its most developed phase in the 18th century, and Europe after the French and the Industrial Revolutions.

In many respects, the 18th century was still very, very much of a transformed medieval society, or at most, an early modern society. In the first part of these comments today, I'm going to be emphasizing forces of continuity, forces of stability. Europe's economic structure was still overwhelmingly agrarian in nature, and scarcity of food was common. Life was still nasty and brutal and short, as Thomas Hobbes had said in the 17th century. Most farming was still subsistence in nature, based around some kind of localized manorial economy, and the most serious problems that the overwhelming majority of people faced were limited crop yields and natural disasters. Hunger and even starvation were realities for large segments of the population everywhere, even in the most developed civilizations.

As a result of this, Europe's social structure was also quite traditional. Most European societies were divided into legal classes, known as *estates.* The first estate was the clergy; the second was the aristocracy or the nobility; the third usually comprised everyone else—the peasantry, urban workers, the middle class. In all the larger societies, even the most well developed, the overwhelming majority of people, were peasants—and that's why the society is so much a transformed medieval society. Seventy-five percent of the people in Great Britain were still peasants. Ninety-seven percent or so in Russia were peasants, and they were the ones whose lives were most difficult.

In most areas, even in western Europe, remnants of feudal obligations remained, while the overwhelming majority of peasants in central and eastern Europe were serfs—a system of obligation and bondage much like slavery in the United States—and that still existed until 1848 in parts of Prussia and in the Austro-Hungarian Empire, and until 1861–1863 in the Russian Empire. Both the clergy and the aristocracy comprised small segments of the population (usually less than 5 percent each) and were bound by different obligations, laws, privileges, and customs. And there was an enormous difference between the upper clergy and the upper aristocracy, generally intermingled, and all the rest of society. The middle classes, part of the third estate, were also a small group, although they were growing in size and in importance in western Europe. While wealth was increasingly important, greater status and access to wealth still came from the accident of birth, rather than from accomplishment or merit.

Europe's political structure was also rather traditional in nature. Most states were sovereign and territorial, but not yet truly "national" in nature. What that means is that a locus of authority known as sovereignty resided in each given territory, but they were not yet nation-states for the most part. The majority of people who lived in these societies were subjects, rather than citizens, and most of the states were also very proprietary. Whether or not Louis XIV said, "I am the state," he could have said it, because he would have meant it. "I am the state; the state is me; it is an extension of my person." A century later, Frederick the Great said, "I am the first servant of the state." At least he understood that there was a differential between his person and the state, but in practice it didn't make much difference. Frederick the Great did pretty much what he wanted to do, and most states were monarchies claiming "divine-right" legitimacy, usually supported by the aristocrats and the middle classes, and certainly by the clergy and the religious authorities in those societies.

Although most monarchs recognized they were subject to some external authority, whether it was God's authority or natural law, again they viewed their states as an extension of themselves as proprietary, and usually there was no separation between their private income and the state's wealth. Again, the majority of most people were subjects, rather than citizens.

By the 18th century, however, several important states were more constitutional in nature, with some form of truly shared governments and promulgated law. The most important of these was Great Britain, which was the best example of a limited, or constitutional, monarchy that developed after the Glorious or Bloodless Revolution of 1688. There was some blood, but not much. Holland was the best example of a republic—a series of elite governments, but without a monarch.

Most Europeans were also enmeshed in a very traditional culture, a very traditional civilization. Most people were profoundly religious and superstitious, as well as illiterate. Even most of the clergy, especially the village priests, were barely literate and deeply superstitious. The overwhelming majority of people lived in a very localized and narrow cultural environment based on family, clan, and village—face-to-face relationships. Anyone outside of that local area, even if coming from a village 10 miles away, was a foreigner—suspected, sometimes mistreated.

However, the 18th century was also the last era in what is called early-modern European history; it was a time of accelerating change, which had actually begun during the Italian Renaissance, in the beginning of the 14th century. The Renaissance lasted from sometime in the early 14th century until the middle of the 16th century. It took place in parts of Italy and then spread to northern Europe, western Europe, and central Europe. It placed a greater emphasis on classical learning, textual criticism, secularism, individualism, and humanism. Let's get one thing clear: The overwhelming majority of people who lived during the Renaissance still had relatively traditional religious beliefs, but what they chose to emphasize and to study (at least primarily in the Italian Renaissance) was the classics and man, and their emphasis on the well-balanced individual. Warrior and thinker, in all ways, and their emphasis on the individual searching for truth using the most modern linguistic techniques that were possible at that time, represented a considerable change. Again, the people who took an active part in the Renaissance overwhelmingly were the elites—those who were wealthy. In fact, in most of early modern European society you basically have two groups of people: those who were more wealthy and those who were poor. And those who were poor didn't have time for learning. And those who were wealthy had more time for learning.

The Reformation (the Protestant Reformation), which began in 1517 and progresses until the middle of the religious wars of the mid-17th century—the Reformation destroyed one of the main areas of unity of medieval civilization, and that was the general medieval Catholic

Church—the unity of religious beliefs. The Reformation shattered that beyond all possible reconciliation. The Reformation led to an enhanced power of "secular" princes over the Catholic Church and over their subjects. It challenged many traditional cultural assumptions, at least for a while. Ironically, some of the people who were rebelling against the authority of the Catholic Church then subjected others to the authority of one branch or another of the Protestant Churches. In the beginning of the Reformation there was still only one truth, and everyone was simply trying to see what that truth was. It would not be until later that people would begin to become comfortable with multiple truths and tolerating others whose truth was different than one's own truth. The fact that neither the Catholics nor the Protestants could destroy the others and overwhelmingly predominate made possible over time the beginning (out of necessity and then out of belief) of concepts of toleration and understanding of multiple truths.

That became all the more prevalent during the Scientific Revolution of the 17th century, sometimes also known as the Age of Reason. The Scientific Revolution was a time period in which the scientific method—a process of learning, a feeling of empowerment based on reason and experimentation, hypothesis, synthesis—first gave a large group of individuals who took part in a world scientific community, based mainly in Europe (in fact, based overwhelmingly in Europe), a sense that they were moving forward and, in fact, that they had gone beyond the ancients. During the Renaissance, people always looked back toward the ancients for wisdom. The scientists of the 17th century recognized that they were revising the ancients and doing better—and that education, learning, reason, a scientific method, could lead to progress and that the future would be better than the past, through education.

By the 18th century, the forces of change were increasingly more numerous and were increasingly more important. This was a time period of accelerating change, and clearly it was a time period of economic change, as well. In fact, we will begin to emphasize at this point in our comments those areas of European civilization that looked forward toward change rather than backward toward continuity and stability. And I want to make it clear that I'm not using terms like "forward" and "backward" as value judgments, but simply statements as to where the basic processes were pointing. In the 18th century, the forces of change were numerous and increasingly important. This was clearly evident in the area of economic change—especially in western Europe, and even more so in the states of Great Britain and Holland and France, where expanding international empires had already begun to be very much a factor in economic development and economic growth. Commerce was expanding, and commerce itself was becoming the greatest source of new, fluid wealth. Land was the basic source of the largest quantity of wealth, but commerce (commercial capitalism) was the greatest source of new, usable, fluid wealth. And wherever commerce was expanding, merchant capitalists were expanding as well, and a larger middle class was developing. And as a rule of thumb, generally speaking, the larger the middle class, the more prevalent the economic change and development that occurs.

During the second half of the 18th century, mainly in the Low Countries and in Great Britain, an agrarian revolution also was underway, yielding surplus food supplies, really for the first time, and making possible even greater urban growth. Rotation of crops and the use of nitrogen-fixating crops made it possible to produce more food, making possible an expansion of the population—making possible a redistribution of the population, which is one of the hallmarks of modernity.

Around 1760–1780 in Great Britain, a process later known by historians as the First Industrial Revolution was already underway, replete with all kinds of implications—far-reaching implications, misunderstood at the time, but very, very real. Economic change brought increasing social change, especially growth in the highly variegated group known as the middle class, or the middle classes (plural) as some historians tend to view them. And again, generally speaking, the more economic development, the larger the middle class. The larger the middle class, the more economic development.

With increased economic dynamism and competition both within states and between states, states were becoming more centralized and more efficient; a number of 18th-century rulers, known as *enlightened despots*, realized that the state was more than their expanded "person". Again, I've indicated that Frederick the Great said, "I am the first servant of the state." They surely were enlightened, primarily in terms of seeking efficiency, but also sometimes even of seeking greater toleration. But let's put this in a context. "Enlightened" Frederick the Great in Prussia and enlightened Catherine the Great in Russia increased serfdom in their areas because they needed the support of the nobility, and the best way to gain the support of the nobility was to give the nobility more power over their peasants or serfs. So "enlightened" leaders, for self-interest, could even make traditional patterns more deeply rooted. The cumulative impact of these economic and cultural changes—beginning during the Renaissance and continuing during the Reformation—very much moved forward during the Scientific Revolution, which produced natural laws of the physical universe and began to also produce the belief that there were natural laws that governed the human condition (human society), such as the natural laws that John Locke, the late-17th-century British philosopher, saw—life, liberty, and property as natural laws. They come from nature. They are inalienable. They can't be taken away. They are inbred in us. The cumulative impact of cultural and other changes produced a rich cultural florescence and synthesis—in the 18th century—generally known as the *Enlightenment*. In many, many respects, the Enlightenment was the popularization and the further spread of the peak thinking of the greats of the 17th-century Scientific Revolution.

Most "enlightened" thinkers (and this becomes very interesting), whether aristocrats, clergy, or members of the middle class, believed that governments existed for the purpose of the governed; I think that's worth repeating. "Enlightened" thinkers were found among the aristocrats and among the clergy, who had the wealth and time to think. And, of course, "enlightened" thinkers were found among an expanding middle class. But progressives during the Enlightenment believed that the purpose of government was the governed—that states should function because of utility. Secondly, they believed that the method of government should be efficiency. In other words, they were pragmatic—more pragmatic in nature. And lastly, coming from the impact of a scientific revolution and from such basic treatises as John Locke's essay on religious toleration, these thinkers increasingly believed that states should be tolerant. The purpose of the government was utility. The method of government should be efficiency, and the spirit of government should be toleration. Most "enlightened" thinkers (in fact almost all of them) believed that progress was possible, desirable—and that all institutions and traditions were subject to rational scrutiny, whether it was the king or the Bible, and that rational scrutiny and education could bring greater happiness to more people. So that even when many members of the Enlightenment still believed in monarchy, they believed that monarchy existed to serve the greater good, rather than just to serve the general interests of the monarch.

As a rule of thumb, the states and societies of western Europe had changed more than those of central Europe; again, not in all areas, but as a rule of thumb—and still more than those of eastern Europe. The same was basically true between the areas of northern Europe and the areas of southern Europe, even within areas that would later become states—so that in Italy, northern Italy was much more well-developed than southern Italy, just as it is, in fact, today. Moreover, the highly competitive and often warring states were aware that they existed in a European state system, with an implicit balance of power—for a balance of power whose main purpose was to prevent what they called "universal monarchy" and what we might call hegemony—the overwhelming power of any one state to affect the rest at its will.

By the second half of the 18th century, there were five recognized great powers: Great Britain, France, Prussia, Austria, and Russia—Great Britain and France in the west, Austria and Prussia in the middle, and Russia in the east. On the eve of the French Revolution, England (or Great Britain, more properly) was the most dynamic European power—indeed, the world's greatest power, with an empire that equaled or surpassed Rome's. England's strength was based largely on a trilogy of commerce, colonies, and sea power. And just think about the meaning of those words: commerce, colonies, and sea power—what they represent and what they don't represent. Britain had clearly bested France in the most important colonial wars of the 18th century, even though France took sweet revenge during the American Revolution (fortunately for us).

France is often known as the *grand nation*, the "great nation." It was the strongest continental power, which had largely dominated the continent militarily and culturally since the age of Louis XIV. Indeed, most of the German aristocracy and the Austrian, and even the Russian aristocracy, preferred to speak French rather than their own languages, which tells you something about the lack of a deep-seated nationalism at that time. France was more than twice as large as Great Britain in population. And on the eve of the French Revolution, even though England had more colonies and more commerce and more sea power, France being so much larger was roughly equivalent in global productivity with Great Britain.

The Austrian Empire, whose Habsburg ruler was still the head of a nearly meaningless structure of 330-plus largely Germanic states known as the *Holy Roman Empire* (Voltaire said it was not holy, nor Roman and not an empire)—the Austrian Empire was the historic counterweight to France in the west and the historic counterweight to the Ottoman Empire in the east. That was quite a burden to their balancing France in the west and the Ottoman Empire, which was still powerful in the east. But now we have a geography lesson—and also, sadly and tragically, a lesson of what not to do. In three successive partitions of Poland, in conjunction with Prussia and Russia—in 1772, 1793, and 1795—Austria regained some of the luster she had lost in a series of defeats at the hands of upstart rival Prussia. Poland disappeared, although Poland was a large nation, because Poland did not create a strong, efficient central government of any kind. But when Austria and Prussia and Russia divided up Poland, guess what they did? They reduced the geography, and now they were contiguous, next to each other. Now Russia was really part of Europe.

On the continent, at least, Prussia was the big winner of the 18th century, especially under Frederick the Great, the last of a series of four very, very powerful Hohenzollern monarchs. Frederick the Great ruled Prussia from 1740–1786. One of my favorite quotes, when he attacked Austria, was: "If duke we must, then let us be the greatest of all scoundrels." And duke he did. He attacked Austria in 1740, and he increased the power of the Prussian state by 50 percent, because Prussia was, before that time, clearly the fifth of the five great powers, with modest economic and demographic resources. But she emerged as a great power in the 18th century as a result of the strenuous efforts of this group of four Hohenzollern monarchs in the end of the 17th century through the 18th century—military success, military conquests, and especially at the expense of Austria under Frederick the Great.

Lastly, Russia first joined the European great power club upon entering the War of Austrian Succession (1740–1748)—that war begun by Frederick the Great when he attacked Austria. Russia then became a permanent fixture of the European balance of power. By far the greatest European power in size and population, especially having recently defeated Sweden and the Ottoman Empire in a series of wars, she became now an immediate neighbor to Prussia and to Austria as a result of their shared partition of Poland.

A number of other states still played a secondary role in the European state system by virtue of their history, their wealth, or their geography. The non-Christian Ottoman Empire, although still of military and economic importance—the Ottoman Empire still besieged Vienna in 1683—the Ottoman Empire, however, was clearly in decline. It had lost much of its power during the early and mid-18th century. European tolerance only went so far. It wasn't part of the club, at least not officially. And Turkey is still having difficulty joining the club today. Tolerance still only goes so far.

In terms of power, the fewer than 3 million citizens of the newly formed United States of America—beacons though they might be— in terms of power they might just as well have been living on the moon. However, by virtue of their ideas and their example, the American colonies and the young United States had begun to make their mark, because the American Revolution, and the French support of America during the American Revolution, was the issue that finally bankrupted the French monarchy and the immediate presage to the French Revolution.

If most Europeans still had a profoundly traditional worldview and way of life, some were already living in a far more modern and dynamic universe; at that point, greater change was virtually inevitable. In other words, this era of the late 18th century is definitely an era of transition. If the overwhelming majority of people were peasants, still living in a very, very traditional way, people who lived in urban areas—the aristocrats, the upper clergy, the middle class—were beginning to live in a new and different world already, before the French Revolution. The pregnancy was well into its gestation. A new world was about to be born.

Thank you.

Lecture Three
The Age of Revolution, 1789–1848

Scope:

Although it is not often that an age can be associated with an historian, British Marxist historian E. J. Hobsbawm merits this respect; his trilogy of studies on 19th-century Europe best explains the manner in which the French and Industrial Revolutions served as the midwives of modern European history and, via the umbilical cord of European imperialism, of modern world history as well.

Terming these two processes a *dual revolution*, Hobsbawm explains how they undermined the Old Regime and ushered in a different world. The French Revolution conceived of its message of liberty, fraternity, and equality in universalistic terms, and its armies and Napoleon's carried these ideas across Europe, temporarily implementing some as well. Among the most important concepts were: uniform laws, civil rights, careers open to talent, a more centralized state, economic policies that facilitated capitalism, and popular sovereignty in the form of nationalism, which became the most powerful secular religion of the 19th century. The shadow of the French Revolution dominated the hopes and fears of Europeans during the first half of the century, providing its primary ideologies and myths.

Simultaneously, an even more profound historical process, the Industrial Revolution, took shape in late 18th-century Britain, gradually spreading to areas of western and central Europe; thereafter, with increasing rapidity, it ushered in a more modern industrial capitalist urban reality that transformed European life.

Outline

I. The years between 1789–1848, often known as the *Age of Revolution*, are captured by British Marxist historian E. J. Hobsbawm in a book aptly titled *The Age of Revolution, 1789–1848*, published in 1962.

    A. Hobsbawm is among the first scholars to have understood how the dual revolutions combined to become the midwives of modern European history, undermining traditional society wherever they spread.

B. Initially, the French Revolution was the more important, casting a shadow over much of the 19th century, especially the years between 1789–1848.

   1. France, when mobilized, was the most powerful state on the continent, both materially and culturally.
   2. The French Revolution became the most radical of all of the late 18th-century revolutions.
   3. Only the French Revolution saw the rise of a Napoleon, who spread many of its fundamental ideas and concepts, even as he ruled as a dictator and conqueror.
   4. By 1815, with the final defeat of Napoleon, not only had many structures of the *Ancien Régime* been uprooted or severely challenged, but a series of modern political ideologies and concepts had taken form, creating much of the political vocabulary of the modern world.
   5. Nineteenth-century liberalism believed in promulgated constitutions, basic civil rights, limited male suffrage, careers open to talent, and the primacy of private property and limited government.
   6. Democracy or radicalism shared many of these concepts but favored universal male suffrage and more state action.
   7. Early forms of socialism were expressed during the revolution as well; socialism saw economic necessity as prior to political necessity and wished to redistribute wealth.
   8. A more modern, "utilitarian" form of conservatism emerged in reaction to the revolution, joining divine-right monarchy with updated armor; Edmund Burke's *Reflections on the French Revolution* (1790) was conservatism's most powerful statement.
   9. Significant strides were made toward formulating arguments for equal rights for women, although the revolutionary and Napoleonic eras saw women's rights neglected and male dominance codified in law.
   10. The concept of nationalism was advanced in concept and reality.
   11. Revolution as a just and efficacious method of change was lodged in the hearts of millions of Europeans.

C. Parallel to the French Revolution came the First Industrial Revolution, which began in late 18th-century Britain, then spread to Belgium, France, and central Europe in the 1830s and thereafter.

1. This "revolution" was the most important development in human history, at least since the development of cities and sedentary life several millennia ago.

2. It made possible comparatively unlimited levels of productivity, partially freeing humankind from the harsh whims of nature.

3. With industrialism came significant accelerating changes in virtually every area of life, including urbanization, education, and the entire social structure of society.

4. Given that industrialism was also synonymous with power, especially with military power, all of the great powers were forced to come to terms with it.

5. Globally, the Industrial Revolution also had a deep impact on politics, ideas, and culture as a whole, challenging traditional patterns.

D. Although the impact of the French Revolution on the continent was greater than that of the Industrial Revolution prior to 1848, by mid-century, this balance was shifting; thereafter, their combined impact increasingly challenged and undermined traditional society, ushering in a modern, urban, industrial civilization.

II. In two later volumes, *The Age of Capital: 1848–1875* (1975) and *The Age of Empire: 1875–1914* (1987), Hobsbawm details the continuation of this process throughout Europe and the rest of the world, either through European migration, European imperialism, or both, eventually leading to the era of anti-colonial revolutions as well, especially after World War I.

III. Although other scholars, such as C. A. Bayly in *The Birth of the Modern World, 1780–1914* (2004), have shown that Hobsbawm's interpretation of modernization was too Eurocentric and that Europeans also were reacting to worldwide developments, the thrust of Hobsbawm's analysis is a useful way of viewing the development of modern civilization.

Essential Reading:

John Carey, *Eyewitness to History*, pp. 246–293.

E. J. Hobsbawm, *The Age of Revolution, 1789–1848*.

Robin Winks and Thomas Kaiser, *Europe, 1648–1815*, pp. 138–187.

Supplementary Reading:

Robert Gildea, *Barricades and Borders, Europe 1800–1914*, pp. 3–33.

Jan Goldstein and John W. Boyer, *Nineteenth-Century Europe*, pp. 1–40 (Introduction, Bentham), pp. 288–336 (Schleiermacher, Wilberforce, Feuerbach).

Victor Hugo, *Les Miserables*.

L. C. B. Seaman, *From Vienna to Versailles*, pp. 1–22.

Questions to Consider:

1. What are the major implications of an industrial revolution?
2. What does it mean to say that one is a Marxist scholar? How might non-Marxists evaluate that scholarship, or challenge it?

Lecture Three—Transcript
The Age of Revolution, 1789–1848

During our last series of comments together, we spoke about the *Ancien Régime* or the Old Regime, delineating the ways in which European society, even during the late 18th century, were still relatively traditional in nature, except for the more urban areas and among the wealthier in those urban areas, who had become more engaged in a more modernized segment of Europe's economy—and who had become deeply engaged in the intellectual movement of the 18th century—the broad intellectual movement of the 18th century known as the *Enlightenment*.

Today we're going to do an introductory set of comments on the first of the ages of the 19th century, the Age of Revolution, from 1789–1848, with a semicolon called the Hobsbawm thesis, perhaps the only time during this whole series of commentaries that I'm going to subtitle an age by the name of a historian who happened to have written about that particular time period; perhaps it's because Hobsbawm was one of the first of the great scholars whose works I read when I entered graduate school in 1965. Interestingly, Hobsbawm is perhaps the greatest of the European historians of the 20th century, writing about the 19th century and the 20th century. He's a British Marxist historian, whose work is so subtle that I've used his work in classes without the students realizing that he is, in fact, a Marxist historian. Even though I have not personally been tempted by Marxism, even though I've been influenced by it, Hobsbawm continues, even today, to be a Marxist scholar long after the collapse of the Soviet Union, but his realm of history is simply brilliant, comprehensive, and on a worldwide scale.

Most importantly for the comments today, he is the first, really, to recognize and to put in place a powerful way of understanding the first half of the 19th century, and then, indeed, of the whole process of modernization thereafter, using what he calls the *dual (or twin) revolution thesis* in a book called *The Age of Revolution, 1789–1848* (first published in 1962). Hobsbawm first realized how the peculiar interaction of the French Revolution and the Industrial Revolution acted as the midwives of modern European history—and then, indeed, through the process of imperialism (which was the umbilical cord between Europe and the rest of the world) world history, as well. It's a fascinating way of viewing the development of civilization globally.

The French Revolution and the Industrial Revolution undermined traditional society wherever they spread, in Europe or worldwide. Initially, the French Revolution was the more important of the two, casting a shadow over much of the 19th century, and especially the years between 1789 and 1848. Many scholars, obviously, understood the importance and the power of the French Revolution. But what Hobsbawm did is to center in on those peculiar ways in which the French Revolution was different from other late-18th-century revolutions (including the American Revolution), and other revolutions that occurred, in fact, during the first half of the 19th century.

France, when mobilized, was the most powerful state on the continent, both materially and culturally. Remember again, the elites (especially the aristocrats) of most of the other countries (except for Great Britain) preferred to speak French rather than their own language. Moreover, the French Revolution became immeasurably more radical than all of the other late-18th-century revolutions, including those of the 13 colonies. Only in France did one segment of the middle class—known henceforth and forever as the *Jacobins*—introduce full male democracy (male suffrage), even at times tinged with state socialism, in order to save the revolution from internal and external enemies. There were conservative counter-revolutions within France, and a war between the French and a number of their neighbors who were against the revolution. These Jacobins sought to harness the power of the masses for the first time, really, in European (and, indeed, in world) history—not because they were inherently so much more radical to begin with, but because they felt they needed to move further in that direction to give the masses a stake so the revolution as a whole could survive.

Indeed, also, only the French Revolution was succeeded by a Napoleon, who spread many of its fundamental ideas and concepts, expanding them. He further developed the centralized power of the state, promulgating laws in his code—even as he broke those laws when he wished to, because he ruled as a dictator and as a conqueror. But the core ideas, especially of the first phase of the French Revolution, were not lost, and they remained there even at the end of the Napoleonic reign. Moreover, unlike the Americans (the colonists) who were, indeed, living on the moon in terms of their isolation, the French saw their revolution (even initially) in universalistic terms—for export. And especially under Napoleon, its army set out to revolutionize the world; its ideas actually did so. Wherever the armies went, the ideas did follow.

By 1815, with the final defeat of Napoleon, not only had many of the structures of the *Ancien Régime* been uprooted or severely challenged and tested, but a series of modern political ideologies and concepts had taken form, creating much of the political vocabulary of the modern world—our world, even.

We start with one of the tougher ones, because the most important prevalent ideology in the early 19th century—and, indeed, after the French Revolution—was 19th-century liberalism. Here, Americans get hung up, because in the 20th century, in America, liberalism means more government, not less government. So, let's emphasize and let's keep in mind through the entire realm of this course that 19th-century liberalism was different. Nineteenth-century liberalism is somewhat like 20th-century conservatism, because 19th-century liberalism believed that that government governs best that governs least. Government was seen by 19th-century liberals as negative and only to be used when necessary because the economic philosophy of 19th-century liberalism was *laissez-faire* economics. Coming from Adam Smith—the invisible hand—remove government power, let the economy flow, have free trade, and it would all work out as we all searched for our own individual self-interest. However, what made 19th-century liberalism moderately radical for its time is that 19th-century liberals believed in promulgated constitutions; basic civil rights; limited male suffrage (limited male right to vote) based on property, how much taxes you paid, and sometimes on education; and careers open to talent, rather than birth—in other words, on some level, equality of opportunity.

19th-century liberals believed in the primacy of private property and limited government. We call that "life, liberty, and the pursuit of happiness." John Locke called it "life, liberty, and property." Our understanding of the "pursuit of happiness" was our right to pursue property unhindered by government—by excessive government. And this 19th-century liberalism had a model during the French Revolution, the Constitution of 1791.

But secondly, as the French Revolution went through phases, and we will trace those phases in excruciating detail next time, but secondly came democracy or radicalism. We would call it democracy; in Europe it was usually called radicalism. It shared many of the concepts of the liberals—promulgated laws, civil rights, et cetera—but favored universal male suffrage, especially once the revolution decreed "*un levee en masse*"—universal military conscription. When did the 18-year-olds get the right to vote in the United States? When they went to Vietnam. You have the right to die for your country; you have the right to vote for your government—so, universal male suffrage. (Ironically, when I was a student it was simply called "universal suffrage." It was understood it was "male suffrage." But we have to remember "universal male suffrage.")

The democrats also allowed for more state action—not as a positive good, necessarily, but when it was necessary. Private property was important and central, but it could give way to the wider communal good—as with the concept of eminent domain—so that during the more radical phase of the French Revolution, associated with the Constitution of 1793 (universal male suffrage), you did have the fixing of prices and wages, universal military conscription, much more state action, because the revolutionaries (the Jacobins) feared that being attacked on the inside by conservative counter-revolutionaries and being attacked from the outside by the Austrians, the Prussians, and others, they needed to harness and mobilize the power of the state, the power of the masses, to maintain and win the revolution and spread it further. And they took the risk, and they did so. The liberalism is most associated with the late-17th-century ideas of John Locke and the 18th-century ideas of Montesquieu in France. The democratic ideas are more associated with Jean-Jacques Rousseau, whose *Social Contract* in 1762 became one of the most important books of the 18th century.

Going even further to the left, although it was not a powerful force during the French Revolution, was an early form of socialism—embryonic. Just as during the 17th-century English revolutions embryonic socialist ideas were expressed, they were also expressed during the course of the French Revolution, as well. Socialists believed in freedom of speech, and freedom of thought, and freedom of the individual. It's just that they saw economic necessity as coming prior to political necessity (these early socialists)—as the right to eat, for example, as being more important than the right to vote. They were more egalitarian, including in the economic realm, in reaction to these three ideas—all of which were viewed as radical and subversive by all those who opposed the revolution, either during it or thereafter. A more modern, "utilitarian," pragmatic form of conservatism emerged in reaction to the revolution, joining divine-right monarchy with the pragmatic reasons why conservatism in and of itself was better for everybody.

And the most powerful statement of that was Edmund Burke's *Reflections on the French Revolution*, written in 1790. At first, Burke was kind of glad when he saw the outbreak of the French Revolution. After all, the French were just doing what the English had done 100 years earlier, and that just showed that they had good taste. But once the revolution began to attack the monarchy, Burke got very, very anxious, and he created the most powerful statement of modern pragmatic conservatism in the late 18th century and indeed for most of the 19th century and thereafter. Burke saw society as a contract between the living, the dead, and those yet to be born. And if you made radical changes and if you uprooted any particular aspect of society, what would happen is chaos and increasing misery for everyone.

It needs to be understood at the same time that Burke, a conservative, would have been liberal among many continental Europeans, because what he was trying to conserve was a British system of government that was already a moderately liberal system of government, a constitutional monarchy. But to real 19th-century continental conservatives, even that was partially anathema, depending on how conservative they were. So, Burke is the best statement for 19th-century utilitarian, pragmatic conservatives. Many others still believed in divine-right monarchy. They may have used Burkian ideas as a best self-defense, but Tsar Nicholas II, until the day he was finally executed, believed that he had been placed on the earth by God to serve as the divine-right monarch of holy Russia.

Significant strides were made toward formulating powerful arguments for equal rights for women, although (ironically here) both the revolutionary and Napoleonic eras saw women's rights neglected—indeed, overturned—and wide male dominance made part of promulgated law, especially during the Napoleonic Code. So, in achieving their own liberty, men did (both metaphorically and directly) enslave women for another 100 years or so. Even in

England, women wouldn't gain more absolute rights over their own self, and their children, and their property—and England was, of course, more advanced than most other states. But we do get powerful, early feminist statements from Olympe De Gouges in France and Mary Wollstonecraft in England—statements about women's equality that would not be fully achieved until after World War I and, indeed, until after World War II. And that famous Napoleonic Code, surely one of the emperor's lasting contributions to European constitutionalism, unfortunately reinforced in stronger form male dominance, owing to women's natural biological inferiority and maintaining social peace.

The concept of modern nationalism was also dramatically advanced, both in concept and reality by the revolutionary ideas—such practices as universal military conscription. Generally liberal in tone at the beginning, some say nationalism began like Sleeping Beauty and ended up like Frankenstein's monster. Liberal in tone because it stressed popular sovereignty, citizenship, and national self-determination of some type, that was the form of European nationalism that tended to predominate during the first half of the 19th century. But in any case, nationalism became the most powerful secular ideology of the 19th century.

In addition, revolution itself as a just and efficacious way to achieve historical progress also became very, very much spread during this process and during this period of time. Even as millions of Europeans were seeing gains that had been made being taken away and conservative legitimists were attempting to re-impose something like the Old Order once again, revolution was seen as a process and as a legitimate procedure by those who opposed this having been done. As one scholar of the period, talking about the succeeding Age of Revolution (in which so many revolutions occurred in Europe between 1820 and 1848) said (and he is one of the readings that I am suggesting you take a look at—L. C. B. Seaman)—Seaman says, "It's idle to consider the causes of the various revolutions in the period after 1815 without realizing that the major cause of them all was the French Revolution of 1789."

Parallel to the French Revolution of 1789 came the First Industrial Revolution in Great Britain—a process of tremendous power, which—as Hobsbawm says directly—"was probably the most important event in world history, at any rate, since the invention of agriculture and cities." This Industrial Revolution made possible comparatively unlimited levels of productivity once it really got underway, partially freeing humankind from the harsh whims of nature. For example, by 1840, Great Britain was producing more iron and utilizing more steam power than the rest of Europe combined— whereas in 1789, the global productivity of France and Great Britain had been about even. With industrialism came significant accelerating changes in virtually every area of life, including urbanization, wider education, and the entire social structure of society.

In fact, one of the things that you might want to do after this lecture at some point, if you have nothing else to do one evening, is to just take a blank piece of paper and write the word "industrialism" on it, and diagram the impact of an industrial revolution anywhere if it really gets underway. What are the implications of industrialism anywhere when it happens?

Since industrialism was also synonymous on some level with power, and especially with military power, all of the great powers were forced to come to terms with it, like it or not. For example, I mentioned in one of the earlier lectures that Russia was defeated by Britain and France in the 1850s because Russia had not industrialized. After that defeat, they began to try to figure out how they could better industrialize. When they did not do it very well, at the end of the 19th century they were defeated once again by Japan, which again had learned how to industrialize. After that defeat you'd better believe they turned their attention to learning better how to industrialize.

What didn't they like about industrializing? Industrialization implicitly uproots traditional society, makes the middle class more important and the aristocrats comparatively less important. If a society is based on the power of nobles and aristocrats, industrialization inherently eats away at the whole foundations of society, the power structure, and many of the basic beliefs.

Globally, the Industrial Revolution had deep impact on politics, ideas, and culture as a whole, always challenging traditional patterns of society. Although the impact of the French Revolution on the continent was greater than that of the Industrial Revolution prior to 1848, by the middle of the century, the balance was beginning to shift; thereafter, their combined impact increasingly challenged and undermined traditional society, ushering in a modern, urban, industrial civilization wherever they really took deep root. In two later volumes, *The Age of Capital: 1848–1875* (1975) and *The Age of Empire: 1875–1914* (1987), Hobsbawm details the continuation of this process throughout the rest of Europe, first from 1850 to 1870 and then from 1870 (or actually 1873) to 1914, and, in fact, the rest of the world, either by European migration, European imperialism, or both, eventually leading to an era of anti-colonial revolutions as well, especially after World War I.

The ideas of the French Revolution and the material forces of the Industrial Revolution were transferred worldwide, disrupting traditional patterns of life as they had done in Europe. After several generations of European domination in many of these colonial areas, native elites and the masses used and adapted European ideas and material power, combined with their own cultural norms, against European domination, much as the European middle class and masses had done in Europe a century or more earlier against their aristocrats and kings.

Although many other scholars, such as C. A. Bayly in a new book, *The Birth of the Modern World, 1780–1914* (just published this year), have shown that Hobsbawm's interpretation of the development of modern civilization worldwide was too Eurocentric (and remember, I alerted you that my view is Eurocentric because that's what I study) and that Europeans were also reacting to developments worldwide rather than instigating them exclusively. There is always an ebb and flow of cultural interchange. The overall power of Hobsbawm's analysis is a useful way of viewing the development of modern civilization, even today. Indeed, if you want to take that even further and study the short 20th century (which I also teach), one of my favorite ways of doing that is to take British Marxist historian Hobsbawm and his additional book on 20th-century world history, juxtapose it with Paul Johnson (British conservative historian), and use the two as a way to see how this 19th-century paradigm continued and was changed during the course of the short 20th century.

In our next set of lectures, on the French Revolution, we will be looking at how the Hobsbawm thesis works, under a microscope, more carefully, with more detail, and thinking through how each of the particular phases of the French Revolution led a peculiar legacy for 19th-century European thought, aspiration, and behavior. The Constitution of 1791 again primarily gave us a model and a legacy of 19th-century European liberalism. The Constitution of 1793, under the power of the Jacobins, gave us a model of what a constitution would look like under radicalism or democracy. Universal male suffrage, the right to work, the right to subsist, and the right to rebel, even, were written into the Constitution of 1793 (all the while excluding women). And then the Constitution of 1795 basically returned to the Constitution of 1791, which was the core legacy that the French Revolution bequeathed to the immediate governmental structure of the post-1789 era.

Following that, we'll be looking more carefully at the way in which Napoleon took, molded, expanded, and detracted from some of those core ideas of the French Revolution. Thereafter, in greater detail, we'll look at the process by which the Industrial Revolution developed, its major impact, and how the French and Industrial Revolutions combined and set the framework for European history, European society, European life, and European culture during the first half of the 19th century—establishing some people's dreams and other people's nightmares, some people's hopes and other people's deepest fears.

I look forward to being with you. Thank you.

Lecture Four
The French Revolution

Scope:

Although scholars debate the causes of the French Revolution, in the context of the socioeconomic, demographic, and ideological changes that occurred in 18th-century France, all agree it was a dramatic event that helped determine the political vocabulary, expectations, and myths of 19th-century Europe.

Part of the power of the French Revolution is that it lasted for at least 10 years in Europe's most powerful state. Moreover, from 1787 until 1799, nearly every segment of society, including the poor and women, played an active role, while one segment of the middle class, forever known as *Jacobins*, implemented radical political and social agendas to save the revolution and to defend France from the wrath of aristocratic Europe. Thus came the Terror of 1793–1794, the most debated revolutionary experience.

In addition, every phase of the revolution represented a political ideology and constitutional/institutional models that spread to other parts of Europe in the "knapsacks" of French soldiers, united by the secular ideology of nationalism. These challenges left a legacy of hope and fear, depending on one's worldview, and opponents of the revolution would need to mimic some of its reforms and passions in order to survive. Part of this legacy was Napoleon Bonaparte himself and the challenges he presented to a frightened and tired European leadership elite.

Outline

I. Although scholars assign different weights to the causes of the French Revolution, most agree they were multiple in nature.

    A. One area always presented is the impact of the Enlightenment.

        1. Great philosophers, such as Montesquieu, Voltaire, and Rousseau, critiqued established institutions and traditions, including the aristocracy, the church, and the functioning of the monarchy.

2. These ideas and many others were given focus by Diderot and d'Alembert, whose multi-volume *Encyclopedia* appeared between 1751–1777.
3. The ideas of the Enlightenment were spread more broadly through many forms of elite and popular culture.
4. Even members of the aristocracy and clergy were affected by potentially incendiary ideas, as were members of the middle classes and many common folk.

B. Many scholars, especially Marxists, stress the contradiction between a growing commercial capitalist economic structure and the bourgeois class, facing the constraints of feudal society, dominated by the aristocracy. Actually, there was much commonality (politically, economically, and culturally) of interest between members of the aristocracy and upper bourgeoisie, although they headed toward a collision course just prior to 1789.

C. Others stress that French institutions were rotten and could not continue to function for long.
1. This was particularly true with respect to tax collection, in which the two wealthiest estates, the clergy and the aristocracy, were exempt from many taxes, while the poorest groups were taxed severely.
2. Most taxes were collected inefficiently and sometimes corruptly by *tax farmers*; on the eve of 1789, half of the revenues garnered were used to fund interest on the debt.
3. Still, French institutions were not notably less efficient than those of several other great powers, especially Austria and Russia; Cardinal Fleury, who managed affairs between 1726–1740, had bequeathed his monarch a balanced budget.

D. Another area of stress, especially on the eve of 1789, was a substantial population increase, not matched by an equivalent agrarian yield.
1. Increasing misery was evident during the 1770s and 1780s and especially during the agrarian depression of 1787–1788.
2. Urban unemployment and hunger paralleled rural crisis.

E. Three costly continental and imperial wars forced the monarchy to live beyond its means, falling deeply in debt.

1. Between 1740 and 1783, France was involved in the War of Austrian Succession (1740–1748) and the Seven Years War, (1756–1763); these two wars were costly economically, and losses in both diminished France's prestige.
2. French support for the American Revolution, in its victorious revenge against Britain, from 1776–1783, finally bankrupted the monarchy and made the vocabulary of the Enlightenment and American revolutionary ideas the rage of the day.

F. Both Louis XV and Louis XVI, either through their persons or their policies, undermined the status of the monarchy and encouraged France's elites to challenge their absolutist claims.
1. With unabashedly dissolute behavior, King Louis XV scandalized even a sex-tolerant Parisian society.
2. Tarnished by rumors of impotence, Louis XVI's inability to consistently support the policies of reforming ministers allowed a crisis to turn into a catastrophe.

G. Matters were brought to a head in 1787 when an Assembly of Notables, called into being to accept taxes on the aristocrats and clergy, refused to do so without sharing authority.
1. This confrontation is often known as the pre-revolution, the aristocratic or feudal reaction, or even the first phase of the revolution.
2. Deadlock and bankruptcy forced King Louis XVI to summon the Estates General, which last met in 1614.

H. The dramatic year between the two assemblies saw widespread debate concerning French institutions and the crisis of the monarchy.

I. Lack of clarity as to how the three estates would function and whether or not the first two would override the wishes of the third estate, which constituted 97 percent of the 25 million people of France, brought tensions to a head between the middle classes (and some liberal aristocrats and clerics) and more conservative elites. When liberal cleric Abbé Sieyès wrote his famous inflammatory pamphlet, "What Is the Third Estate?" (1789), claiming the masses represented the nation while the aristocrats were parasites, the die was cast.

II. Owing to a complex set of forces (including the king's weakness, class and ideological conflict, continued economic distress and financial instability, painful decisions concerning the role of the church in France, urban and rural violence, and foreign wars), the revolution unfolded in a series of phases, between 1789 and 1799, each with its own leadership elite, accomplishments, failures, and tone.

A. The first phase, lasting roughly between 1789 and 1792, saw an uneasy balance between an increasingly weakened monarch and an increasingly powerful legislature.

    1. Among its famous early hallmarks were the Tennis Court Oath (June 20, 1789), the storming of the Bastille (July 14), and the Great Fear in the countryside (July–August).

    2. Between 1789 and 1791, the main remnants of feudalism were destroyed and a constitutional monarchy was established.

    3. The Declaration of the Rights of Man and Citizen (August 26, 1789) was somewhat more radical than the American Bill of Rights.

    4. The confiscation of church property and Civil Constitution of the Clergy, requiring a loyalty oath, deeply divided Catholics and left a legacy of church-state conflict.

    5. The suppression of guilds and prohibition of workers' organizations signified support for a capitalist economy.

    6. The flight and capture of the royal family in June 1791 raised further questions about the possibility of monarchical compromise.

    7. The mostly bourgeois members of the Legislative Assembly, which convened in October 1791, took stronger measures against non-juring priests and émigré nobles, declared war against Austria in April 1792, and abolished the monarchy in August 1792.

B. A second phase between September 1792 and July 1794 saw the radicalization of the revolution, expanded foreign war, and Robespierre's Reign of Terror.

1. Urban and rural masses continued to be active, and revolts against the revolution also occurred.
2. France now found itself at war with Austria, Prussia, Holland, and Britain.
3. The king was tried and executed (December 1792–January 1793).
4. A more democratic Constitution of 1793 was adopted in late June, proclaiming universal male suffrage, the right to work, the right to subsistence, and even the right to rebel against tyranny.
5. Faced with internal civil war (the Vendée), foreign defeat, severe inflation, and shortages, Robespierre came to dominate the newly established Committee of Public Safety and take even more radical measures, including universal military conscription, wage and price controls, revolutionary tribunals and the Reign of Terror, and state centralization.
6. Following the execution of thousands of real and purported enemies of the revolution, along with republican victories against foreign opponents and numerous internal rebellions, Robespierre and his closest Jacobin allies were overthrown and executed at the end of July 1794.

C. Following a transitional year known as the *Thermidorian Reaction*, lasting from late summer 1794 to fall 1795, a five-person Directory was established between November 1795 and 1799; both represented a return to the moderate, constitutional phase of the revolution and the search for order and stability internally, although with increasing cynicism.
1. Moderate deputies and surviving Girondins reentered the legislature.
2. Most forms of public protest, whether republican or royalist, and independent political organizations were repressed.
3. The Constitution of 1795, similar to that of 1791, was adopted in early October, with a Directory of five members serving as the executive branch of government, in conjunction with a two-house parliament.

4. Increasingly, the army and its new heroes were used not only to do battle with France's foreign foes but to maintain order.

5. Continued foreign conquest, often now more traditional in manner, and continued political disunity led to a decline in support for the Directory and to the meteoric rise to power of France's most popular general, Napoleon Bonaparte, in a new form of government known as the *Consulate*, in 1799.

Essential Reading:

John Carey, *Eyewitness to History*, pp. 246–255.

John Merriman, *A History of Modern Europe*, volume II, pp. 467–516.

Jeremy D. Popkin, A *Short History of the French Revolution*, pp. 1–98, 148–164.

Supplementary Reading:

James Collins, *The Ancien Régime and the French Revolution*.

Ronald Schechter, ed., *The French Revolution*.

Questions to Consider:

1. Why did the French Revolution become so much more radical than the American Revolution?

2. Overall, was the French Revolution a positive event in human history?

Lecture Four—Transcript
The French Revolution

Good morning! Having encountered E. J. Hobsbawm in our last commentary, with his wonderful book *The Age of Revolution, 1789–1848*, we now take a step backward and talk about the French Revolution itself. The first part of this era, basically from 1789 to 1799, when Napoleon Bonaparte came into power, ended that segment of the French Revolution. Although scholars assign different weights to the causes of the French Revolution (and we'll deal with the causes first, in some detail), and those weights and the description of those causes changes about every 20 years, most would agree that they were multiple in nature.

One area always presented by scholars is the impact of the Enlightenment, whose most powerful proponents lived in France. A long time ago, it tended to be conservative scholars who criticized the Enlightenment for eating away at the structures of the Old Regime by criticizing its basic institutions. Great philosophers such as Montesquieu, Voltaire, Rousseau, and many others critiqued established institutions and traditions including the aristocracy—even the church—and the functioning of the monarchy with a clear sense that improvements were both possible and necessary. These ideas, and many similar ones, were given focus in the mammoth efforts of editors Diderot and d'Alembert, whose multi-volume *Encyclopedia* appeared between 1751–1777.

More recently, once again emphasizing the impact of ideas in setting the preconditions for the revolution (even if they weren't the absolute immediate causes), a newer generation of scholars has studied how the ideas of the Enlightenment, in fact, were also spread more broadly via various forms of elite culture, *salons* and reading rooms, and even popular culture, in pamphleteers and in oral tradition in an age of a somewhat larger middle class and a somewhat expanded literacy. Ironically, even members of the aristocracy and clergy were affected by the potentially incendiary forms of thought, as were members of the middle classes or the *bourgeois*, and many of the urban common folk. In fact, many members of the aristocracy used the ideas of the Enlightenment to attempt to get the monarch to share power with them, not recognizing that they were beginning to dig their own graves.

An earlier generation of Marxist scholars (and there are still scholars who see things this way) stress the contradiction between the growing commercial, bourgeois, fluid economy, capitalist economy of 18th-century France and the constraints placed on it by the aristocratic control of the state from the top down, with the monarchy in charge. That is to say that one class was predominating over another, newer, growing class—preventing it from getting its part of the pie. Scholars today emphasize more the commonality between the aristocrats and the upper middle class in terms of self-interest, economic concern, and even ideas. However, both of these groups were concerned that their elements of modern economic orientation were simply not being supported in any rational way by the economic structure of the Old Regime and the monarchy. All wanted some say in determining the kind of economic policy that the regime would pursue. In other words, even when one has an economic cause, the emphasis is in some ways even more political than economic, because it's the political manifestation of it that becomes more powerful.

However, at the last moment, on the very eve of the revolution, the aristocracy and the *bourgeoisie* did head to a collision over who would have more of a say in determining what the actual policy would be in determination with the monarch. Others have stressed that the French institutions were simply rotten—not functioning well, in need of some real updating. At the same time, there were other societies whose institutions were not more well developed than those of France; I want you to think of Russia and Austria. But the difficulty in France did pertain most directly to the method of tax collection, in which the two wealthiest groups (the first estate, the clergy; and the second, the aristocracy) were exempt from any taxes, which meant that the middle class and sometimes the very poorest (when they could, at least) paid more in taxes than perhaps they should have been doing. In either case, the taxes were collected inefficiently and sometimes corruptly by *tax farmers*. So much so, that on the eve of the revolution, half of the revenues garnered were used to fund interest on the accumulated debt, and it was becoming more and more difficult for the French state to get loans, and they paid a high percent for those loans—double the percent that the British or the Dutch paid, for example, at the same time.

However, as of 1740 this had not been the case, because the financial minister between 1726 and 1740 had actually left the monarchy a balanced budget by keeping expenditure in tow with requirements. So, the issue, again, on a certain level, becomes political. How much does a regime spend, versus how much does it take in? The problem becomes when there is a discrepancy between what you spend and what you take in. That discrepancy becomes most predominant when a regime enters into a series of wars. And, in fact, that is precisely what happened when the French monarchy in its colonial disputes with Great Britain entered into three colonial wars between 1740 and 1783. The first of these wars was the War of Austrian Succession, between 1740 and 1748. The second was the Seven Years War or the Nine Years War, the French and Indian War, or the war that began between 1756 and 1763 on the continent. And the most important thing about these wars is that France lost both of them, losing many of its colonies to the British.

This did two things. On the one hand, it was very costly. On the other hand, it took away from national legitimacy, because the very most important thing that any regime needs to do is to defend the state against its enemies, and Great Britain was an enemy, and France did not effectively defend the state, the patrimony, the colonies. And this took away from the legitimacy of the monarchy.

Plans for reforming the tax code were under consideration during the regime of Louis XV, which ended in 1774, and also during the regime of Louis XVI after 1774 until the eve of the French Revolution. These plans, posited by successive finance ministers, continued to be discussed, throughout, until the very eve of the revolution, and were, in fact, the reason why the Assembly of Notables was called in 1787 and the Estates General in 1789. Factions around the king and factions within the Parliament de Paris (the Parisian law court that had to register these laws) fighting one another and the weakness of the king in seeing a straight path and supporting his ministers, almost all of whom came up with similar policies, that the nobles and the clergy had to pay taxes, caused the regime to fail to deal with this increasingly burdensome, pressing issue.

That's when the last of the wars broke the bank. French support for the American Revolution in its victorious revenge against the British, between 1778 when France joined and 1783, not only bankrupted the monarchy, but made the vocabulary of the Enlightenment and

American revolutionary ideas the rage of the day. In Hobsbawm's words: "war and debt broke the back of the monarchy."

Furthermore, both Louis XV and Louis XVI, through their persons, their policies, and their behavior, encouraged French elites to challenge their absolutist claims to authority and divine-right rule, because there didn't seem to be much divine about their behavior. Louis XV, even in a Parisian society that was not bashful about sex, scandalized society with his behavior and his mistresses—and even the political power that some of his mistresses seemed to have. Louis XVI at first seemed to be impotent, and his wife, the Austrian princess Marie Antoinette, carried on. The French didn't like either of these extremes. This also took away from the legitimacy and the weight of the monarchy, which just wasn't taken quite seriously enough anymore.

Matters were brought to a head in 1787 when an Assembly of Notables was called to discuss taxes on the aristocrats and clergy. They refused to do so without sharing authority in some manner with the monarchy, and they suggested that the Estates General, which had not met—a kind of Parliament that had not met since 1614— should be called. This confrontation is often known as the pre-revolution, or the aristocratic or feudal reaction, or even the first phase of the revolution. Deadlock and bankruptcy forced the king to summon the Estates General.

However, this occurred at the same time, unfortunately for the regime, of a dramatic agrarian crisis. There were food shortages, which pushed peasants into the city, with unemployment and turmoil—in other words, before the outbreak of the French Revolution, people were hurting. Workers were hurting. Artisans were hurting. Peasants were hurting. The same thing would occur before 1848 and the revolutions, and the same would occur before the Russian Revolution. In other words, there was an immediate, additional burden of economic hardship on the masses, while at the same time there was a burden of political incapacity between the elites and the monarchy. What finally happens is that that political incapacity spreads within the elites, as well.

The people, as a whole, are asked to devise a list of grievances— *cahiers de doleances*. Those *cahiers* tell us clearly what the state of France was at that time. They give us an excellent view of the time. But that view shows us also how different groups wanted different things. The clergy wanted the Estates General to meet, but they wanted to ensure the predominance of Catholicism as the exclusive public religion of the state. The nobility wanted to make sure that the Estates would meet, but they wanted more power for themselves, as well. And much of the rest of the nations, increasingly, wanted recognition of the fact that they did represent the majority of the nation. That was brought to a boiling point and a head by a powerful pamphlet written by a cleric, the Abbé Sieyès, on the eve of the revolution, "What Is the Third Estate?" Sieyès said—dramatically and inflammatorily—the third estate is the nation. What are the rest, if they are not willing to join the third estate—essentially they're parasites on the nation. And the die was cast.

The die was further cast because the decision had to be made over how would the estates meet? Would they meet as they had done in 1614, in which the two upper estates could overwhelm and outvote the third estate? Or would they meet together, in which some of the liberal aristocrats and some of the liberal clergy joining the third estate would enable the third estate (which, after all, represented 95 to 97 percent of France) to outvote the aristocrats and clergy in a more liberal constitutional regime? That issue brought matters to a boiling point. And that issue is why, in 1789, the French Revolution really began to get out of control.

Owing to a series of complex forces, including the king's weakness, increasing class and ideological conflict even more so; continued economic distress, both in terms of food and in terms of runaway inflation; financial instability; painful decisions concerning the future role of the church in France; urban and rural violence that broke out increasingly all over, both on the part of pro-revolutionaries and anti-revolutionaries; and foreign wars among the European powers who didn't like anything that was happening in France, and wanted it to stop and wanted to preserve the monarchy (because what was done to the king in France could be done to them just as easily). This forced the revolution to unfold in a series of phases between 1789 and 1799. Each phase had its own leadership elite. Each phase had its own accomplishments. Each phase had its own set of failures or excesses. And each phase had its own distinct tone—cultural included—even dress, music, art.

The first phase, lasting roughly between 1789 and 1792, saw an uneasy balance between an increasingly weakened monarch and an increasingly more powerful legislature, known first as the National Assembly, and then (later) as the Legislative Assembly, in which the representatives of the three estates sat together, at least in theory. Which meant that, after a brief period of time, some liberal aristocrats, some liberal clerics, and the middle class sat together. The overwhelming majority of people came from the third estate, obviously.

It had a number of famous hallmarks that many people remember from high school or college: the Tennis Court Oath in June of 1789, when the third estate refuses to abandon until it achieves its goals; the storming of the Bastille by urban artisans in Paris; and the Great Fear in the countryside in the summer of 1789, in which peasants burned manor rolls and tax rolls and records, and executed some nobility. And even the women of Paris going to Versailles to bring the king the baker and the baker's wife and the baker's kid back to Paris where they could do the business of the people rather than their own funny business in Versailles.

Think for a minute what these hallmarks represent: the entrance of the middle class, the entrance of peasants, the entrance of urban artisans, and the action of women—all different groups that were part of the nation.

Between 1789 and 1791, the main remnants of feudalism were destroyed and a constitutional monarchy was established. The Declaration of the Rights of Man and Citizen in August of 1789 was somewhat more radical and universalist than our recently issued American Bill of Rights. These first gains in the revolution, including the emancipation of Protestants and then the emancipation of Jews, including careers open to talent, including a constitutional monarchy, promulgated law, trial by jury—these were reflected in the Constitution of 1791.

In 19th-century liberal terms, this was a moderate, liberal constitution, something like what the British have themselves. And, indeed, many people feel that this was by far the most important, the most positive, period of the revolution, and the core of this, in fact, did really survive even the rest of the revolution and even Napoleon himself.

The confiscation of church property and Civil Constitution of the Clergy, requiring the clergy to take loyalty oaths to the revolution and the nation, deeply divided Catholics and left a bitter legacy of church-state conflict that lasted in France even until after World War II and is finally, seemingly, becoming just something of the past (thankfully!). Indeed, I remember seeing masses in France on television in which Catholic priests urged their parishioners to go out and find people who were different (Protestants, Jews, Moslems) and to get to know them because they were all part of France. These programs brought tears to my eyes.

The suppression of guilds and the prohibition of worker's organizations signified support for a capitalist economy, while giving only male taxpayers the right to vote indicated the limited and the moderate nature of the changes foreseen.

The flight and capture of the royal family in June 1791 raised further questions about the possibility of coping and compromising with the monarchy—especially in the face of counter-revolution conservative and Catholic counter-revolution, unfortunately, and the external opposition of the nations on France's borders. The mostly bourgeois members of the Legislative Assembly who convened in October of 1791 took stronger measures against priests who wouldn't take the oath and nobles who fled from France, increasingly taking all of their property, and they declared war against Austria in April of 1792. They finally abolished the monarchy in August of 1792, ushering in yet another phase or another segment in this revolutionary turmoil.

The second equally complicated phase between September of 1792 and July of 1794 saw the further radicalization of the revolution, expanded foreign war, and Maximilien Robespierre's Reign of Terror. All of the revolutionary emphasis was pushed further by internal counter-revolution, foreign war initially being lost by France, urban and rural masses being active continuously because food was still short and the currency was still depreciating terribly, and revolts against the regime. France now found itself at war with Austria, Prussia, Holland, and Britain, and they weren't doing well. In this context, the king was tried and executed in January of 1793— actually dying with more strength and more dignity than he had lived. However, in the face of all these internal problems, a more democratic Constitution of 1793 was adopted under the pressure of the now-dominant group of Jacobin radicals, proclaiming universal male suffrage, the right to work (wouldn't we like to have that?), the right to subsistence, and even the right to rebel against tyranny.

In other words, the Jacobins understood, and they were middle class, and they did respect property, but they understood that the power of the French people, the power of the revolution, had to be harnessed or the revolution would unravel and fail. Faced with internal civil war (in the Vendée, especially), foreign defeats, severe inflation, and food shortages, Robespierre came to dominate the newly established Committee of Public Safety and take even more radical and extreme measures to defend the revolution and to defeat France's internal and external enemies. In doing so, Robespierre suspended the constitution. First we will defend the revolution, then we will defend civil liberties.

Tragically, they did defeat internal enemies, with the loss—I've seen numbers of between 100,000 and even a quarter of a million in the internal counter-revolutionary revolts. I have seen numbers as high as 40,000 on the guillotine, of people who had lost their heads, including a number of people who did so for no reason whatsoever. People who were actually part of the revolution, but in some way disagreed with Robespierre. It got out of control. The Jacobin era got out of control, even though it was in support of democracy, and even though it was in support of the French nation, and even though it was successful militarily, and even though it harnessed the power of the nation more completely than any regime had ever done (probably in history). It just got out of control.

As it is said sometimes, the revolution began to devour its own children. At that point, no one knew who was safe. Because with the guillotine functioning at such a rapid pace, who would be next?

During this time period, state centralization was expanded even further as the power of Paris over the rest of France was expanded. Centralization occurred in lots of ways. There were a variety of revolutionary cultural manifestations—the cult of the Supreme Being. A new system of months was introduced. New forms of dress became popular. During this time period—ironically, with extreme male democracy—came the suppression of women's organizations, and women's right to be part of that revolutionary enterprise, even though they had played a dramatic role more than once, and affected the outcome, and claimed their rights in written and oral meetings, just as the men had done—the Declaration of the Rights of Woman and Man.

Following the execution of thousands of real and purported enemies of the revolution, along with republican victories—both against foreign opponents and numerous internal rebellions—Robespierre and his closest allies were overthrown. The Jacobins themselves were executed by the same means by which they had executed their enemies (imagined or real) during July 1794.

Following a transitional year known as the *Thermidorian Reaction*, in late summer 1794 through fall 1795, a five-person Directory was established, and it governed in place between November 1795 and 1799. The Directory represented a return to the moderate, constitutional phase of the revolution. It represented the search for order, the search for stability, internally. However, at the same time, there was increasing cynicism. There was increasing corruption. There was increasing jockeying for power.

Most of the severe controls that had been put into place during the Jacobin era, including wage and price controls, were abandoned. A constitution was issued—the Constitution of 1795—somewhat like the Constitution of 1791, except that now the Directory replaced the monarchy as the executive part of the government. Many other popular mechanisms of expression—including the Jacobin clubs themselves, and any other worker's organizations, or any other feminist groups—were suppressed. Censorship was reintroduced. An increased police presence was there. Increasingly, the army and its new heroes were used not only to do battle with France's foreign foes but used to maintain order itself—order against internal enemies; order against any manifestations of domestic discontent, or rebellion, either from the left (those who really preferred the 1793 variety) or from the right (returning émigré nobles or clergy who still wanted to have the whole thing unravel).

The Directory provided a relatively competent government and did establish a certain level of stability. It did establish a certain number of newer cultural institutions and schools that reflected the major social gains of the revolution—especially those of the middle class.

However, continued war—now more for foreign conquest and more traditional than, really, on behalf of the revolution—continued political disunity, jockeying for power, corruption, cynicism, and led to a decline in the legitimacy of the Directory, and made possible the meteoric rise in power of France's young and by then most popular general, Napoleon Bonaparte. Ironically, he was called into play by our old friend Abbé Sieyès, who had written "What Is the Third Estate?" in 1789, helping to spark the revolution itself. Sieyès brought in Bonaparte as part of a triumvirate, the *Consulate*, in 1799. They overthrew the Directory. Sieyès thought he would teach Bonaparte. Few people ever taught Bonaparte. He devoured them, and he devoured them easily.

We will turn to him, both for the positive and for the negative, in our next series of comments. Thank you.

Lecture Five
The Napoleonic Era, 1799–1815

Scope:

An adventurer of enormous talent and capacity for work and intrigue, Napoleon Bonaparte dominated Europe's historical imagination like no other "great man" until Adolf Hitler. However, unlike Hitler, Napoleon represented much that was best in his era—promulgated law, careers open to talent, administrative efficiency, and religious toleration—although his legacy was marred by a monumental ego and penchant toward conquest.

A child of the Enlightenment, a son of the revolution, and an enlightened despot, Napoleon was an epoch-making figure. His 16-year reign ensured that many revolutionary accomplishments would be retained, while his desire to dominate Europe virtually ensured that his opponents would unite. In the process, millions died, France lost its position as Europe's dominant power, the Old Regime temporarily reasserted its ascendancy, and the British maximized their economic and imperial dominance. Still, when the powers met in Vienna in 1814–1815 to reassert the principles of legitimacy, anti-revolutionary solidarity, and the balance of power, the ideologies of the revolutionary epoch had taken form: Liberalism, radicalism, socialism, nationalism, the myth of revolutionary possibility, and more modern conservatism were locked in mortal combat.

Outline

I. Napoleon Bonaparte's rise to power was based on opportunities presented by the French Revolution and his outstanding political and military talents and powerful ambition.

   A. Born into a poor Corsican noble family in 1769, he received military training in France, specializing in artillery.

   B. Somewhat out of place, he was influenced by Enlightenment thought and threw in his lot with the revolution, joining the Jacobins.

   C. He showed unusual talents in military engagements, especially in lifting the British siege of Toulon in December 1793, and made political connections, switching his support to the Thermidorians and marrying the well-placed Josephine de Beauharnais.

D. As one of the youngest generals in the French army and after changing his name to Napoleon Bonaparte, he won military victories against the Piedmontese and Austrians in Italy in 1796 and 1797, negotiating treaties and gaining fame.

E. This was followed by a dramatic campaign in Egypt and Syria, but soon Napoleon's military victories were undermined by Admiral Nelson's destruction of his fleet.

F. Napoleon returned from Egypt in October 1799, in time to join Abbé Sieyès in overthrowing the Directory.

II. Iron-willed, ambitious, and popular, Napoleon assumed overall control of France's political and military destiny, achieving success during more than four years of the Consulate.

A. Napoleon became consul-for-life in 1802, then emperor in May 1804.

B. He consolidated a number of the moderate gains of the revolution, healed some of its worst tensions, and continued to expand the power and efficiency of the state.

    1. He implemented a constitution with a strong executive and a complicated set of three chambers.

    2. Although maintaining "careers open to talent," Napoleon used highly competent individuals from all political backgrounds, including royalists.

    3. Powerful and effective prefects were appointed in each of France's departments.

    4. A Concordat with the papacy was reached in July 1801, appeasing most Catholics, while establishing the better part of state control over the church.

    5. Gains made by Protestants and Jews during the first years of the revolution were maintained.

    6. A semi-private Bank of France was established in 1800 and France's currency was stabilized by 1803.

    7. The major property changes that occurred during the revolution were maintained.

    8. Other institutions were created, such as an expanded secondary and university system for the elites and the Legion of Honor, especially for prominent state service.

C. During the early years, France was able to defeat all its military opponents fairly easily, even getting the British to sign the Peace of Amiens in 1802.

    1. France was now not only at peace but in a dominant position in Europe, having made considerable gains along its borders.

    2. A large part of the war costs were paid by the vanquished and by armies that lived off the land.

III. The second phase of Napoleon's rule, from the early years of his emperorship until the Grand Army invaded Russia in June 1812, can be divided into two periods.

  A. Between 1804 and 1808, Napoleon continued to experience great success.

    1. These were the years during which most of the articles of the famous Napoleonic Code were devised and implemented, guaranteeing equality under the law for men—and the subordination of women—the predominance of contracts and the security of property, and careers, in theory, open to talent rather than to preferred birth.

    2. France continued to be relatively prosperous, because most of Napoleon's battles were still paid for by France's neighbors.

    3. Although Admiral Nelson's second decisive victory at the Battle of Trafalgar (October 1805) prevented a French invasion of Britain, Napoleon achieved his greatest military victories against Austria, Russia, and Prussia at Ulm in October 1805; Austerlitz in December 1805; and Jena and Auerstädt in October 1806.

    4. These decisive victories and the Peace of Tilsit, signed with Russia in July 1807, marked French predominance over western and central Europe.

    5. France annexed much territory and established satellite states; most significant was the creation of the Confederation of the Rhine in 1806, followed by the abolition of the meaningless Holy Roman Empire, reducing the number of German states.

    6. Still, the Continental System of 1806, set up to exclude British goods, raised problems in Europe and France.

B. Between 1808 and 1812, French predominance began to unravel, even though Napoleon won decisive victories.

    1. The Peninsular War, France's conquest of Portugal and Spain in 1808, became an open sore; 350,000 soldiers could not destroy the Spanish guerrilla nationalist movement, aided by British money and men.

    2. Nationalist reactions against French imperialism became prominent in Germany, while Prussian reforms prepared them for upcoming conflict.

    3. The Continental System was leaking all over, including in Russia, also ready for conflict.

IV. More irascible and increasingly impetuous, Napoleon "gambled" on the destruction of Russia in order to finally bring Britain to heel.

    A. The Grand Army of 600,000 soldiers invading Russia in June 1812 became the tattered remnants of 40,000 troops returning to France in December, defeated by severe weather and the Russians.

    B. Sensing the possibility of finally defeating Napoleon, the more battle-tested Russians, Prussians, Austrians, and British cooperated more effectively.

        1. Severely outnumbered, Napoleon was badly defeated in the Battle of the Nations (Leipzig) in October 1813.

        2. The Allies entered Paris at the end of March 1814, followed by Napoleon's abdication and "comfortable" exile to the Island of Elba in the Mediterranean.

        3. The Allies, negotiating with French Prince Talleyrand, agreed on a non-punitive treaty; King Louis XVIII was placed on the throne but accepted a charter; and France kept the borders of 1792, its "natural" frontiers.

        4. Napoleon made a dramatic return to France but was defeated on June 18, 1815, at Waterloo, and packed off to St. Helena in the South Atlantic.

        5. Louis XVIII returned to France, stripped of its territorial gains, but mostly glad to be at peace.

V. Although the Allies reached an intelligent postwar settlement at the Congress of Vienna, Europe would never be the same again.

    A. A number of the revolutionary changes were maintained in France and elsewhere.

B. Constitutional and national ways of thinking could not be erased.

C. Industrial forces, advancing in Britain, soon spread to the continent.

Essential Reading:

John Carey, *Eyewitness to History*, pp. 256–293.

John Merriman, *A History of Modern Europe*, pp. 517–552.

Jeremy D. Popkin, *A Short History of the French Revolution*, pp. 99–142, 165–167.

Supplementary Readings:

Robert Gildea, *Barricades and Borders, Europe 1800–1914*, pp. 34–54.

Alistair Horne, *The Age of Napoleon*.

Paul Johnson, *Napoleon*.

Questions to Consider:

1. Why was Napoleon so successful in maintaining his power internally?

2. How does one explain his military triumphs, facing so many enemies?

Lecture Five—Transcript
The Napoleonic Era, 1799–1815

Having just recently traveled with the French through the many phases of the first 10 years of their revolution, and wishing that somehow they could possibly have stopped somewhere between 1792 and 1793, we enter onto another roller coaster together with Napoleon from 1799 to 1815, with all of Europe being in one of the cars.

Napoleon Bonaparte's rise to power was based on a combination of opportunities presented by the disruptions of the French Revolution and his outstanding political and military talents and powerful ambition. Born into a poor Corsican noble family in 1769—just after France acquired the island from Genoa, named Napoleone Buonaparte—he received his military training in France prior to the revolution, specializing in artillery, and being embarrassed by his name and his accent and his lack of wealth, and changing his name and his affectation along the way, as best he could—always somewhat out of place and needy and, therefore, on the make. He was influenced, however, by Enlightenment thought, and he quickly threw in his lot with the revolution, even joining the Jacobins in 1792—placing a good bet, because they were about to take power and to have their run.

Napoleon quickly showed unusual talents in a series of military engagements, especially in lifting the British siege of Toulon in December 1793, with his use of artillery. And he also made excellent political connections, switching his support to the Thermidorians and marrying the well-placed Josephine de Beauharnais, who was a mistress of one of the Directors, Barras. He then became one of the youngest generals in the French army, changed his name fully, and won significant military victories against the Piedmontese and the Austrians in Italy in 1796 and 1797. He did what he did best, in a sense, when off on his own, going beyond his orders, negotiating treaties on his own accord, but gaining considerable fame and notoriety in Paris as well—both from elites, but also from the masses.

This was followed by a dramatic campaign in Egypt. When he went back to Paris, they wanted to send him off, because he was dangerous, in a sense, in Paris. But soon Napoleon's daring military victories were undermined by Admiral Nelson's destruction of his fleet, which would become a recurring scene for the next part of his career as well, because Nelson would do the same thing as well in 1805 at Trafalgar. One can wonder what would have happened if the French fleets were not destroyed? And what would have happened to Great Britain?

Napoleon returned home from Egypt in October 1799, just in time to join our old friend Abbé Sieyès in overthrowing the Directory, in a move that the other conspirators thought would lead to them being in the driving seat, and Napoleon following. However, iron-willed, ambitious, a general, popular, holding better cards if he chose to play them—which he did—Napoleon quickly assumed overall control of France's political and military destiny, increasingly expanding his power and achieving considerable success during more than four years of what was called the Consulate. He was the first consul among the three, making himself such. He made himself consul-for-life in 1802, and then he took the crown from the hands of Pope Pius VII in May 1804 and crowned himself emperor, rather than having the pope crown him emperor, as Charlemagne had allowed himself to do centuries and centuries before.

During this early segment of his rule, Bonaparte consolidated a number of the moderate gains of the revolution, and he also healed some of its worst tensions, and he continued to expand the power and the efficiency of the state. If only that had been what his real person was. France was making gains. Napoleon oversaw the implementation and acceptance by plebiscite of a constitution with a strong executive and a complicated set of three chambers. The Council of State was the most important. Its members were chosen by Napoleon, and it was the main action body, where laws were proposed and formulated, often with his participation. This is one of the things that not everyone is aware of when thinking about Napoleon. We always see him on horseback, but he was also a workhorse himself, and he took an active part in the debates dealing with important issues, and he also would be very, very conscious of detail as well.

Although maintaining the possibility and the reality of "careers open to talent" (one of the main gains of the revolution, especially for the middle class), Napoleon accepted and promoted highly competent individuals from all political backgrounds, including royalists, and including royalists who had emigrated and returned. He encouraged real debate as long as his primacy was uncontested. Powerful and effective, prefects were appointed in each of France's departments—further centralizing power in Paris, and strengthened by an effective police presence as well. The name Fouchet, as head of the police is a name that was feared, just as the name Talleyrand as the brilliant foreign minister is a name that continues to be respected. One of the things that Napoleon was able to do is to get people like Fouchet and Talleyrand to serve him as they had served others and would continue to serve others after him.

Very importantly, because France was a Catholic country, a Concordat with the papacy was reached in July 1801. That was one of the legacies of the revolution that was most destabilizing and troubling. This was able to appease most Catholics, while still establishing the better part of state control over the church, with Catholicism now being the religion of the majority of Frenchmen. The state would nominate the bishop; the pope would invest the bishop. The issue of religion brings up the whole sense of Napoleon, who himself was very much a skeptic, but a skeptic who had big plans for the role of religion in society—because, as he said, "I see in religion not the mysteries of heaven, but the mysteries of the social order on Earth. Without religion, one would have anarchy."

And it was this opportunistic and utilitarian attitude toward religion that also was so true to so many other things that were part of his makeup. Gains made by Protestants and Jews—both very small minorities—during the first years of the revolution were also maintained.

Turning to the financial structure, and one of the issues that had plagued the revolution during most of its time prior to that point, was inflation and financial instability. A semi-private Bank of France was established in 1800 and France's currency was stabilized by 1803, ending (for a time) the economic instability that had characterized many of the previous years. To compare that with Great Britain, Great Britain already had a semi-private bank in the 1690s that worked on stabilizing its currency as much as was possible. But, of course, with greater technology through the 18th century, it was easier to do this as well.

Significantly, the major property changes that had occurred during the revolution were also maintained. This further ensured the support of most Frenchmen, including large numbers of the middle class who had acquired property, but including also most of the peasants, who had acquired more absolute rights over their small property, which was just as important, and even more important to them, because it was a question of survival.

Equality under the law, another major revolutionary gain, was also maintained and was of extreme importance. During this early phase, a number of other state-supporting institutions were created, such as some expanded secondary education and a university system for the elites, as well as the establishment of the Legion of Honor, especially for prominent state service, and especially for military service. Again, with his cynicism, Napoleon said, "It is by baubles that men are governed." He gave out more than 30,000 of those baubles to people he thought were deserving.

During the early years, France was able to defeat all of its military opponents fairly easily, even getting the British to sign an unequal Peace of Amiens in 1802. France was now not only at peace but in a dominant position in Europe, having made considerable gains along all of its borders. And remember, if those borders are in Switzerland, if they are in Belgium, if they are in western Germany, if they are in northern and southern Italy—wherever the French go, their new laws and ways of doing things go with them.

Since a large part of the war costs, at least in the early phase, were paid by the vanquished and by armies that lived off the land, and since security and order had been restored and maintained in France, the early phase of combat had been "cost effective" and largely very popular in France. This was not always to be the case, and certainly not at the end of Napoleon's regime. However, the second phase of his rule, from the early years of his emperorship until the Grand Army invaded Russia in June 1812, can be divided into two periods. Between 1804 and 1808, Napoleon continued to experience great success in almost all areas. *2 periods 1804-08*

These were the years during which most of the articles of the famous Napoleonic Code were devised and implemented. Often seen as the most meaningful gain of the revolution because it encapsulated all of the previous gains, it in effect guaranteed equality under the law for all men, and the subordination of women, property-like. It guaranteed contracts (including contracts over women) and the security of property, and it guaranteed careers, in theory, open to talent rather than to preferred birth. It was many volumes and excruciatingly detailed, and its positive elements were really positive—and its negative elements were negative. These laws were implemented for free men in French colonies; slavery was re-imposed where it had existed earlier in the French colonies. In many areas occupied by France or satellite to it, these laws became the normative goals for male constitutionalists for most of the 19th century. We need to remember there were already female constitutionalists also fighting to get their voices heard at the same time, and not having a very good time of it. Their arguments made complete sense as we look at them today, and we can wonder at how modern their arguments were and how sensible they were, and how much men did not want to go along with them. Protestants and Jews maintained equal rights, although Jews were shown both the carrot and the stick by Napoleon.

France continued to be relatively prosperous, as most of Napoleon's battles were still paid for by France's neighbors, including forced and voluntary recruiting into the French army. Now you wonder how Napoleon could have fought most of the rest of Europe (sometimes all at once). One of the ways he did it was by recruiting others. If Adolf Hitler had had that same wisdom, I really shudder to think of what he could have accomplished if he had been willing to recruit Poles and Ukrainians and turned them against Russians, instead of subduing them and mistreating them immediately. I don't even want to go there.

Although Admiral Nelson's second decisive victory at the Battle of Trafalgar (in October 1805)—and as he lay dying he kept on repeating, "I have done my duty. I have done my duty." And he knew his duty was to save England—prevented a French invasion of Great Britain, still, Napoleon achieved his greatest military victories in the next several years against Austria and Russia and Prussia at this time. He combined daring speed, a vision that allowed him to see the whole battlefield, massing forces and concentrating them at the enemy's weakness, outflanking them, moving in secret, using his artillery and (very, very importantly) enormous courage—standing in the front of the battlefield sometimes, or just behind—in front of his men and they knew he was there, and they knew he was with them—at least still during these earlier periods. We can go back to something he had said to his troops in 1796, just to get a sense of the vocabulary he used:

Soldiers, in two weeks you have won six victories; you have made 15,000 prisoners; you have killed or wounded more than 10,000 men. Deprived of everything, you have accomplished everything. You have won battles without cannons. Negotiated rivers without bridges. Made forced marches without shoes. Encamped without brandy, and often without bread.

The man knew how to speak to his troops, even if he would abuse them by overusing them from this point on. Napoleon defeated the Austrians at Ulm in 1805 and further crushed the Austro-Russian army at Austerlitz in December 1805. He defeated the Prussians at Jena and Auerstadt in 1806. He followed that up at the Battle of Friedland against the Russians in 1807. And then he dictated, in concert with Alexander I, the Peace of Tilsit, which marked French predominance over all of western and central Europe, allowing the Russians their predominance over eastern Europe. The reason I am emphasizing the geography is because, again, every extension of French power is an extension of French ideas and French procedures.

France annexed much territory and created satellite states that were mostly governed by Napoleon's brothers and other relatives, which allowed Napoleon to redraw much of the map of Europe. Significantly, in 1805 and in 1806, twice he redrew the map of Germany, reducing the number of states from more than 300 to about 19, followed by the abolition of the (by then) meaningless Holy Roman Empire. And without realizing it, by reducing the number of German states, he would be preparing the way for later German unification at France's discomfiture. But, of course, that's not how he thought history was going to proceed.

Still, even at the peak of his power during this time period, the Continental System he set up in 1806 to exclude British goods from Europe and make Britain accept French dominance was troubling, unenforceable, and raised problems throughout Europe, including in France. He had to try to beat England economically, since without a fleet that was strong enough, he could not invade her. He would gladly have done so—he would have preferred to have done so—if he could have created a fleet sufficient to do so. It might have been wise for him to have taken some time and done that, as well, rather than to have attacked Russia later. But again, that's another story, and Adolf Hitler was to make the same mistake 140 years later.

Between 1808 and 1812, French predominance began to unravel, even though Napoleon still won many decisive victories and continued to annex more territory. The Peninsular War, France's conquest of Portugal and Spain in 1808, became an open sore. When the French introduced into Spain things like ending the Inquisition and ending particular rights for nobles and ending the particular place of the church, this was so much contrary to Spanish cultural acceptance that they rebelled. And they rebelled effectively. Three hundred and fifty thousand French soldiers still could not destroy the Spanish guerrilla nationalist movement, supported by British money and then by British soldiers. This is where Wellington learned how to be a commander—a real commander, in action.

Nationalist reactions against French imperialism became even more prominent in parts of Germany, while military and other reforms in Prussia better prepared Prussia for the next round of conflict. Names like Stein, Hardenburg, Scharnhurst, and Nieschenelle become these very powerful German names as nationalism is spread and reform is spread in Prussia, and elsewhere in Germany as well. In other words, one of the things about the French armies and the Napoleonic armies that forced the pace of change is if the surrounding states didn't copy some of their procedures and reforms and offer something to their own people, even if only temporarily, they could not compete. They could not garner the passions of their own people without doing what the French were doing at the same time. And even afterwards, when they tried to take back many of those gains that had been made, it was in the memory bank, and it could never be totally rolled back.

Even with further defeats of Austria at Vagram in 1809, followed by the French annexation of the Netherlands and even more German territory, things continued to be resented. These exactions and taxations and billeting were resented, including in France. It was simply going on too long—too much of the same thing. He just didn't know when to stop.

The Continental System was leaking all over, including in Russia, and Russia was now ready for another round of conflict. Seemingly more irascible and divorced from reality, throwing caution to the wind, Napoleon "gambled" on the destruction of Russia, again, in order to finally bring Britain to heel—this time, going too far. There are different estimates on the size of the Grand Army, and there are different estimates of how many people actually returned to Paris when it was defeated. Some say it was more than 600,000. Others say it was 700,000. But it was a huge army that invaded Russia from Warsaw in June 1812. Tattered remnants returned to France months later. Some say 40,000 troops survived. Some say a larger number of men survived, but they were tattered and in terrible disarray by December of the same year, defeated by General Summer, even more by General Winter, General Space, and the Russians and the burning of Moscow. It seems that the Russians set Moscow afire, preventing the French from having respite there. This is the first time the man was really put to flight in the field.

Sensing the possibility of finally defeating Napoleon, the more battle-tested Russians, Prussians, Austrians, and British now cooperated more effectively in the final campaigns, ending Napoleon's dominance. Again, this is one of the things that Napoleon was able to do; he was able to divide them to reach treaties separately with them, so that they would get the best deal that they could get while they could, leaving others in the lurch. This time they had come to realize "He has to be stopped. And the only way to do it is for all of us to do it together, and hang in until the very end." And this is what they did.

Severely outnumbered, Napoleon was badly defeated in the Battle of the Nations (at Leipzig) in October 1813. The Allies then entered Paris at the end of March 1814, which was followed by Napoleon's abdication and his "comfortable" exile (at first) to the Island of Elba in the Mediterranean. Negotiating with Prince Talleyrand, who now was switching sides, the Allies wisely agreed on a non-punitive treaty for France. Even though nationalism was being born in this age, it was not yet an age of complete nationalism. The aristocratic monarchies did not have to worry about public opinion when they restored France to what it was and, in fact, even allowed it to have some of its early conquests. King Louis XVIII was placed on the throne, but he accepted a charter guaranteeing shared governance and many of the most important gains of the revolution. And, of course, this is what is so important about keeping those gains all the way throughout, even with a monarchical restoration. The clock could not be simply turned back. In this first phase, France kept the early territorial gains of 1792, which is known as its "natural" frontiers.

However, eluding the British, secretly Napoleon made a dramatic return to France. Incredibly, the army sent to subdue him melted in front of him, including marshals who embraced him when they were supposed to arrest him. The person's magnetism and charisma must have been extraordinary. But more overwhelmingly outnumbered, Napoleon was defeated on June 18, 1815, at Waterloo, outside of Brussels—packed off this time to hard exile on St. Helena in the South Atlantic, and apparently poisoned six years later in 1821.

Louis XVIII returned to France, now stripped of all of its territorial gains, but staying whole, and the French overwhelmingly were mostly glad to finally be at peace—and so was the rest of Europe. At peace, the Allies reached an intelligent postwar settlement at the Congress of Vienna. However, Europe would never be the same again. A number of revolutionary changes were maintained in France and even in some parts of Germany and elsewhere. Constitutional and national ways of thinking could not be erased, even if they could be temporarily suppressed.

At the same time—parallel to what was going on in France—more subtle, slower changes had begun to take place in England from the 1760s on—the early phase of what's known as the First British Industrial Revolution. By 1815, this change in England was advancing more quickly, and it would soon spread to the continent as well, certainly by the 1830s in Belgium first, and then in France, and then in other parts of Germany and northern Italy and several parts of the Austrian Empire (Bohemia, Moravia—Czechoslovakia, essentially). In other words, by the time that the Napoleonic reign ended, still the impact of the French Revolution was being felt everywhere—the fuller impact of the British Industrial Revolution joined it, to be the midwives of modern European history for the rest of the 19th century and, indeed, thereafter.

So, in our next set of comments, we will turn to the second major and even more massive development in human history, the First Industrial Revolution. Thank you.

Lecture Six
The First Industrial Revolution, 1760–1850

Scope:

Although scholars debate the origins of the Industrial "Revolution," all agree it was the main force propelling Europe's modernization and urbanization. Now understood more as a process, rather than a radical break, the Industrial Revolution transformed much of Britain's urban landscape over several generations; by 1850, Britain was the workshop of the world, with a greater productivity than the rest of Europe combined.

Sometimes referred to as the *classical* or *English Industrial Revolution*, concentrated largely in textiles and other consumer goods, it developed with less governmental involvement than the "heavy" industrial changes that occurred after 1850. Still, British preeminence was not accidental. The Isles benefited from nearly unique circumstances, including a relatively stable and tolerant political system; a more well-developed commercial and banking system; a more fluid social structure, including a large middle class; an expanded food supply derived from agrarian improvements; ample natural resources; colonial and European markets protected by the world's premier navy; a widespread "entrepreneurial" spirit; and a series of new inventions that facilitated the machine age.

Once this process took on momentum, it set Britain apart from its neighbors, who sought to catch up, following the hiatus of the Napoleonic wars. Although industrial productivity brought disruption, it brought wealth and power for states that followed suit; the converse was also true.

Outline

I. Although the Industrial Revolution, which can be traced to late 18th-century Britain, was more of a process than a historical event, it was the most powerful force of historical change in modern history.

    A. Involving the replacement of tools by machines with built-in guidance and energy, this revolution made possible undreamt-of levels of productivity, eventually mostly in large factories, and other great changes.

B. Included in these changes were revolutions in transportation and communications, rapid urbanization, mass literacy, a changed class structure, and eventually, a higher standard of living for most.

C. Industrialism also made possible the process of national integration of citizens into modern nation-states and changes in the European and global balance of power.

II. Although scholars disagree over the conjuncture of forces that caused or made possible the acceleration of industrial productivity in late 18th-century Britain (1760–1780), many apparent preconditions were most prominent there.

A. Relatively small in size and having had a "successful" political revolution in the late 17th century, Britain was relatively well governed and politically stable.

    1. There was acceptance of Britain's basic institutions, especially of shared governance.

    2. Government was relatively cheap and unobtrusive, yet favored policies conducive to all levels of economic expansion, including agriculture, commerce, and manufacturing.

    3. There was a high level of trust in the stability and durability of the system and even a belief in British exceptionalism.

    4. With the establishment of a private National Bank of England in 1694, acceptance of universal low-level taxation, and the sense that the national debt was guaranteed by the elites, Britain's financial and banking structure was comparatively well developed.

B. Britain's national success was based on the trilogy of commerce, colonies, and sea power, all giving economic advantages and inducements.

    1. Britain's colonial and commercial preeminence, closely connected, gave her excess capital for investment, as well as markets and sources of raw material.

    2. Trade in Britain conferred status, rather than being detested; not only did Britain have a diverse middle class, but there was social mobility among the wealthy elites.

3. Naval supremacy protected British commerce and blocked invasion, thus obviating an expensive standing army.

C. As with the Low Countries, Britain experienced a moderate agrarian revolution in the 18th century.

   1. Britain had larger farms, more efficient and intelligent forms of cultivation, and the use of fertilizer and nitrogen-fixating crops.

   2. Greater agrarian productivity led to more liquid capital.

   3. Agrarian revolution facilitated a significant population increase and expanding urban industrial labor force.

D. Britain was well endowed with coal and iron ore and had relatively well developed internal transportation.

E. British artisans and inventors produced a series of technological advances relating to the manufacture of textiles, putting them to industrial use.

F. The same was true with respect to steam power, linked with textiles and railroads, the sinews of British supremacy.

   1. Railroads for industrial use began in 1820; for passengers, in 1830.

   2. Britain first used steam for cross-Atlantic voyages in 1816.

III. Although scholars emphasize the gradual nature of early industrial changes, their aggregate impact was tremendous.

A. Although in 1780, the total value of British trade was slightly above France's, in 1840, British trade was double France's.

B. In 1850, Britain was producing about five times more coal than France and all the states of the Germanic Confederation and more steam power than the rest of Europe.

C. Inasmuch as the destabilization of the French Revolution and Napoleonic eras may have retarded industrial growth on the continent, while accelerating it in Britain, by 1815, Britain was the workshop and financial center of the world.

IV. Although the long-term impact of the Industrial Revolution(s) led to a better standard of living for most Europeans, this was probably not true until the second half of the 19th century.

A. Even if the process created more middling-level jobs, living conditions for most workers were terrible and almost totally unregulated until the 1830s, when some unions formed and more public attention was given to the situation; this was particularly true with respect to working conditions for women and children.

B. By the second quarter of the 19th century, British working and living conditions began to improve somewhat and would continue to do so after most workers obtained the right to vote in 1867 and expanded unions.

C. Religious and humanitarian reform efforts also played central roles in ameliorating conditions.

D. Most important was increasing productivity, making possible both profit and better living conditions.

V. If the first phase of the Industrial Revolution was largely a British affair, during the 1830s and 1840s, it spread to parts of France, Belgium, the Rhineland, the Ruhr region, Silesia, Bohemia, and parts of northern Italy.

Essential Reading:

Jan Goldstein and John W. Boyer, *Nineteenth-Century Europe*, pp. 62–82 (British Debates, Factory Legislation), pp. 202–215 (Artisans in France).

Karl Marx, *The Communist Manifesto*.

John Merriman, *A History of Modern Europe*, pp. 553–597.

Supplementary Reading:

C. A. Bayly, *The Birth of the Modern World*, pp. 49–83, 170–198.

Charles Dickens, *Hard Times*.

Questions to Consider:

1. What were the major gains and losses during the First Industrial Revolution?

2. What are the major political implications of this type of economic change?

Lecture Six—Transcript
The First Industrial Revolution, 1760–1850

Having spent the last two sessions together considering the rebellious and then militarily dominant French, we're going to turn today to an equally important, and indeed perhaps an even more important, event in human history (or process in human history). We turn our attention to the British, who, during the second half of the 18th century, became involved in a process known as the Industrial Revolution (or the First Industrial Revolution, the Classical Industrial Revolution, the British Industrial Revolution), which then spread to the rest of Europe after the 1830s and the second half of the 19th century. Our friend Eric Hobsbawm has called this probably the most important event in world history, at any rate since the invention of agriculture and cities—meaning it's pretty darn important.

Although the Industrial Revolution, which can be traced to late 18th-century Britain, was more of a process than a historical event or even a series of events, it was to be the most powerful force of historical change in modern history. Essentially involving the replacement of tools by machines with built-in guidance and energy, this long-term revolution made possible previously undreamt-of levels of productivity, eventually mostly in large factories, in large cities (new) with collective, dramatic impact on almost every aspect of society. Included in these changes were revolutions in transportation and communications, rapid urbanization, growing and then mass literacy, a changed class structure—a greatly changed class structure over time—and, during the second half of the 19th century, even higher standards of living for most who lived in industrialized societies, including the working class and peasants.

Industrialism also made possible the gradual process of national integration, including most citizens in modern nation-states. It made possible radical changes in the European and global balance of power. It made possible industrial warfare. It made possible mostly European control over the greater part of the globe until after World War II—joined at the end of the 19th century by the newer, non-European industrial powers of the United States and Japan.

Although scholars disagree over the precise conjuncture of forces that caused or made possible this acceleration of industrial productivity in late-18th-century Great Britain, from, say, 1760 to 1780 or so, many seeming preconditions were more prominent there than anywhere else. Scholars debate this, and now have come to realize that some of those preconditions (in fact, many of them) were also present in places such as areas of China or areas of India, but not in the same entire conjuncture as occurred in Great Britain at that time. Relatively small in size and having had a "successful" political revolution in the late 17th century (the so-called "Glorious Revolution" of 1688), Britain was relatively well governed and politically stable. Again, this is very ironic because in the 17th century, the English were looked down upon as revolutionaries, people who engaged in terrible civil war and then murdered their king—regicides. But by the end of the century, they had put this in their past—as it turned out, establishing a stable political system. There was general acceptance on the part of a broad spectrum of opinion on Britain's basic institutions, including (and sometimes even especially) shared governance—constitutional monarchy. Governance was relatively cheap and relatively unobtrusive, yet it favored policies conducive to all levels of economic expansion—from agriculture to commerce and manufacturing. A series of enclosure laws during the 18th century, for example, made possible the development of larger farms under the control of aristocrats not pleasing the tenant farmers or the other day laborers who were pushed off the common lands, but eventually making possible greater productivity and work for almost everyone.

There was a high level of trust in the stability and durability of the system. By the 18th century, there was even a belief in British exceptionalism. She had defeated the Spanish at the end of the 16th century. She had defeated the Dutch at the end of the 17th century. And, during the course of the 18th century, she defeated the French, primarily, as well, especially in areas relating to navy, commerce, and colonies. With the establishment of a private National Bank of England in 1694, there occurred greater acceptance of universal low-level taxation because the economy was stable, basically, and a sense that the national debt was guaranteed by the nation's elites, collectively. Therefore, Britain's financial and banking structure was comparatively well developed and sound.

The Dutch had achieved a similar circumstance, and both the Dutch and the Brits could get loans at about half of the interest of what the French government was forced to pay for loans, or other French business enterprises would pay for loans. Britain's national success was based on a trilogy of commerce, colonies, and sea power—

commerce, colonies, and sea power—all giving her economic advantages in an interrelated way, and all giving her inducements for further development. Britain's colonial and commercial preeminence, which were closely connected, gave her excess capital for investment. It also gave her markets and sources of raw material. Capital. Markets. Raw material. Three of the main things needed for industry.

There was a different kind of attitude in England, even on the part of the elites. Trade in Britain conferred status, as the 18th-century novelist Daniel Defoe said, "Trade in England makes gentlemen." In most parts of the world, an aristocrat would not touch trade, and didn't really want to work for money, but rather inherited wealth. The British aristocrats were not above earning more money and expanding their wealth by labor, even—all right, not physical labor, but labor. Not only did Great Britain have a relatively large, diverse, and growing middle class, but there was greater social mobility and intercourse among the wealthy elites, including even many of the aristocrats.

Naval supremacy protected British commerce, protected Britain from invasion, and also protected her against having to maintain continental-style expensive and dangerous standing armies— dangerous because the king can use those armies (if the commanders are loyal to him) against the Parliament and against the achieved acceptance of shared governance. And it also costs less.

As with the Low Countries, Britain experienced a moderate agrarian revolution in the 18th century as well, with names like "Turnip" Townshend being remembered. Britain had larger farms, more efficient and intelligent forms of cultivation than crop rotation, and the use of fertilizer and nitrogen-fixating crops. And, of course, greater agrarian productivity led to higher profits, and therefore even to more liquid capital.

However, greater agrarian productivity also led to the possibility and the reality of an increased population and an increased labor supply. And that labor supply is another one of those essentials for any industrial revolution. So the agrarian revolution not only facilitated a significant increase in population, but the capacity to support an expanding urban industrial labor force as well.

Britain was well endowed with such natural resources as coal and iron ore. Britain already had a relatively well-developed internal transportation system—comparatively better roads, lots of rivers, always being close to the ocean. So, even its smaller size gave it an advantage in terms of movement and in terms of the conjunction of all of these separate forces coming together at one point and feeding off of each other. By the mid-18th century, British artisans and inventors were producing a series of technological advantages— advances mainly relating to the manufacture of textiles—while they and other entrepreneurs were putting them to good and wider industrial use, especially with steam engines and then later with railroads. So, you have names like Hargraves, Arkwright, Crompton, and Cartwright in terms of textiles; you have names like Watt, Boulton, and Stephenson in terms of steam engines and the like and other industrial processes. And then you have names like Adam Smith, Malthus, and Ricardo—people who stepped back and thought about what was the meaning of all of these changes that were occurring. It's not accidental that *The Wealth of Nations*, this great economic tract, was published by an Englishman in 1776.

So, the same was soon to be true in the mysteries of steam power, which had already been true in terms of the mysteries of expanding textile production, and they were linked with textiles and railroads, which were the joint sinews of British industrial supremacy. In fact, most of the First Industrial Revolution occurred mainly in textiles, in cottons, and woolens and things that poorer people also needed, and they were transported by railroads, which for industrial use began in 1820 and then expanded during the 1820s. Those for passengers were first employed in 1830, and in that particular area, the continental Europeans did catch up fairly quickly. Germany had its first railroads in 1835. But the British still had a lead even in that domain, and if you want to think about the importance of the railroad in all of this, pick up any of Charles Dickens's novels. The Iron Horse dominates the age. Britain first used steam for cross-Atlantic voyages in 1816, and the use of steamboats spread to the continent in the 1820s and thereafter.

Although scholars now emphasize the gradual nature of early industrial changes even in Britain, their aggregate impact was becoming important toward the end of the 18th century, and becoming dramatic during the second quarter of the 19th century. While in 1780, the total value of British trade was perhaps slightly above French trade, in 1840, Britain's trade was double France's, although France's population was still basically double Britain's. This signifies a considerable, indeed a radical, change.

In 1850, Britain was producing about five times the amount of coal as France and all the states of the Germanic Confederation combined, including Austria, and was in fact utilizing more steam power—double the amount of steam power—as the rest of Europe combined. By 1850, nearly half of the largest 10 cities in Europe were in Britain—those new, industrial cities. And by 1850, Britain was also already 50 percent urban—the only other state in that category was Belgium, not surprisingly, which became the second industrializing power in the 1830s, while France was only 25 percent urban, and would not become 50 percent urban until either right before or right after World War I, 1914–1918.

Inasmuch as the collective uprootedness and instability of the French Revolution and the Napoleonic years may have retarded the Industrial Revolution on the continent, while accelerating it in Britain, by 1815, Britain was clearly the workshop and the financial center of the world.

Although the long-term impact of the Industrial Revolution (or Revolutions, because it is a continuous process) led to a better standard of living for most Europeans, this was probably not true until the second half of the 19th century. Even if the process created more middling-level jobs, brutal living conditions for most workers were terrible and in an almost totally unregulated system until the 1830s—and even then the regulation was insufficient and not applied—when some unions finally began to form in the 1830s, the union laws finally having facilitated that when the combination acts preventing unions were finally repealed in 1824, and when more public attention was given to the horrendous situation of workers—and most particularly to women and children, who were more easily manipulated and forced to work under grueling conditions with less resistance than men. In many cases, some of the men used to break machinery—the Luddites, especially artisans, sometimes even in an organized fashion, and sometimes even during the Napoleonic wars themselves.

So, many of these tasks, especially in textiles, could be more easily done by women and children. In fact, as one apologist for this early industrial process (Andrew Ewer) said, it is almost impossible to get children adjusted to the timing, constraints, and discipline of the factory system once they enter puberty. So, it's much better to deal with them when they are six and seven years old. In fact, he said further, the main difficulty above all was in training human beings to renounce their desultory habit of work, and to identify themselves with the unswerving regularity of complex automation. That doesn't sound like much fun.

Even if the quantity of living conditions may have improved somewhat for some people, the quality of life probably declined at first. Separation of family members probably increased; communal support structures probably declined; and adjusting to the tempo of machine labor and the growing ubiquitousness of the clock must have been extremely difficult. Even some of the hardest critics of early industrial society still ring true today, such as Karl Marx, "Capitalism came into the world steeped in mire, from top to toe, and oozing blood from every pore." Or the Hammonds, who studied the Industrial Revolution in the earlier 20th century, who said the curse of Midas was on this society.

The British began to even investigate this as early as 1815, in Parliamentary committees. One investigation went this way, as a young Elizabeth Bentley was queried:

> What age are you?
> Twenty-three.
> Where do you live?
> Leeds.
> What time did you begin work at the factory?
> When I was six years old.
> What were your hours of labor in the mill?
> From five in the morning until nine at night.
> What time were you allowed for meals?
> Forty minutes at noon.
> Did they keep you constantly on your feet?
> Yes. There are so many frames and they run so quick your labor is very excessive. Yes, you have not time for anything.
> Suppose you flagged a little, or were late. What would they do?
> Strap us or beat us.
> And they are in the habit of strapping those who are last in their work?

Yes.

Constantly?

Yes.

Girls and boys?

Yes.

Have you ever been strapped?

Yes.

Severely?

Yes.

And it continued and continued.

But at least the British began to ask those questions as early as 1815. And what we have to remember in terms of this particular industrial process is that this was the first. And the firsts are always more difficult because there was no past tense. There was no history. We also have to remember that subsistence-level rural life was not pretty, and it could never be pretty because it was based on the whims of nature. So, without some kind of industrial, mechanized, agrarian productivity, most people lived on the brink of starvation and would always live on the brink of starvation.

By the second quarter of the 19th century, British working and living conditions began to improve somewhat, and they certainly would do so after most workers obtained the right to vote in 1867, and increasingly joined unions as well. Religious and humanitarian and political reform efforts also played central roles in ameliorating conditions. For example, in 1843, William J. Fox made a speech to the Anti-Corn-Law League. Fox was a radical. He was a friend of Bentham and a friend of John Stuart Mill. He was making a speech that helped in the end to destroy the Corn Laws and make possible free trade in grain, which lowered the price of food for these very workers. So, he's not an apologist for any of this industrial development. But he talked about machinery at the same time in this speech to this crowd of people. He said the following:

> When machinery is employed in manufacture, what is the natural result? Production is cheaper. Goods, apparel of various kinds, are brought to market at a lower rate. The use of it is diffused more extensively in society. People have enjoyments and accommodation which they did not possess. The demand has increased, and this again reacts on production. More hands are employed, and in the natural

course of things, there is found to be more work, more wages, and more enjoyment.

It can't be clearer than that. What happened is that issues like this were not only debated outside of Parliament in civil society, by tribunes of the people, but they were debated in Parliament as well, after the meeting of commissions, leading to a series of regulatory legislation from the early 1830s throughout the whole rest of the century. For example, the debates over factory laws in 1846 and 1847. Thomas Babbington McCauley, who earlier had championed voting rights for the middle class and for some workers, talking about child labor laws concerning women and children. Remember, that is contrary to *laissez-faire*; that is contrary to government non-intervention, which was like a religion. So, they are criticizing their own religion in a sense, their own secular religion.

> Is there a single gentleman so zealous for the principles of free trade as to admit that he might consent to the restriction of commercial transactions when higher and other considerations are concerned? Take questions of police.

Or:

> Why do you interfere with free contract between two people? The answer would be that a boy of immature age cannot secure himself from injury, and the state is his guardian. But the property of the poor and the young lies in his health and strength and skill—the health both of his body and of his mind.

In other words, before 1850 you're beginning to get not only extra-Parliamentary beacons and unions beginning to form, but more responsible, articulate people within the British Parliament coming out and saying, "This needs to be regulated. The state needs to get involved. *Laissez-faire* be damned, at least in this particular instance"—even though *laissez-faire* remained one of the secular religions of Great Britain until after World War I.

Even more important, however, was the simple fact of increasing productivity, making possible both profit and better living conditions. The worst thing in a society is disruption caused by rioting, striking, breaking machinery. And the British figured out a way during the course of the 19th century to modify and lessen those three things, although they still continued to happen.

If the first phase of the Industrial Revolution was largely a British affair, during the 1830s and 1840s, it spread to parts of Belgium; France; the Rhineland and the Ruhr in the Germanys; Silesia, which also had become part of Prussia; and Bohemia and Moravia, which were part of the Austro-Hungarian or Austrian Empire (now Czechoslovakia). In many cases, aware of the British lead, continental governments played a greater role in stimulating the process, particularly in areas with potential military application, as in the transportation sector, or even in banking and the beginning of protective tariffs, or anything having to do with military hardware. The British had an incredible lead in 1850. And this world was more and more interconnected, and others were aware of that. Their awareness radically expanded during the British First Universal Exposition in 1851, with that magnificent Crystal Palace that showed the world where Britain had come and what they had better do if they wanted to keep pace in this competitive state system. The central European and west European states understood it quickly, caught on, and began to press ahead in these areas. Russia did not because they understood also, implicitly, that this industrialization would change the whole very fabric and assumptions of their entire civilization, based primarily on agrarianism, tradition, and continuity.

Still, after the 1850s, the British lead was monumental. And the predominant questions that faced the continent before 1850, especially in western and central Europe, were the unresolved issues from the French Revolution and the Napoleonic era. In other words, in the 1830s and even more in the 1840s, growing urbanization, the growth of the beginning of factories, the transference of industry and railroads, became issues of concern and change in western Europe. The most burning issues in western Europe between 1815 and the revolutions of 1848 were still the unresolved issues of the French Revolution and the Napoleonic era: issues of constitutionalism, issues of nationalism and national identity, issues of equal opportunity (career open to talent), and what place would the middle class have in society during this whole process.

Thank you.

Lecture Seven
The Era of Metternich, 1815–1848

Scope:

The years between the Congress of Vienna and the outbreak of revolutions in 1848 were turbulent, characterized by tensions between the forces of order and the forces of change. The forces of order, represented by Prince Clemens von Metternich, generally dominated, especially in Austria, Prussia, and Russia. However, in Britain and France, a more liberal, constitutional world emerged, far more naturally in "England" and via revolution, in 1830, in France.

In the aftermath of the revolutionary and Napoleonic wars, European statesmen, at Vienna and thereafter, established a more stable international order, dominated by the great powers, including France, in a loose *Concert of Europe*. Conflict and tensions existed, but they were kept in bounds. Meanwhile, constitutional and nationalist revolutions broke out, mostly in 1820 and 1830, as dreams inspired by the French Revolution, especially among urban populations, went largely unfulfilled. Still, this era saw peace and material progress, and its romantic temper was dominated by those who thought ideas mattered.

With the hungry 1840s, particularly the agrarian and urban crises of 1846–1847, tensions came to a head, especially when revolt broke out in Paris in February 1848. Barricades, violence, and mystical expectations dominated, and King Louis Philippe and Prince Metternich took flight.

Outline

I. The Congress of Vienna (November 1814–June 1815) served as a dividing line between the Revolutionary and Restoration eras.

   A. Dominated by Prince Clemens von Metternich of Austria and, to a lesser extent, by Count Robert Castlereagh of Britain, the great powers sought to restore the old order, using the principles of legitimacy, compensation, and balance to ensure stability and peace.

   B. Their goals were to prevent the revival of French expansion, to preserve a general balance of power in Europe, and to prevent the outbreak of further revolutions and wars.

C. Although there were tensions and fears among the victorious powers— including fear that Russia could replace France as hegemon—intelligent decision making and the desire for peace often prevailed.
1. With the connivance of Prince Talleyrand, France was "rehabilitated" as a member of the balance of power. The Peace of Paris was not Punic, and France joined the postwar *Concert of Europe,* or *Congress system,* including the Holy Alliance, championed by Tsar Alexander I.
2. The four victorious great powers found ways to compromise and to divide the spoils of war; monarchs were "returned" to states or states were "invented" for them.
3. The powers created a 39-member Germanic Confederation, or *Bund,* to stabilize the German states, where Napoleon had wreaked havoc.
4. Except for Britain, the powers placated the more mystical/ romantic Tsar Alexander I, joining his proposed Holy Alliance and adding a Christian dimension to the "sacred" tasks of peace and stability.

D. Most decisions reached at the Congress of Vienna helped facilitate peace among the great powers, the most prominent marker of the 1815–1848 era, even during the revolutions of 1848.

E. Still, not only were there disagreements between powers, but meaningful and "legitimate" desires of many of the peoples of Europe were ignored, especially with respect to constitutional and national issues.
1. The British, unsympathetic toward repression in Europe and with respect to rebellions in Latin America, soon withdrew from the Congress system.
2. Following the "liberal" French revolution of 1830, the French often sided with the British against the more conservative Austro-Prussia-Russian alliance.
3. "Old Europe" could not be reconstructed; not even an alliance between throne and altar (monarchy and church) could prevent change.

Revolutionary Legacy

II. The impact of the revolutionary legacy (ideas, experiences) and of industrial changes (more in Britain) made change or conflict inevitable.

    A. Internally, and sometimes externally, European society was loosely divided between the forces of change and the forces of order.

        1. The active forces of order included monarchs, aristocrats, and most churchmen, especially on the continent and even more so in Austria, Prussia, and Russia.

        2. Although moderate conservatives, more so in France and Britain, accepted slow change, Metternichians lumped constitutional or national change into the same basket—*verboten* ("forbidden").

        3. The forces of order used military and bureaucratic power to repress forces of change.

        4. Depending on the issue or the place, artisans, peasants, workers, or members of the middle class could also crave some form of "order."

    B. The active forces of change consisted of various proponents, mostly but not exclusively among members of an expanding middle class.

        1. Liberals, radicals (democrats), and some socialists sought constitutional changes, along the lines of the French Revolution or the British experience.

        2. Nationalists, usually liberal or radical, sought independence from "foreign" occupiers, or in the case of "Germans" and "Italians," a wider unification of their compatriots, defined by language, culture, and history.

        3. Middle-class elements sought the ideal of careers open to talent.

        4. The poor sought more food, protection, the removal of repressive laws, or in central and eastern Europe, the removal of the remnants of feudalism or serfdom.

III. As a result of the obvious clash of interests and worldviews and the inability of conservatives, except in Britain, to reach compromises, especially with the growing members of the middle class, riots and revolutions occurred repeatedly between 1815–1848.

A. Sometimes they occurred in spasms, with increasing range and intensity in 1820, 1830, and 1848.

B. Although most were repressed, there were a number of "successes" from 1815–1848.

   1. Greece gained independence from the Ottoman Empire during the 1820s, formally accepted in 1832.

   2. Belgium gained independence from Holland in 1830, formally guaranteed in 1839.

   3. A number of Latin American nations gained independence from Spain and Portugal in the 1820s.

C. The best example of an intelligent avoidance of violent revolution and a co-opting of the middle class was the British Reform Bill of 1832.

IV. Other major themes were prominent during the 1815–1848 era.

A. The humanities, especially philosophy and history, were held in great esteem.

B. Continentals stressed the power of ideas as the main source of meaning and change, in the work of such German philosophers as Kant and especially Hegel.

C. Early "utopian" socialists included Charles Fourier, Henri de Saint Simon, Louis Blanc, Robert Owen, and others, and the anarchism of Pierre-Joseph Proudhon.

D. There was also a religious revival during this era.

E. All these tendencies were related to the dominant Romantic tone of the epoch, evident in literature, art, and music.

F. The 1815–1848 era was often an age of frustration. Constitutionalist and liberal nationalist expectations were often dashed.

G. Until the mid-1840s, it was a time of economic improvement and of the gradual spread of industrial advances to parts of western and central Europe.

V. Severe agrarian depression, from traditional crop failures in 1845–1847, led to urban recession, as well, placing many areas of society in a situation of "overload," ripe for rebellion and violence.

Essential Reading:

John Carey, *Eyewitness to History*, pp. 293–320.

Robert Gildea, *Barricades and Borders, Europe 1800–1914*, pp. 55–79.

John Merriman, *A History of Modern Europe*, pp. 598–661.

Supplementary Reading:

Charles Breunig and Matthew Levinger, *The Revolutionary Era, 1789–1850*, pp. 127–265.

Barbara Caine and Glenda Sluga, *Gendering European History*, pp. 1–86.

Questions to Consider:

1. Why were the conservative elites so resistant to change during this era?

2. What seem to be the wider implications of the Romantic movement?

Lecture Seven—Transcript
The Era of Metternich, 1815–1848

Having put the great Napoleon to rest (although he still is going to jump forward and disturb our dreams for a moment or two this morning), and having also considered the Industrial Revolution that was taking place in Britain, parallel to the time period we're going to discuss today, we now turn to what is usually called Restoration Europe, or sometimes simply just the era of Metternich, between 1815 and 1848.

The Congress of Vienna, which met from November 1814 to June 1815, and the settlement it created served as a dividing line between the Revolutionary era and the era of the Restoration. Dominated by Prince Clemens von Metternich of Austria and, to a lesser extent, by Count Robert Castlereagh of Great Britain, and also occasionally by Alexander I of Russia, the great powers sought to restore the old order—as much as was possible—using the principles of legitimacy, compensation, and balance in order to ensure stability and preserve the peace. They used those principles advisedly, discarding them when it was in their interest to do so. Their most important goals were to prevent the revival of French expansionism and revolution, to preserve a general balance of power in Europe, and to prevent the outbreak of further revolutions and wars, intimately connected as they were. By 1815, almost everyone understood implicitly how closely tied were war and revolution, and how revolutionary actually was war as a human experience.

Although there were many tensions and fears among the victorious powers—including the seemingly justifiable fear that Russia could now replace France as the new hegemon (the new dominant power)—generally intelligent decision-making and an understandable desire for peace and stability often prevailed. And Metternich was a master at that, as also was Prince Talleyrand, who was representing France and who helped "rehabilitate" France in an essential manner in the balance of power, playing an active role in the negotiations. Indeed, the meeting at Vienna is sometimes compared to the meetings at Versailles, an entire 100 years later, to show how much more intelligently it was done at Vienna than later at Versailles, although the Napoleonic wars and World War I were two totally different kinds of human experiences.

Talleyrand did serve many masters, including the revolution and Napoleon, and he basically was a wily and brilliant diplomat—one of the true greats of the age. Although France gave up additional territory following Napoleon's Hundred Days (he comes back to haunt us), accepting the lesser boundary that was its in 1789, rather than the more expanded boundary of the Revolution of 1792, the Peace of Paris was not Punic in nature, especially when it concerned France. Although there was an Allied occupation for three years, the Allied troops left by 1818. Shortly thereafter France joined the postwar *Concert of Europe*, or *Congress system*, including the Holy Alliance championed by the somewhat mystic and somewhat more romantic Tsar Alexander I of Russia, to which the British were not willing to agree.

Although there were tensions, the four initial great powers (Great Britain, Russia, Austria, and Prussia) found ways to compromise and to divide the spoils of war in a reasonable way (at least to them), and at least in terms of immediate stability. For example, Austria gave up the Austrian Netherlands (Belgium) to Holland, but they took control of northern Italy (Lombardy and Venetia)—a fair trade. Monarchs were either "returned" to states or states were "invented" for them.

Austria, under Metternich's tutelage, for the whole era until 1848, which is why this era is justly known as the Age of Metternich—Austria was primarily responsible for overseeing security in the states of Italy, both in northern Italy and also in Naples and Sicily. Austria and Prussia would provide stability with respect to the settlements in the German states, and a Germanic *Bund* was recreated—a confederation of 39 states, in which Austria was always the president, and Prussia was always the vice-president. And they worked well together until 1848, generally accepting that relationship because they had so much in common.

Austria, Prussia, and Russia agreed on a settlement to maintain their annexations of Polish territory. How easy it is to agree when what you are agreeing on doesn't really belong to you. The powers also agreed more or less on several other mechanisms with which to ensure peace and to maintain the status quo. The powers agreed to hold a series of Congresses in order to further discuss issues and problems that might arise. The powers formed a loosely defined Concert of Europe of the great powers, for the same purpose. And even after the Concert of Europe ceased to function by the Crimean

War in any really important way, as late as the end of the century, statesmen were still discussing the Concert of Europe in their diplomatic dispatches.

As I indicated earlier, the powers created a 39-member Germanic Confederation, or a Bund, in order to stabilize the Germanic states, where Napoleon had wreaked havoc. Before the French Revolution there had been more than 300 separate states in Germany—everything from bishoprics, to cities, to full-size states. Napoleon took a look at that madness and reduced it to below 20. At Vienna, they reestablished it at a nice number of 39.

Except for Great Britain, the powers placated the more mystical and romantic Tsar Alexander I, joining in his proposed Holy Alliance and adding a Christian additional dimension to the "sacred" tasks of peace and stability. For the British, religious though they were, this was too corny, and they didn't want to be involved in it.

Most decisions reached at the Congress of Vienna helped facilitate a generation of peace among the great powers. And indeed, this peace between 1815 and 1848 is one of the most prominent markers of the entire era, which even held during the revolutions of 1848. That tells us how much they had suffered from the continuous wars of the French Revolution and the Napoleonic era. It was not just the wisdom at Vienna, but the clear understanding that war and revolution were to be avoided at almost any cost that helps us understand how that peace was able to be maintained during the first half of the 19th century.

Still, not only were there disagreements between powers, but meaningful and "legitimate" desires of many of the peoples of Europe were ignored by the Viennese statesmen, or the statesmen at Vienna, especially with respect to constitutional and national issues. And here we come to some of the negative elements and even hypocritical elements of the Congress of Vienna. The feelings of the Belgians were not consulted, nor were the Czechs, or the Hungarians, or the Poles, or the Serbs, or the Greeks. And the feelings of middle-class liberals or democrats, for whom the French Revolution had represented hope and a future—they were not consulted either.

The British—who were far more liberal than any of the other continental powers, unsympathetic to the repeated anti-revolutionary repressions, both in Europe and with respect to the rebellions in Latin America—soon withdrew from the Congress system because they just really didn't want to be part of it. Indeed, the famous Monroe Doctrine is also part of that. Rebellions in Latin America after 1815, especially in the 1820s—the European states were considering how to overcome those rebellions and restore these colonies to their rightful European masters. We issued the Monroe Doctrine, but what backed it up was the power of the British fleet—who wanted no part and made it clear that they did not want and would not countenance any part of a re-conquest, because their economic interests then were primarily involved in maintaining the newer structure in Latin America.

Following the "liberal" French Revolution of 1830, in which Louis Philippe (sometimes known as "The *Bourgeois* King" or "The Citizen King") became a constitutional monarch, the French often sided with the British against the more conservative Austro-Prussia-Russian alliance. But we should not make too much of this ideology in politics during this time period. The British and the French also quarreled over issues in Egypt and the Ottoman Empire, so their liberalism only brought them together just so far. And politics was not that ideological during this age. That would be one of the areas in which the revolutions of 1848 would add an additional ideological resonance, separating liberalism and conservatism in the great powers themselves.

However, "Old Europe" could not simply be reconstructed by a series of diplomats meeting in Vienna, or even by a series of diplomats meeting occasionally thereafter. Even the alliance between throne and altar, monarchy and church and aristocracy could not always prevent change. Change was there implicitly throughout, and change and continuity, and forces of change and forces of continuity, were always in tension—quite frequently during this era in direct conflict. The continued impact of the revolutionary legacy (ideas, experiences, myths, memories, practitioners) and the slow impact of industrial changes—far more dramatic in Great Britain, but after 1830 working their way into France, Belgium, northern Italy, the Ruhr, the Rhineland, Silesia, and Bohemia—also made change or conflict (indeed, both) virtually inevitable. Both internally and sometimes externally, European society was loosely divided between the forces of change and the forces of order. The active forces of order were symbolized most prominently by Metternich and his system. It included the monarchs, the aristocrats, and most of the clergy (although there were liberal clergy—usually told to keep quiet), especially on the continent and even more so in Austria, Prussia, and Russia, where this alliance was maintained throughout. Although moderate conservatives, more so in France and Britain, accepted slow change, Metternichians lumped any constitutional or national change into the same basket—*verboten* ("forbidden"). And what they didn't understand (and this is really their weakness, which is surprising given Metternich's intelligence) is by putting liberals, democrats, socialists, and nationalists all in the same basket, you can't co-opt any of them. Liberals were fairly moderate, but they were no more accepted by Metternichians than were democrats, socialists, and radical nationalists. So, by failing to distinguish between their opponents, they could not co-opt them; they made conflict all the more likely. Indeed, it occurred.

The forces of order willingly used military and bureaucratic power to repress the forces of change—internally or elsewhere, whenever possible. They used spies; they used censorship; they used militias; they used the army; they used whatever they needed. And occasionally this even happened in England, as in 1819 in the Peterloo Massacres, when troops charged on horses a crowd of people demonstrating the reform of Parliament, killing a number and wounding 500, and leaving the poet Shelley to pronounce:

> I met Murder on the way—
> He had a mask like Castlereagh—

So, even in Great Britain, things like this happened—all the more so in Italy and in the states of Germany and in Poland. Depending on the issue and the place, however, even artisans, peasants, workers, or members of the middle class could also crave "order," depending on how one defines it and depending on what their self-interest was at that particular time. For example, artisans—who generally belonged to guilds that protected their terms of labor—were not very happy about the newer mechanization of industry that was beginning to seep into the continent. In fact, they liked to break those new machines because it cost them jobs. Peasants, once they had some land, wanted stability and less contact with the state. So, any group could be conservative or traditional at a particular moment in time.

But, generally speaking, the active forces of change consisted of a larger array of elements—mostly, but not exclusively, among expanding numbers of the middle class, which continued to grow even when there wasn't predominant industrial change. There was continued urban, commercial expansion by and large during this time period, at least until 1847 or so. Moderate constitutional liberals, radical democrats (and even they were not so radical—not in our terms), and some early socialists sought constitutional changes along the lines of those suggested earlier in the French Revolution or in Great Britain. Great Britain continued to be a model for this change as well. Nationalists, usually liberal or radical, sought either independence from "foreign" occupiers, or in the case of "Germans" (middle class mainly) and "Italians" (more middle class), a wider unification of their compatriots, either in a confederation or some sort of union that would make Germany look more like France and Great Britain, and give it the power of France and Great Britain— defined by language, culture, and history, and sometimes also in more conservative nationalism defined by ethnicity.

Middle-class elements continued to seek jobs, careers open to talent, not preserved for petty nobles and great aristocrats. Remember, when aristocrats controlled the state, it was socialism for the rich, or socialism for the well born. It was aristocrats, and children of aristocrats, and petty nobles who got placement, where harder-working, newer-learned members of the middle class couldn't get access if they didn't have contacts—or, if they had improper opinions.

The poor sought more food, always. They still lived on the margin— protection, removal of repressive laws, and in central and eastern Europe, the removal of the remnants of feudalism or of actual serfdom, which continued to exist in Austria, parts of Prussia, and throughout the Russian Empire, where half the people were still serfs—slaves, bondage. As a result of the obvious clash of interests and worldviews and the inability of conservatives, except in Great Britain, to reach compromises, especially with the growing members of the middle class—including merchants, lawyers, journalists, and students—riots and/or revolutions occurred repeatedly throughout Europe between 1815 and 1848. Sometimes they occurred in spasms, with increasing range: in 1820 and the early 1820s somewhat limited, in 1830 and the early 1830s even more widespread—*Les Miserables*, Victor Hugo, *Consuma*, a riot that actually took place in Lyons—the second city of France—in the early 1830s, and especially in 1848, known as "the springtime of the peoples," in which riots, rebellions, and revolution broke out in almost all of the major cities on the continent in western and central Europe, although not in Russia and not in England.

Although most of these riots, rebellions, strikes, protests, and gatherings were repressed, and sometimes severely, there were a number of major "successes" between 1815 and 1848, for the forces of change. Greece gained independence from the Ottoman Empire during the 1820s, in its rebellion, formally accepted in 1832. Now Greece, Athens, Athens! Freedom! The Olympics. The Ottoman Empire. The powers were caught in a bind there because they wanted the stability of the Ottoman Empire. They didn't want it destabilized. That could be dangerous. But the Greeks were Christian, and the Ottomans were Moslem. The Greeks were the source of western identity. The Moslems were not. The Ottomans were not. So the populists supported the Greeks.

Belgium—mainly Catholic—gained independence from Holland— mainly Protestant—in 1830, formally guaranteed in 1839. And let us remember that Protestant and Catholic mattered a lot in the 19th century. A number of Latin American nations, as I've already indicated, gained independence from the Spanish Empire in the 1820s, and from the Portuguese Empire as well, the mammoth state of Brazil.

The classic and best example of an intelligent avoidance of violent revolution and the co-opting of the middle class was obviously the British Reform Bill of 1832, although it was presaged by some violence as well. The king actually threatened to create more peers, but the House of Lords wouldn't pass the bill. And the great historian/parliamentarian Macaulay got up and said, "We drive over to the forces of revolution those who we keep out of power." In other words, let's co-opt members of the middle class. They will become members of order and not members of revolution. Push them in a corner. Don't give them their due. No taxation without representation. You're going to cause a revolution. The British learned how to do without that problem, even though there was still plenty of violence in British society.

There were a number of other major themes and tendencies during this era that were extremely, extremely important. And kindly for us historians, it was an age in which the humanities, especially philosophy and history, were held in great esteem. Ideas were held to be extremely important—the time of Kant and Goethe in the earlier period, of Hegel, and many, many others—a time in which the power of ideas was held to be really significant. This also comes from the ideas that were represented during the French Revolution and the Napoleonic era, and that were also widely dispersed throughout the Romantic era and that predominated in that post-Napoleonic time period as well.

The age even saw the development of a number of "utopian" socialist theories, such as those of Charles Fourier, Henri de Saint Simon, Louis Blanc, Robert Owen in Great Britain, and the early anarchism of Pierre-Joseph Proudhon in his pamphlet, "What Is Property?" "Property is theft," he said. Now let's stop for a minute here. Who gave us the idea that these people were utopian? None other than Uncle Karl—Karl Marx. Why were they utopian? Because they weren't blood thirsty. They didn't understand that there had to be a class struggle. They didn't understand that there had to be violence. Some of them thought that persuasion would work. Some of them thought that you could communicate with the capitalists and humanitarians. Some of them thought you could form unions. Some of them thought you could form cooperatives. They don't sound all that utopian to me, although there would be violence, to be sure, but not the kind that Marx thought was absolutely essential. And as we will see later, Marx had a good streak of utopianism in his thinking and his worldview as well.

In contrast, there was also a widespread religious revival during this era. There was the pietism in Germany, throughout the German states. There was the spread of Methodism or Wesleyanism in Great Britain. Some scholars even think that the spread of Methodism (of Wesleyanism) helped prevent revolution in England because it absorbed so much of the pain and suffering, hopes, and aspirations of the poor and even lower-middle-class. In that sense, Marx wasn't totally wrong. Religion can function as the opiate of the masses to the extent that people who are deeply religious and who believe that they have to suffer through their human condition and are suffering in this world because the better world is to come, that can lead people to put off going after changes that maybe they should be going after, and even more basically those religious opportunities can give people a sense of belonging. Joining unions also gives people a sense of belonging—but a different kind of a sense of belonging. So, religious revivalism also occurred within the domain of Protestantism and also within the domain of Catholicism as well. Catholicism did recover powerfully from the revolutionary and Napoleonic era, especially associated with the forces of order. And there were liberal Catholic thinkers that were very prominent during this time period as well.

All of these tendencies were generally related to the dominant Romantic tone of the epoch, also evident in literature, in art, and in music. Scholars disagree as to whether or not there actually was a Romantic movement. And the reason they are able to do so is they indicate that so many different members of that so-called movement had different areas of intentionality and of concentration. So, for example, sometimes the Romantic movement is associated with emotion, spontaneity, a return to nature, past-oriented (especially the medieval epics, the Brothers Grimm, folk tales). Some emphasize its anti-rationalist or anti-Enlightenment stress—at least in the sense that the Enlightenment had been so mechanistic that the Romantics rejected the man-machine element of the Enlightenment.

Most Romantics did not share all of those particular qualities, although those qualities run throughout the movement through many of its more important representatives. However, what most scholars do agree is that during this era there was such a thing as a Romantic tone. There was a striving to create new ways of viewing reality— new systems of thought out of the collapse of the old, through the French Revolution. There was a desire to bridge the gap between the real and the ideal—between man's aspirations and man's limitations and suffering.

The period of 1815 to 1848 was also an age of frustration, in which constitutionalists and liberal nationalist aspirations and expectations were dashed by the powers that be—in which expectations for the possibility of achieving immediate and direct change outran the possibility of actually achieving that change against the forces of order. Until the mid-1840s, this time period was also a time period of general economic improvement and of the gradual spread of industrial advances to parts of western and central Europe. These advances were still disruptive, leading to urban growth and tensions, especially on the part of artisans and many others, among the real urban poor. Severe agrarian depression, from crop failures in 1846 and 1847 (which actually had begun in Ireland, tragically, in 1845), led to an urban recession, as well, placing many areas of society in a real situation of "overload," ripe for rebellion and violence. In February of 1848, as the saying goes, "Paris sneezed, and the rest of Europe caught a cold." The revolutions of 1848 had begun. We'll turn to them next time.

Thank you.

(motive)

national
constitutional
socioeconomic

Change effects
emancipation from serfdom

Lecture Eight
The Revolutions of 1848

Scope:

The year 1848 has rightly been called "the springtime of the peoples," analogous to 1989 but with different results. Sparked by an "unintended" revolution in Paris, outbreaks involving middle-class elements, workers, and artisans erupted in urban areas in the Germanic states, the Austrian Empire, and the Italian states, leading to a temporary collapse of established authority and hasty concessions.

If the causes of these revolutions involved a combination of national, constitutional, and socioeconomic grievances, the early success of the "revolutionaries" was attributable more to the incompetence and lack of nerve of rulers in France, Prussia, and Austria than to the power of revolutionary leaders, who were divorced from the urban and rural masses. Unlike 1789, neither great-power conflict nor successful Jacobin-like revolutionary responses emerged.

If revolutions saw success from February to May, they stalled and were eclipsed during 1849 and 1850. Once the elites, supported by armies and Russian intervention, regained composure, the disunited revolutionaries were no match; on the surface, the old order was largely reestablished by the end of 1850.

However, some things had changed. The peasants of Prussia and the Austrian Empire had been "emancipated" from serfdom; moderate constitutions remained in force in Prussia and Piedmont; many monarchs, including the pope, had seen their legitimacy undermined; a series of class and ethno-national tensions had worsened; and elements of the reformist middle class, disabused of "Romantic" sentiments, drew closer to the forces of order. The disillusionment of 1848–1850 and the advent of industrial civilization ushered in a different age.

Outline

I. The revolutions in areas of western and central Europe had a number of causes.

A. Participants, especially in the states of Italy and Germany, but also large ethnic minorities in the Austrian Empire, had nationalist and constitutional frustrations.

B. In France, the issues were primarily political (constitutional) but also social.

C. A growing number of middle-class individuals in expanding urban areas also sought careers open to talent.

D. In central Europe, feudalism or feudal remnants still afflicted large sections of the peasantry.

E. Agrarian depression in 1846–1847, leading to urban recession, brought grievances to a boiling point.

F. Political elites were insensitive, unimaginative, and unprepared for the outbreaks that occurred following the "signal" given by Paris in February 1848.

G. The overall legacy of 1789, in the minds of both revolutionaries and their opponents, was often decisive as well.

II. The revolutions of 1848 generally developed in three phases.

A. From February to May, many revolutions appeared to be successful and obtained major concessions from terrified monarchs.

1. Following outbreaks in Paris, Louis Philippe abdicated and a republic was proclaimed, with universal male suffrage; national workshops were also established, mainly in Paris and Lyon.

2. On March 4, King Charles Albert of Piedmont issued a moderate constitution.

3. After riots in Prague, Vienna, and Budapest, on March 13, Metternich resigned, a constitution was promised, and Hungary became virtually independent.

4. A similar series of events occurred in Berlin and elsewhere in Germany, leading to a more liberal ministry and a military evacuation of the city; King Frederick William IV promised a constitution and support for German unity.

5. The Austrians were ousted from Milan, a republic was proclaimed in Venetia, and Piedmont declared war on Austria.

6. At the end of March, an all-German pre-parliament assembled in Frankfurt, followed by the full Frankfurt Parliament in May, to achieve German unity.

7. In April, a constitution was promised for the Czechs, riots spread to other sections of the Austrian Empire, revolts for independence began in Poland, and Pope Pius IX declared neutrality.

1 stage
une-Dec 1848

B. During the second stage, between June and December 1848, the revolutions were in trouble.

1. Following the meeting of a Pan-Slav Congress in Prague, Austrian General Windischgratz bombarded Prague, crushing the Czechs.

2. During the *June Days* in Paris, following the closing of national workshops, radical republicans and socialists were suppressed, leading to wider reaction; Prince Louis Napoleon was elected president in December, defeating republicans.

3. In July, the Austrians reoccupied Milan and Lombardy; in the end of October, General Windischgratz reoccupied Vienna, while Franz Joseph replaced his weak-willed father.

4. Meanwhile, Hungarian forces invaded Austria, while the pope fled following insurrections in November.

1 stage
49-51

C. During the third stage, from 1849 to 1851, reaction succeeded in most areas.

1. In Italy, during 1849, the Roman Republic was overthrown by French troops, while Austria defeated Charles Albert's Piedmontese forces.

2. In the Austrian Empire, in 1849, with the aid of Russian armies, Hungarian independence ended, while the Austrian Parliament was dissolved in 1851.

3. Following a long debate, the Frankfurt Parliament offered a federal crown to King Frederick William of Prussia, who turned it down. Although his attempt to form a Union of North German states was quashed in 1850 by Austria, backed by Russia, Frederick William maintained the limited constitution granted in 1849.

4. Following attempts to change the French constitution to allow more than a one-term presidency, Louis Napoleon, establishing a dictatorship, proclaimed himself president

for 10 years in December 1851 and emperor-for-life in December 1852.

III. After several years of turmoil, not much seemed to have changed.

    A. Limited constitutions were established in Piedmont and Prussia.

    B. The peasants were emancipated in Prussia and the Austrian Empire.

    C. King Victor Emmanuel I replaced King Charles Albert in Piedmont, Emperor Franz Joseph replaced Franz Ferdinand in Austria, and a Napoleonic restoration occurred.

IV. Although complicated factors explain these limited gains, several general tendencies are clear.

    A. The initial widespread success of the revolutions was based on the weakness of regimes, rather than on the strength and unity of revolutionaries, who did not offer a real economic or social program to the masses; Jacobin-like elements did not emerge successfully, as they had in 1792–1793.

        1. Especially in the German states and in Austria, most revolutionary leaders were more nationalist than constitutionalist, with little sympathy for the aspirations of Slavic, Hungarian, Italian, or Danish claims to self-determination or autonomy.

        2. In Prussia and Austria, the military and bureaucracy, dominated by aristocrats, remained loyal to the regimes, and Russia served as the policeman of central Europe.

        3. The British, generally favoring liberal constitutional changes, did not intervene, while the French concentrated on their own problems.

    B. On some basic level, the Concert of Europe sustained itself; remembering the impact of 1789, the powers had no interest in wars of conquest.

V. Still, the impact of the events and even failures was profound.

    A. The revolutions led to new leaders in France, Austria, Prussia, and Italy, less attuned to established ways of governing internally, including the Concert of Europe.

    B. The revolutions exacerbated nationalist feelings, between both states and peoples.

1. Italian and German patriots were upset with Austria.
2. British and French liberals were upset with Russia and Austria, while Napoleon III was angry with the Russians, who refused to recognize him.
3. Antagonisms between Germans and Slavs were exacerbated, while Hungarians wanted independence.
4. Austro-Prussian tensions were raised, while Austrian elites felt threatened because they were forced to rely on Russia.

C. Class tensions were raised as the middle class and the more self-conscious working class (*proletariat*) came into greater conflict.

D. The failure of the revolutions undermined idealistic or utopian "Romantic" conceptions, at least in terms of achieving national, constitutional, or socioeconomic aims, using contemporary methods.

E. However, the revolutions led elites to realize that they needed to placate the middle classes and the masses, by one means or another, including expanding the military, police, and the paternalistic power of the states and by harnessing nationalism.

F. Constitutional and nationalist ideas continued to spread throughout Italy, Germany, and the Austrian Empire.

G. Both the emancipation of the serfs in central Europe and greater state attention, facilitating economic growth, accelerated the spread of capitalism and industrialism throughout much of Europe, except for in Russia.

Essential Reading:

Robert Gildea, *Barricades and Borders, Europe 1800–1914*, pp. 80–134.

John Merriman, *A History of Modern Europe*, pp. 670–701.

L. C. B. Seaman, *From Vienna to Versailles*, pp. 49–54.

Supplementary Reading:

Peter Jones, *The 1848 Revolutions*.

Jonathan Sperber, *The European Revolutions, 1848–1851*.

Questions to Consider:

1. How does one explain both the early success and the later failure of most of the 1848 revolutions?

2. What tools might the elites use to avoid such disruptions in the future?

Lecture Eight—Transcript
The Revolutions of 1848

Good afternoon, ladies and gentlemen. Let's begin Lecture Eight with a direct historiographic confrontation. One great historian, G. M. Trevelyan, says the following about the revolutions of 1848, "1848 was the turning point at which modern history failed to turn." Another great historian, Hans Rothfels, says virtually exactly the opposite, "Failure or not, 1848 was a genuine turning point."

What did they mean, exactly? Trevelyan was a liberal. The year 1848 is sometimes known as "the springtime of the peoples"—great hopes and great expectations. What he meant is that European history should have turned for the better. And since it failed to turn, in some ways it turned for the worst. And that's what Rothfels implicitly understood. Turning point or not, 1848 indeed had a dramatic, dramatic impact. The revolutions that broke out in many areas of western and central Europe during the early months of 1848 had a number of causes. And now we're talking about causes that are clear, rather than about preconditions as with the French Revolution of 1789. *[Causes]*

A number of participants, especially in the states of Italy and Germany, but also large ethnic minorities in the Austrian Empire—such as Hungarians, or Czechs, or Poles—had both nationalist and constitutionalist issues that had been long suppressed. In France, the issues were more political (constitutional) but also social in nature, demonstrating the further leftist adventure that France had taken with all of those utopian socialists, and we could name a number of others as well. The French example also had some national implications, but in a different way than in the Austrian Empire or in Germany or in Italy. That is to say that the regime of Louis Philippe from 1830 to 1848 just wasn't very exciting to French nationalists. And when Louis Philippe brought back Napoleon's ashes and put them in the *Invalids*, what he did was bring attention to the deficit he shared when compared with Napoleon as a nationalist. This upset a number of French people as well.

A growing number of middle-class individuals in expanding urban areas also sought careers open to talent. They wanted better jobs. In central Europe, feudalism or feudal remnants still rankled large sections of the peasantry—this human bondage.

Then there was agrarian depression in 1846 and 1847 on the continent, which led to urban recession as well. This exacerbated a host of grievances and brought them to a boiling point. Faced with these concerns, political elites in most areas were minimally insensitive, unimaginative, and surprisingly unprepared for the sort of outbreaks that occurred following the "signal" given by Paris in the end of February 1848. Indeed, the great French liberal constitutionalist Alexis de Tocqueville, before 1848, on the eve of the revolution, said publicly, "France is a nation that is bored. Can't you feel the breath of revolution in the air?" The overall legacy of 1789, both in the minds of "revolutionaries" and their opponents, was often decisive.

The revolutions of 1848 generally developed in three phases, and we have just considered their causes. We will consider their course, and then we will consider their impact.

During the first phase, from February to May, many revolutions appeared to be successful and initially obtained major concessions from terrified monarchs and political elites. Following outbreaks in Paris in mid- to late-February (February 22–24), King Louis Philippe abdicated and a republic was proclaimed, with universal male suffrage; national workshops were also established. Interestingly, again, these national workshops harkened back to the Constitution of 1793, which guaranteed the right to work. Most of the people who were part of the committees that put these things in place in Paris and Lyons had wanted nothing to do with national workshops, but once the people set up barricades, they wanted nothing to do with more urban violence, either. So they placated the people, hoping to take back what they were giving, later. So there were some real radicals and some even moderate socialists involved, but most really wanted a more reformist monarchy, like Great Britain.

Spreading very quickly to northern Italy, although there had earlier been rebellions in southern Italy, which didn't hit the map hard because it wasn't Paris. On March 4, King Charles Albert of Piedmont, in the midst of riots, issued a moderate constitution.

After riots in Prague, Vienna, and Budapest—three great cities in the Austrian Empire—on March 13, our friend Prince Clemens von Metternich resigned and fled to London. He said, "I can tell the difference between a passing illness and a terminal malady. We are in the throes of the latter." And he left, happy to have his head. A constitution was promised, and Hungary became virtually independent.

Shortly thereafter, a similar series of events occurred in Berlin and elsewhere in Germany—in many major cities, as well—leading to a more liberal ministry and a military evacuation of the city. The military did not want to evacuate the city, but King Frederick William IV did want to evacuate the city, because, as with Louis Philippe, he was afraid of too much violence. The military kept its head better than the monarchs. They knew they had the power to repress if the will to use the power was there. King Frederick William also promised a constitution and support for German unity in one way. Again, constitutionalism, some form of support for nationalism—these are the big issues in most of the states of Germany.

Almost simultaneously, the Austrians were ousted from Milan, a republic was proclaimed in Venetia (Venice), and Piedmont declared war on Austria. So, all that Austrian inheritance from the Congress of Vienna is now being put in jeopardy. At the end of March, an all-German pre-parliament assembled in Frankfurt, followed by the opening of the full Frankfurt Parliament—which debated, and debated, and debated about what was the best way to achieve German unity.

In April, a constitution was promised for the Czechs, in Bohemia—again, one of the more industrialized areas of the Austrian Empire. Riots spread to other sections of the Austrian Empire. Revolts for independence even began in Poland, including Russian Poland. And Pope Pius IX declared neutrality in a war between Catholics against Catholics, losing much of his earlier support. Coming into power in 1846, he looked and began to speak like a more reformist pope, until the revolutionary outbreaks occurred.

2 stage

During the second stage of the revolutions, between June and December 1848, the revolutions were clearly in trouble, almost on all fronts. Following the meeting of a Pan-Slav Congress in Prague, Austrian General Windischgratz (if you can spell it, extra credit comes to you) bombards Prague, crushing the Czechs. Again, German nationalists at Frankfurt were happy that this occurred—Czechs versus Germans.

During the *June Days* in Paris, following the closing of those national workshops, radical republicans and some socialists were suppressed in the bloody June Days leaving a legacy of class hatred, and leading to reaction. Moderate liberals didn't want a radical republic, let alone a fully democratic republic. Prince Louis Napoleon, nephew of our Napoleon, was elected president of the republic in December, easily defeating all of his republican rivals, including Lamartine the poet and General Cavignac, who had repressed the workers in the June Days.

In July, the Austrians reoccupied Milan and Lombardy; at the end of October, our friend General Windischgratz reoccupied Vienna, while Franz Joseph replaced his weak-willed father in December. Meanwhile, Hungarian forces trying to make good on their independence invade Austria, while the pope is forced to flee Rome, following insurrections in November.

During 1848 as well, and this was important, in Prussia and in Austria, the regimes did have the intelligence to free the peasants from serfdom. Once the peasants were freed, they became a conservative force.

Moving to the third stage of the revolutions, from 1849 to 1851, reaction really seemed to succeed almost everywhere, albeit not completely. In Italy, during 1849, the Roman Republic was overthrown. By whom? By the French, because French Catholics didn't want the pope in exile. This happened while Austria defeated Charles Albert's Piedmontese forces, and republican forces throughout northern Italy, taking back what had been lost. And Charles Albert has to resign, and his son Victor Emmanuel becomes King of Piedmont. Within the Austrian Empire, in 1849, with the aid (very interesting) of Russian armies, the Austrians allowed Russian armies to come in and help them put down Hungarian independence and other ethnic nationalist movements. This is the conservative part of the *Concert of Europe* working, while the Austrian Parliament was then dissolved—incredible that the Russians didn't take territory as a result of having been of help—but again, this is the remarkable Concert of Europe at that time, at least between the Austrians and the Russians, although the Russians don't get much thanks for it later. The very limited Austrian constitution granted in 1849 was abrogated at the end of 1851. The forces are put down, and the constitution is taken away.

At the same time, following a lengthy debate, the delegates at the Frankfurt Parliament, mostly middle class, offer a federal crown to King Frederick William of Prussia, who turns it down a month later. "I would rather chop wood than reign in the manner of the King of England," he said. Although his attempt to form a Union of North German states on behalf of the princes was quashed in 1850 by Austria, backed again by Russia, Frederick William maintained the limited constitution he had granted in 1849. His word was better than that of the Austrians. The same was true in Piedmont: the limited constitution was maintained. This was going to be important.

Following attempts to change the French constitution, allowing Louis Napoleon to be president for more than one term, Louis Napoleon established a dictatorship. He proclaimed himself president for 10 years in 1851 and emperor-for-life in 1852. Those who had been at Vienna were rolling over in their graves. One of the primary elements in the settlement of the Congress of Vienna was that no scion of Napoleon could ever inhabit the throne of France again. And he's there. And one of the reasons he's there is because the Russians were too occupied, and everyone else is too occupied, to do anything about it, although they did not like it. Napoleon said, *"Mon empire est la paix"* ("The empire is peace"). Huh. He didn't keep his promise, either. No one did anything about it, even though he had to struggle to achieve his legitimacy. Therefore, after several years of substantial turmoil, great instability, fear, not much appears to have changed, at least not in a very concrete way.

Limited constitutions are established in Piedmont and Prussia. They will be important. The peasants are "emancipated" from serfdom in Prussia and the Austrian Empire. That would be important in a different way. On the one hand, it would make the peasants more of a conservative force. On the other hand, it would allow them the freedom to migrate to cities, enhancing and facilitating the spread of a more fluid capitalist economy, and a larger labor force necessary for industrialization. One of the problems of serfdom that was later realized in Russia at the same time, is if you don't have a mobile labor force, it's harder to industrialize. It's harder to achieve economic development. Indeed, that's one of the reasons they emancipated the peasants anyway—not just really to satisfy them and keep them quiet, but because it was recognized that serfdom should have been a thing of the past. We were about to fight our wars over slavery and other issues.

King Victor Emmanuel I replaced King Charles Albert in Piedmont, Emperor Franz Joseph replaced Franz Ferdinand in Austria, and a Napoleonic restoration occurred in France. Although a variety of complicated factors explain these limited gains, several general tendencies are clear. The initial widespread success of the revolutions was based far more on the weaknesses of the established regimes and especially of the kings of France, Prussia, and Austria, rather than on the strength and unity of revolutionaries. Their ideas were strong, but fuzzy, and they were disunited and had no power. The divided revolutionaries were generally more liberal than radical—which means that they couldn't offer real economic or social programs to the masses, whether the urban masses, or the artisans, or the rural masses. Jacobin-like elements did not emerge successfully, as they had during 1792–1794 in France, which tells us how unique that Jacobin phase was—whether you like it and think it was positive, or whether you think it was absolutely horrendous and unimaginable. But when nothing is given to the masses, what you have is middle-class revolutionary elites who are chiefs without Indian followers and, therefore, they lack real authority and real power.

Concerned about disorder and the loss of security for property, the middle classes in fact feared both the urban poor and the peasants, and liberal members of the middle class feared radical members of the middle class. Both liberal and radical republican members of the middle class feared socialist members of the middle class. Especially in the German states and in Austria, most revolutionary leaders, in a crunch, were more nationalist than constitutionalist. The delegates of the Frankfurt Parliament had little sympathy for the aspirations of Slavic, Hungarian, Italian, or Danish claims to self-determination, autonomy, or having their grievances dealt with appropriately at any case. And they supported Prussian, Austrian, and Russian repression of these claims, not realizing that those same Prussian, Austrian, and Russian troops could then easily be turned directly on them. Especially in Prussia and in Austria, the military and the bureaucracy, dominated by the aristocrats, clearly remained loyal to the regimes, anxious to repress the revolutionaries—while Russia served very, very effectively as the policeman of central Europe without asking for any real payment. Incredible.

The British—while generally favoring liberal constitutional changes on the continent as long as they didn't get out of control, and while opposing very much Russian intervention—did not themselves intervene, while the French, even during their revolutionary phase, were also content to concentrate on their own problems, the recreation of order and stability. When the French did act, as I mentioned before, they intervened to restore the pope to authority in Rome, in the Papal States, in the states ruled by the pope, who was both a temporal and a spiritual leader.

Moreover, on some basis, and a clear basis, the Concert of Europe sustained itself during this widespread cauldron of disruptiveness; remembering the impact of 1789, remembering the wars, the powers had no interest in going at one another again. These were people who still remembered the past. Incredibly, they had lived long enough to do so, and that's not where they wanted to go—not even the generals.

Still, the overall impact of the events and even of the failures of these revolutions was profound. The revolutions did lead to the replacement of many key traditional leaders in areas (states) that were most affected by those revolutions: in France, in Austria, in Prussia, and even in Italy. The newer leaders were less attuned to established ways of governing internally, and they were less committed to the Concert of Europe. These were not people who remembered the wars of Napoleon and the wars of the French Revolution. And especially with Metternich gone, a vacuum was there, and the vacuum was filled by a new generation of people who turned out to be very intense, powerful, action-oriented states people known as *realpolitikers*, who favored realism in politics. They were like Frederick the Great: "If duke we must, let us be the greatest of all scoundrels." They were not wedded to the Concert of Europe. What did the Concert of Europe mean to Napoleon III? It meant a lack of his legitimacy. What did the Concert of Europe mean to Bismarck? Or to Cavour in Prussia or Piedmont, later? These were people for whom the ends justified the means, and war itself was not all that great of a risk.

The next era would be a totally different era, under the leadership of this new group of younger people who took power after the elders went into abeyance during the revolutions of 1848. Even the new monarchs were prepared to take greater risks. Moreover, adding to this risk-taking intensification was the fact that intensified and exacerbated nationalist feelings, both between states, and now, more dangerously, even between peoples, was also a part of this revolution of 1848, and all of the violence and mayhem associated with putting down the revolutions all over the core of Europe, except for Great Britain and except for Russia. Russia had a rebellion in Poland, but not in Russia proper. Great Britain sat this one out, because they had already reformed enough that they could sit this one out.

Many Italian and German patriots were incensed with Austria's behavior. That's clear in Italy, because northern Italy was re-occupied by the Austrian forces, and the old elites returned and traditional regimes were set up once again. But the same was true with respect to Prussia, in which many Prussian liberals looked at the Austrian quashing, and even more Prussian nationalists and other German nationalists looked at the Austrian quashing of a wider union (with the support of Russia, of all things) as being very, very negative.

British and French liberals were clearly upset with Russia and with Austria. British liberals did not cotton to the Russian playing of the policeman of Europe, putting down the great liberal patriots such as Kossuth in Hungary, while Napoleon III was especially incensed with the Russians, who refused to recognize him as an emperor. They refused to recognize his legitimacy whatsoever. And he knew that if they had had their druthers, and if they had been able to march across Europe with the Prussians and/or the Austrians to put down Napoleon in Paris, they would have been glad to do so.

Antagonisms between Germans and Slavs were also exacerbated, while Hungarians still wanted independence from Austria, in one form or another. Austro-Prussian tensions were raised, while the Austrian elites also felt threatened because they were forced to rely on Russian intervention. Let's stay there for a while. Even the Austrians were tense, because the Russians had to be called in to help them do their own business. What this meant is that these elites would try to do something about this afterwards in both Prussia and in Austria.

Class tensions were also raised in a number of states, and by 1848, we can begin to talk about class consciousness in a more meaningful way. The year 1848 is when Marx writes the *Communist Manifesto*. The year 1851 is when Marx writes *The 18th of Brumaire: The Rise of Louis Napoleon*. But significantly, 1848 sees de Toqueville publish his *Souvenir*, his memoirs. And in de Toqueville's memoirs he is even more emphatic about the nature of the class struggle he saw on the streets of Paris than Marx was. He's more frightened by it because he's a liberal constitutionalist. Marx is happy for it. To Marx, this 1848 revolution is a presage of what is to come, and what he wants.

However, looking at the violence, disruption, instability, and the workshops even, the middle classes increasingly favored property rights and stability over substantive change. Prior to the revolution, the middle classes tended to speak in the name of everyone else, as well, and think that that was for real—and they were liberal, and sometimes democratic, and sometimes experimental. Now they faced the violence, and they, generally speaking, become somewhat more conservative and somewhat less critical of any order that can establish stability or authority, although this will differ from place to place.

The masses, however, urban masses using violence, demonstrated that their needs had to be considered by the elites—whether aristocratic, or middle class, or both—and they had achieved a greater sense of class consciousness in doing battle, even in defeat. The fact that they had done this forces the elites (if they have any sense of realism or intelligence) to be more attentive to the needs of the masses and the middle classes, through some kind of reform or by greater implements of repression, including a more modern police force. Also it leads them to understand that, like it or not, nationalism is a powerful force. They better learn how to deal with it. This is the beginning of a time period during which some more intelligent members of the conservative elites, including the aristocrats, would know how to co-opt nationalism and use it on behalf of conservatism against liberalism and democracy.

At the same time, the failure of the revolutions of 1848 to establish any dramatic changes except in those moderate constitutions very, very much discredited the power of ideas themselves—that "Romantic" temperament. As A. J. P. Taylor has indicated:

> Never has there been a revolution so inspired by a limitless space than the power of ideas. Never has a revolution so discredited the power of ideas as a result.

The discrediting of the ideas and the myths of revolution—paralleled by the evident material gains and impact of the Industrial Revolution symbolized by the first Universal Expo that took place in London in 1851—usher in a new paradigm, a new historic era. A clear transition has occurred. The period from 1850 to 1870 would be remarkably different than the one that came before it.

Thank you.

Lecture Nine
Europe, 1850–1871—An Overview

Scope:

The dashed expectations of those who had fought for change in 1848, combined with expanding urban industrial civilization, ushered in a new age. The disruptions of 1848 facilitated the rise of a new generation of statesmen known as *realpolitikers* (Napoleon III, Count Camillo di Cavour, Otto von Bismarck) and engendered a series of national antagonisms and hardening class lines. Equally important, the Second Industrial Revolution, characterized by steam, steel, heavier producer goods, and more state guidance, strengthened states that were able to use the new technologies. Once the Crimean War removed the "stabilizing" influence of Russia and Great Britain, by the mid-1850s, the *realpolitikers* went to work; by 1871, Italy and Germany were "united," Austria and France were humiliated, and a very different balance of power emerged.

Simultaneously, the 1850s and 1860s saw scientific and materialist explanations capture the European imagination, while Realism replaced Romanticism as the dominant cultural form. Sometimes known as the age of Darwin, Marx, and Wagner, it was an era of remarkable scientific, economic, and urban advancement, of nationalist and class-based antagonism, and of social Darwinism and "modern" racist thought.

Outline

I. The 1850–1871 era has a coherence of its own quite different from that of 1815–1848; many of its components accelerated, at least for several decades after 1870.

II. A number of forces seem to explain this substantial change.

   A. The revolutions of 1848 had a widespread impact on a number of areas of European life.

   B. More important, expanding industrialization began to dramatically affect western and parts of central Europe, especially Germany.

   C. As with the changed emphasis from mid-17th-century to late 18th-century classicism or Enlightenment rationalism to the

Romantic era, another generational mood swing came to predominate in the social sciences and humanities from the 1850s to the 1880s, at least.

D. A combination of these developments, as well as the further spread of the "ideas of 1789" into eastern Europe and the Balkans, helps explain the changed nature of European civilization from 1850–1871.

III. What, then, are the major components of this epoch?

A. Perhaps the most important marker is the Second Industrial Revolution.

1. Propelled by new technologies in heavy industry, especially steam and steel, the epoch saw revolutions in urbanization, transportations, communications, capital expansion (banking), and so on.

2. Increasingly, governments sought to guide the path of the Industrial Revolution, especially because of the military implications of industrial technology.

3. More and more production took place in larger factories, with obvious implications.

4. Where industrialism spread, the middle class expanded, as did the increasingly self-conscious proletariat, while artisans, peasants, and even aristocrats needed to adjust somewhat.

B. The second dominant force in this epoch was an expanding and changing nationalism, within countries and between them.

1. The more liberal and tolerant nationalism of the first half of the century became more exclusivist and began to be co-opted by conservative elites in their struggle to maintain power.

2. By the 1860s, nationalism began to combine with the newer forces of social Darwinism and "scientific" racism, both against external and internal enemies, often "imagined."

3. This era saw a number of nationalist-related wars, including the Crimean War (1853–1856), a war between France and Piedmont versus Austria (1859–1860), the Austro-Prussian War (1866), and the Franco-Prussian War (1870–1871), leading to the "unification" of Italy

and Germany in the 1860s and to the defeat of Russia, Austria, and France.

4. By 1871, "united" Germany or "expanded" Prussia had become the strongest continental power.

C. These changes marked the breakdown of the Concert of Europe and collaborative diplomacy; the era was dominated by new statesmen, such as Napoleon III, Count Camillo di Cavour, and Otto von Bismarck, and a new style of diplomacy, known as *realpolitik*. Machiavellian and self-satisfied, statesmen made secret treaties and planned for wars, without shame.

D. In place of Romanticism, idealism, philosophy, and history, this was an age of cultural Realism, materialism, and above all, science, all of which reinforced one another and reinforced the changing nature of nationalism and diplomacy.

1. It was the age of Charles Darwin, Karl Marx, and Richard Wagner, as even Marx and Wagner, and others, thought they had discovered or revealed the "scientific" laws governing society, the economy, and race—indeed, the whole evolution of life and civilization.

2. Traditional religions were on the defensive during this era; the Catholic Church's main response was Pope Pius IX's 1864 encyclical, *The Syllabus of Errors*.

E. In many areas, this was an age of expanded constitutionalism (both liberal and democratic) and remarkable economic development.

1. One can begin to speak of "mass society" during the 1860s in the most developed nations.

2. Even tsarist Russia, faced with defeat in the Crimean War, experienced reform from the mid-1850s to the mid-1860s.

F. The era witnessed the expansion of state action on many levels, as well as a dramatic change in the world balance of power. Although not an age of "self-conscious" imperialism, the British and French rather easily increased their power at the expense of India and China and in Southeast Asia, while the increasingly industrialized United States "opened up" Japan in the 1850s, just prior to the American Civil War.

IV. Although a number of these tendencies continued into the next era, the completion of the processes of Italian and German "unification" in 1870–1871 and the emergence of Germany as the new hegemon, replacing France, mark a transition to a new era, not surprisingly known as the *Age of Bismarck* (1870–1890).

Essential Reading:

John Carey, *Eyewitness to History*, pp. 321–379.

Robert Gildea, *Barricades and Borders, Europe 1800–1914*, pp. 137–264.

Jan Goldstein and John W. Boyer, *Nineteenth-Century Europe*, pp. 336–351 (Renan).

Supplementary Reading:

E. J. Hobsbawm, *The Age of Capital*.

James A. Winders, *European Culture Since 1848*, pp. 1–74.

Questions to Consider:

1. How does one explain the substantial "discontinuities" between this era and the 1789–1848 era?

2. What seem to have been the major carryovers?

Lecture Nine—Transcript
Europe, 1850–1871—An Overview

Good morning, ladies and gentlemen. I can't believe it, but we're actually beginning section two in our encounter together. I hope during the course of our comments dealing with the era from 1850 to 1871, your sense of the material will be deepened, your comfort will be enhanced, and you will begin to take ownership of these materials.

In a remarkable way, the period from 1850 to 1871 not only has a coherence of its own, but is one that is relatively different from that of the 1815 to 1848 era. Moreover, many of the major components accelerated, at least for several decades after 1870. In other words, there will be more continuity between this era and the rest of the course than between this era and what has preceded it. There are a number of forces that seem to explain this substantial historical change. As discussed in the previous lecture, the revolutions of 1848 had a widespread impact on a number of areas of European life. As a result of 1848, failure or not, a new generation of states people came into power, with a different sensibility, a different agenda, a different set of expectations. Constitutionalism was spread—at least in both Prussia and Piedmont. The serfs were also freed in both Prussia and in the Austrian Empire, enhancing the possibility of greater capitalist expansion. Extremely important, national antagonisms were deepened as a result of the revolutions of 1848, on a number of areas.

In addition to all of this, the cultural expectations of the previous era—especially the emphasis on the role of ideas and the mythic sense that change was relatively easy if you believed in something and were prepared to risk and act—this was dashed in the failed revolutions of 1848.

Perhaps even more important, expanding industrialization (now often called the Second Industrial Revolution) began to dramatically affect western and parts of central Europe, and spread continuously from that point on to the rest of the continent. This was especially prominent in areas of Germany in the 1850s and the 1860s, but equally prominent in France, and certainly continuously in England and in a number of other areas. This spread of industrialism on a deeper, more rapid area—steam and steel—would affect every element of European civilization.

As with the changed emphasis from the period of the 18th-century Enlightenment to the period of early 19th-century Romanticism, there is also a generational thrust in all of this. In our own day, we should certainly be aware that things change so quickly—that what was new 10 years ago is old. Newness doesn't really mean that much to us. But every generation or so does see a mood swing inherent to itself. And there was a very, big mood swing that took place from the first half of the 19th century into the second half of the 19th century, and then another cultural mood swing would begin actually around the 1890s and then pick up steam thereafter. And the emphasis would change from the social sciences, humanities, ideas, and philosophy in the first half, to science and social science pretending to be science in the second half of the century.

A combination of these developments, as well as the further spread of the "ideas of 1789" into deeper reaches of eastern Europe and the Balkans, helps explain the changed nature of European civilization from 1850–1871. What, then, are the major components of this new epoch? Obviously some of them are the very causes that we just discussed and that we now have to embellish somewhat.

2d Industrial Revolution

Again, perhaps the most important marker is the Second Industrial Revolution and all of its implications. Propelled by new technologies in heavy industry, especially in the realms of steam and steel, this epoch saw revolutions in the domain of urbanization, transportations, communications, capital expansion (real banking). And I would urge you, in thinking about this time period, to pick up any of the books of Charles Dickens, but most particularly *Hard Times*.

Increasingly, governments sought to guide the path of the Industrial Revolution, especially because of the military implications of industrial technology, and especially in the fields of railroads, navies, artillery, weapons, and munitions of all sorts. Remember, this is also the time period (in the 1860s) of the American Civil War, and just think about the confrontation between the *Monitor* and the *Merrimack*. If one had ironclads, the other needed ironclads, because the other ships of the line were no longer any good if you were facing an ironclad. Governments understood this, and they needed to industrialize simply to maintain pace. It was clarified even more directly during the Crimean War, which we will discuss soon.

Although not overnight, more and more production took place in larger factories, with obvious implications. We can really, really begin to talk about a factory system here. Large numbers of workers being in the same place—under still very, very difficult conditions—led to increased class consciousness. Where industrialism spread, the middle class expanded, as did the self-conscious proletariat, while artisans, peasants, and even aristocrats needed to adjust somewhat to the new environment. And not all of them were very comfortable with it—especially aristocrats, the old elite, when they become uncomfortable with a new environment, you could have a problem—as with artisans, who are very, very prone sometimes to take matters into their own hands.

One can also properly begin to talk about class consciousness in a deeper level during this era, and even about an incipient class struggle (as long as this is done with moderation). Even in the growing working class proletariat there were deep divisions and multiple loyalties between skilled, and semi-skilled, and unskilled workers—part-time workers. Karl Marx notwithstanding, but this was the age of Marx—the *Communist Manifesto* and then *Das Kapital* at the end of this particular period. ②
Not Econocles —

This leads naturally to the second dominant force in this epoch, an expanding and changing nationalism, both within countries and between them. The more liberal, tolerant, and universalist nationalism of the first half of the century, signified by the early phase of the French Revolution and by the Italian patriot Mazzini, became sharpened and exclusivist and began to be co-opted by conservative elites as well, in order to maintain their power. Whether Napoleon III, Bismarck, or Cavour, elites began to learn—elites had to learn, moreover—how to use nationalism if they wanted to remain ③ in power. *social Darwinis —*
• scientific racism

Worse, by the 1860s, changed nationalism began to combine with newer forces of social Darwinism and so-called "scientific" racism, both against external and internal enemies, often (usually, in fact) "imagined." Not surprisingly, this era also saw a number of nationalist-related wars, including the Crimean War between 1853 and 1856; a Franco-Piedmontese war against Austria at the end of the 1850s; the war between Austria and Prussia in 1866, which represented a significant change in the balance of power; and then the most important war of all, at least in terms of actually changing the balance of power, the Franco-Prussian War of 1870–1871, in which the new German Empire defeated France and became the strongest power on the continent. These wars led to the so-called "unification" of Italy and Germany in the 1860s and to the defeat of Russia, Austria, and France.

By 1871, a "united" Germany or "expanded" Prussia (however you look at it) had become the strongest continental power, both militarily and industrially. And that was only to accelerate in the period thereafter, especially in the realm of economics, in which the new German Empire would begin to rapidly outstrip the economic power of France, and then catch and begin to outstrip the industrial economic power even of Great Britain. In fact, the only state whose industry expanded more rapidly than Germany's at the end of the 19th century in real terms was actually the United States.

(4) Realpolitik

Obviously, these changes marked the breakdown of the Concert of Europe and the general idea of collaborative diplomacy itself. Indeed, a series of new statesmen who came into power after 1848, such as Napoleon III, Count Camillo di Cavour, and Otto von Bismarck, were governed by a new style of diplomacy known as *realpolitik*. Machiavellian and self-satisfied, statesmen made secret treaties and planned for wars—secret treaties specifically, indeed, to plan for wars, and without shame. If this succeeded, so be it. If it didn't, lie about it in your memoirs. As historian Jacques Barzun has said of *realpolitik*:

> There was nothing really new. But when the practice became the rule, and the rule was preached as moral duty, sanctioned by science, that was something new.

In place of Romanticism, idealism, philosophy, and history (although history still remained very prominent, but in a different way), this was an age of increasing cultural Realism, materialism, and above all, of science, all of which reinforced one another and also reinforced the changing nature of nationalism and diplomacy. Let's stop for a second and think about this. Realism—what is important is what is hard and fast, and touchable, quantifiable. Materialism—again, not ideas, but material forces are what determine history. Think of Karl Marx's material determinism, and also science—all of it undergirded by the powerful presence of science. And this was seen to play out in diplomacy, industrial enterprise, the existence of people and their relationships with one another.

It was the quintessential age of Charles Darwin, Karl Marx, and Richard Wagner, as even Marx and Wagner, and many others, thought they had discovered or revealed the "scientific" laws governing society, the economy, and race—indeed, the whole evolution of life and civilization. Let's stop for a moment and consider what this meant a little bit more carefully. One of the most important books of the entire century (of the entire modern era) was obviously Charles Darwin's 1859 *On the Origin of Species*. Or should we give the full title? *On the Origin of Species by Means of Natural Selection; or the Preservation of Favored Races in the Struggle for Life.*

Darwin was a gentle scientist. He continued to do his research thereafter and published *The Descent of Man*, even more powerful, at the end of this time period, in 1870–1871. And he had worked at his labors scientifically standing on the shoulders of many, many others, as well, carefully, carefully thinking about the implications of his evidence. And, in fact, he waited on the publication of his manuscript because he knew it would challenge established religious beliefs, and he was still somewhat religious himself, and he knew it could be put to bad use, as indeed it was put to bad use. Listen to him more carefully:

> Thus from the war of Nature, from famine and death, the most exalted object of which we are capable of conceiving, namely the production of the higher animals, directly follows. There is grandeur in this view of life. Let me continue. The idea of struggle is as old as life itself. For life is only preserved because other things perish through struggle. In this struggle, the stronger, more able, win; while the less able (the weak) lose. Struggle is the father of all things.

Oops! I made a mistake. That was 100 years later, somewhat. That was Adolf Hitler speaking, but the language is remarkably similar, at least thus far. Hitler would continue:

> Struggle is the father of all things. It is not by the principles of humanities that men live or is able to preserve himself above the animal world, but solely by means of the brutal struggle. If you do not fight for life, then life will never be won.

Well, let's redeem Darwin. Darwin would never have gone ahead with that second half, because Darwin would have wanted to compensate for human decency. During his research, he even said when he was on the Galapagos Islands, "It would appear that the birds in this archipelago have not yet learned that man is a more dangerous animal than the tortoise."

Not surprisingly, traditional religions were on the defensive during this era—both the Catholic and the Protestant churches, and even more so the Catholic Church because it was more centralized.

Darwin found many people who took his arguments and supported them, and generally speaking, arguing both against Protestants and Catholics at Oxford and elsewhere, they won the day. As Huxley said:

> If I had to choose, I would prefer to be the descendant of a humble monkey rather than of a man who employs his knowledge and eloquence in misrepresenting those who are wearing out their lives in searching for truth.

Cardinal Manning retorted, "The ape is our Adam?"

But these were the implications of all of this cultural conflict. It is not accidental that in 1863, Ernest Renan, a French philosopher and historian, published a very, very important book called *The Life of Jesus*, in which, for the first time, a secular biography, done by what was formerly a believing Catholic, concluded that Jesus was a magnificent human being. Of course, all of that spread conflict even further. In the midst of all of this, Pope Pius IX issued, in 1864, a code called *The Syllabus of Errors*, sadly, in which he said the following:

> Error: Every man is free to embrace and profess the religion he shall believe true, guided by the light of reason. Error: Man may find the way of eternal salvation and obtain eternal salvation in any religion. Error: Protestantism is nothing more than another form of the same true Christian religion, a form in which men may be as pleasing to God as in the Catholic Church.

Think of how far we have come and how far we have yet to go.

These were really, really important issues because people based their whole life's assumptions of ground that was shaking and changing right underneath their feet during these two decades. And many of the terrible things that happened in these decades and thereafter are a result of these challenges to the very, very foundations of European civilization occurring during this era.

In the case of Karl Marx, all history is the history of class struggle. We have another direct challenge—the scientific laws of history that Marx thought he had uncovered, that would be true in all places and at all times.

Count Arthur de Gobeneau in France, in 1853–1855, had actually four volumes on *The Origins of Inequality Among the Human Races*, in which he posited that the single most important determinant of history in any period of time was the racial component of the dominant group in its conflicts with other groups—and that each of the races had peculiar biological (again, Darwinian), scientifically valid, racial characteristics. And you can't move from one race to another. You are what you are. And then he categorized them by means of their characteristics. Who was higher. Who was lower. Who was fit to rule. Who was fit to be a slave. Ironically, in Gobeneau's analysis, Jews were as capable as Europeans. Others would see it otherwise. But blacks, Africans, Asians, yellows, were fit to be ruled and had no inherent considerable value—and the worst thing of all was race mixing.

By the end of this period in 1870, we would also begin to get the germ theory of disease as medicine itself would become more powerful. The germ theory of disease, race mixing—you know where we're going.

In many ways, it was also an age of expanded constitutionalism (both liberal and democratic) and remarkable economic development. In fact, one can begin to speak of "mass society" during the 1860s in the most developed nations. Stopping here for a moment to think again about the implications of all of this, this economic development was again inherently related to the Second Industrial Revolution. It was inherently related to the expanded middle class and to the expanded larger numbers of workers in large cities—all of which helped pressure regimes to respond to the constitutional as well as to the national desires of these larger numbers of people. And during this second period, larger numbers of people were also beginning to live better where that industrialization and that constitutional expansion had occurred, as governments very,

very much had to respond to their middle class, and even sometimes to their working class. Governments were learning how to do this quite well during this time period, which is one of the reasons, in addition to the failures of the revolutions of 1848, it's one of the reasons why there was less revolution from below during this time period, even as Karl Marx had thought that the revolutionary era was about to begin. But governments had learned how to adapt. They needed to know how to adapt. They had also, during this time period, even with increased constitutionalism, increased the size and the power and the organization of their police forces (professionalized police forces) for the first time, as well as expanded state apparatus on every level—again, linked to the possibility of transportation and communications revolutions. All of this is impossible if you don't know what's happening in wider spheres of your own country.

Even tsarist Russia, faced with defeat in the Crimean War, experienced considerable, if insufficient, reform from the mid-1850s to the mid-1860s. During the Crimean War (and this in some manner was the most important of the wars because it made possible the unification of Italy and the unification of Germany) it was so obvious that Russia was industrially ill-equipped—but not only industrially ill-equipped. Russia could not mobilize the will of its own people, the passion of its own people, and therefore the new Tsar, Alexander II, first emancipated the serfs and then began a whole series of other reforms that we will talk about in much greater detail in succeeding commentaries, which helped to begin to modernize the whole structure and nature of the Russian state, in the face of what was so clearly its comparative backwardness. Remember again, at each stage, the word "comparative" is central. If France, Britain, and Germany had not progressed, the actual structure of Russia at that time would not have meant such a disparity. It is the comparative and uneven process of all of this change between countries and within countries that is so dramatically important.

The era witnessing this expansion and maturation of state action on so many levels internally also witnessed a dramatic change in the world balance of power as well—obviously, inherently, to the advantage of Europe. Although not an age of "self-conscious" imperialism, the British and the French rather easily increased their power at the expense of India and China and in Southeast Asia, while the increasingly industrialized United States "opened up" Japan in the 1850s, just prior to the American Civil War. And indeed, isn't that how all of us were taught about this confrontation? We "opened up" Japan, doing them a favor; a favor that they didn't want? We came back another year with a larger fleet, and they opened up, and they learned (supposedly inferior yellow races, the Japanese, put a finish to that, if people only had eyes that would see). But that just shows you how clouded our vision can be when we hold to fixed ideas.

Indeed, the American Civil War would be the real harbinger of the future potential of industrial warfare that would occur at the end of this time period between relatively equal combatants. The American Civil War would be a real foretaste of World War I. But again, America, 3,000 miles away, on a certain level might still almost have been on the moon. People didn't study the American Civil War. They studied the Franco-Prussian War; they studied the Austro-Prussian War—wars that took place quickly; limited costs; great advantage to the victor—very, very different than the American Civil War.

Although a number of the major tendencies of these two decades continued into the next era, the completion of the processes of Italian and German "unification" in 1870–1871 and the emergence of Germany as the new hegemon, the new dominant power, replacing France—in the gendered language of the early 20th century, scholars used to say Europe had lost a mistress (France) and gained a master (Germany)—this marks a transition to a new era, not surprisingly known as the *age of Bismarck* (1870–1890), which we will cover in our succeeding lectures.

Other scholars may take different tacks to end this particular epoch. Some feel that the epoch really ends with the beginning of the depression of 1873, until 1893. Don't take the word "depression" to mean 1929. It wasn't that kind of depression, but it was disorienting, and it was powerful. And even our friend Hobsbawm in his book *The Age of Empire* begins with that date and not with the German defeat of France in 1870. Others—scholars whose main emphasis is imperialism—may even start in 1880, when the newer European imperialism really, really dramatically accelerated and led to depredation in Africa and in Asia. I think that the rise of a modern German state under Bismarck, and that state's defeat of France, was the most important political development of the 19th century. France had recovered, and in the 1850s and even the first half of the 1860s,

France seemed to be the dominant power. The Crimean War ended at the Peace of Paris. Where the peace conference takes place frequently is significant because it shows who the dominant power is.

The unification of Germany and the breakaway power of German industrialism and military potential thereafter, I believe, really bring this era to a transition, together with the unification of Italy at the same time. Many of the issues that we have talked about today—from the *realpolitik,* to the materialism, to the science, to the antagonistic, enhanced social Darwinian and frequently racialist nationalism, to the spread and the deepening of the Industrial Revolution—will, in fact, continue into the next time period, the time period between 1870 and 1914, which saw both the zenith and the beginning of the demise of European ascendancy.

Thank you.

Lecture Ten
The Crimean War, 1853–1856

Scope:

Sometimes considered the most senseless of Europe's 19th-century wars, the Crimean War made possible the structural changes Europe experienced from the late 1850s through the Franco-Prussian War (1870–1871). Scholars disagree with respect to the causes of this bloody conflict. Surely the Concert of Europe had been undermined by the national and ideological tensions unleashed by 1848 and especially by Russia's repressive role. This left ill will on the part of liberal leaders' opinions in Great Britain and France, convincing many that Europe's "policeman" needed to be taught a lesson. A more enduring cause of conflict involved the status of the weakened Ottoman Empire, a serious concern for statesmen since the late 18th century and a particular bone of contention between Great Britain and Russia, as well as for France and Austria (versus Russia).

When misperception and poor leadership led to war between the Ottoman Empire and Russia and to an Anglo-French siege of the Russian port of Sebastopol on the Black Sea, Anglo-French industrial power forced Russia to accept the humiliating Treaty of Paris in 1856. However, not only had Russia been stung, but Austria and Prussia had their status diminished, while Cavour, leading Piedmont into the war to curry Anglo-French favor, placed the plight of Italy on Europe's agenda.

Although the Concert seemingly acted in Paris, guaranteeing the independence of the Ottoman Empire, the forces that gave the Concert reality were undermined, and the path was cleared for adventuresome statesmen.

Outline

I.   Although scholars agree that the Crimean War "need not have occurred," at least not in the 1850s, this does not mean it did not have significant causes.

    A.   The Concert of Europe generally functioned until after 1848, because such diplomats as Metternich and British Prime Minister and Foreign Minister Sir Robert Palmerston sought to preserve peace and the balance of power.

B. Although the avoidance of war between the great powers during the revolutions of 1848 reflected these concerns, the year 1848 undermined the Concert in important ways.

1. It raised a number of specific nationalist antagonisms (Prussia versus Austria, Prussia versus Russia).
2. It heightened ideological resentments, especially on the part of liberal British and French opinion against Russia.
3. It saw the demise of Metternich and the rise of Louis Napoleon/ Napoleon III, whose very name was an affront to the Vienna system.

C. Even under the best of circumstances, an "eastern question" existed, given the weakness of the Ottoman Empire, as symbolized by the successful Greek War of Independence in the 1820s, the first of many nationalist Christian independence movements in the Balkans.

1. Given this reality, the Russians wanted as much control over Constantinople as possible and sought exclusive military access through the Straits of the Bosphorous and the Dardanelles, linking the Black and Mediterranean Seas, while the British and French wanted the reverse of these designs, either the status quo or greater influence at the Porte.
2. Russia also had divergent interests with the Austrians in terms of military and economic control of the Danube region.

D. During the crisis leading to the outbreak of war between Russia and the Ottoman Empire in 1853, followed by an Anglo-French coalition war against Russia in 1854, shortsighted, inconsistent, and incompetent diplomacy often prevailed.

1. During 1852, Napoleon III successfully pressed the Ottomans to expand the rights of Latin Christians in the Holy Land.
2. Tsar Nicholas I sought not only a reversal but the formal right to protect Orthodox Christians throughout the Ottoman Empire; in June 1853, Russian troops occupied the Ottoman provinces of Moldavia and Wallachia (Rumania), as hostages.

3. Receiving conflicting indications from British diplomats, the Sultan declared war against Russia, followed by the Russian destruction of the Ottoman fleet.

4. Outrage in the west, and especially on the part of the British, convinced the tsar to change course and to suggest a compromise agreement to the powers meeting at Vienna in February 1854.

5. Anglo-French refusal to accept these offers represents a breakdown of the Concert and the will for peace—and the desire to teach the Russians a lesson.

II. Although the Crimean War was localized, it was bloody and pregnant with consequences.

A. Between September 1854 and December 1855, Anglo-French forces besieged Sebastopol, the most important Russian Black Sea naval base.

1. Although superior western technology allowed their forces to concentrate more effectively than the Russians, lacking adequate railroads, all of the armies performed poorly, although the French performed less poorly. Approximately 500,000 combatants died, including large numbers from disease and exposure.

2. During the course of the war, Prussia, Austria, and Piedmont—the states most affected by 1848—further jockeyed for position and advantage. Austria, though pressed by Britain and France to engage, was unable to get Prussian acquiescence to intervene in the meetings of the Germanic Confederation. Austria, sending an ultimatum to Russia in December 1855, angered Russia without gaining Anglo-French good will.

B. Although the Peace of Paris, negotiated between February and April 1856, seemed to demonstrate the power of collective European action, this was more apparent than real.

1. Russia agreed to a number of demands made by the other great powers, including demilitarization and free trade in the Black Sea (no warships there), a European commission's control of the Danube River (free navigation), the complete independence of the Ottoman Empire (now a member of the Concert), and the loss of any Russian rights over Moldavia and Wallachia; however, Russian compliance was a product of force.

2. Count Camillo di Cavour of Piedmont was given the opportunity to bring the plight of Italy before the powers, to the discomfiture of Austria.

3. Prussia and Austria were concerned about their great-power status and at odds.

4. Napoleon III, having gained by gamesmanship, was encouraged to play again.

5. Most important, both Britain and Russia, chastened, entered into an era of internal reform, creating a vacuum of power used by *realpolitikers* in France, Piedmont, and Prussia to redraw the map of Europe.

Essential Reading:

Ralph Menning, *The Art of the Possible: Documents on Great Power Diplomacy, 1814–1914*, pp. 45–67, pp. 94–110.

John Merriman, *A History of Modern Europe*, pp. 751–755.

L. C. B. Seaman, *From Vienna to Versailles*, pp. 23–31.

Supplementary Reading:

David Goldfrank, *The Origins of the Crimean War*.

Ralph Menning, *The Art of the Possible: Documents on Great Power Diplomacy, 1814–1914*, pp. xix–44, 68–93.

Questions to Consider:

1. What seem to have been the major causes and consequences of the Crimean War?

2. What does the war tell us about the functioning of the Concert of Europe, and what impact did it have on this institution?

Lecture Ten—Transcript
The Crimean War, 1853–1856

This is a slightly different kind of lecture than that which we have been hearing. We're going to be talking today about the Crimean War, following the introductory lecture to this second section of our series. Not because the war in and of itself was so important, or even so dramatic—although it is always dramatic when a half a million people die unnecessarily—but because of what the Crimean War made possible.

In order to understand this more completely, we're going to go back to an organization that I've mentioned several times before, called the Concert of Europe. There is even an argument over whether there was such a thing as the Concert of Europe. Indeed, one of the historians whose books I have suggested that you look at, L.C.B.Seaman, *From Vienna to Versailles*, says essentially that the Concert of Europe is a figment and a creation of historians, rather than an organization that actually existed and had some reality. Other historians, such as David Thompson and Gordon Craig, have said that the Concert of Europe meant no annexation without ratification, or that the Concert of Europe became actual and operative after the Congress of Vienna. It is obviously that particular interpretation that I hold more closely to my soul, specifically since the diplomatic documents that I looked at for my Ph.D. thesis 35 years ago at the end of the 19th century continuously do refer to the functioning or the malfunctioning of the Concert of Europe. So, if diplomats were talking about the malfunctioning of the Concert of Europe at the end of the 19th century, it must have existed at some point at an earlier time, and indeed it did.

So what was the Concert of Europe? The Concert of Europe was the acceptance of the concept of one Europe, of a common Europe, at least on the part of the great powers, and that they had some clear responsibility, indeed, even a conscience (even a conscience on the part of Metternich) to maintain the peace. The Concert of Europe believed that the balance of power was essential to maintain—that no one state should be allowed to expand without compensation with others, and it would be better if none of the great powers expanded at all. The Concert of Europe believed that less-secret diplomacy was better. The Concert of Europe believed in a certain level of self-restraint, compromise, and acceptance of the status quo, in the geography and in the balance of power of Europe. The Concert of Europe also agreed that any power that stepped out of that environment should be constrained by the others—a very, very important concept that all held in mind.

Why was this possible? Why was it possible to function for so long, even during the revolutions of 1848? The men. The time period. Their previous experience. British Prime Minister and Foreign Minister Sir Robert Palmerston, Metternich, Nicholas I of Russia, and many of the other leaders remembered the Napoleonic wars— their ravages, the revolutions, the disruptions that they had caused. They didn't want to see that again in their lifetime. The milieu was also important. This was not a real age of ideology for statesmen, as yet, and especially most of these statesmen surely were not really nationalists. In addition, it was an age in which public opinion could be less important and was less important, and did not disturb the tranquility of statesmen to do their business as they saw fit, among themselves, in their own great-power club.

And most importantly, the Concert of Europe, the balance of power, the maintenance of peace, suited the self-interest of all of the great powers, and that's what you really need for an institution to function, and function indeed it did.

Although the avoidance of war between the great powers during the revolutions of 1848 reflected these continuous concerns, 1848 surely undermined the Concert in several profound ways. As mentioned earlier, it raised a number of specific nationalist antagonisms—some of which became very, very deep—antagonisms between Prussia and Austria, between Prussia and Russia, between France and Russia. These national antagonisms also had ideological ramifications— ideological components—resentments, especially on the part of liberal British and French opinion elites, and sometimes common, against Russian police action in central Europe, let alone against the Austrian repression of what seemed to be reasonable aspirations of very, very large ethnic minorities in the Austrian Empire for some greater degree of autonomy, or say in the conditions that governed their own lives, after all.

Extremely important, once again, it saw the demise of Metternich, the most consistent and powerful conservative presence in the first half of the 19th century, and the rise of Louis Napoleon, who became Napoleon III in 1852, whose very name was an affront to the Vienna system and all that it represented, and who had good reason to resent the Russians, as well, and to resent the Vienna system. The more he could uproot every memory of that system, the greater his own legitimacy would be.

Even if the war did not have to occur, what some folks sometimes forget is that even under the best of circumstances, there was an "eastern question." It already existed. There was the issue of the growing weakness of the Ottoman Empire, near Russia, symbolized by the successful Greek War of Independence in the 1820s, which was the first of many, or the first really successful of many, nationalist Christian independence movements in the Balkan regions, which Russia itself was not opposed to because it wanted more authority over the Ottoman Empire, a historic enemy it had recently defeated a number of times. And, on the other hand, the British wanted to preserve the status quo of the Ottoman Empire because the Ottoman Empire was a bulwark against Russia in Constantinople, protecting the Straits of the Bosporus and the Dardanelles, which would allow Russia to pass from the Black Sea into the Mediterranean Sea. The Mediterranean Sea was the British lifeline to all of its trade in India and in other parts of its empire. Both the British and the French wanted to either retain, maintain, the status quo in the Ottoman Empire, or to increase their influence there, while the Russians wanted to increase their interests there if any change was going to take place. That issue already existed and was a subject of continuous discussion.

There were also divergent interests between the Russians and the Austrians in terms of the whole economic region of the Danube. So, that, too, was an area of tension and concern. Russia now butted up against the other great powers' self-interest.

During the course of the crisis leading to the outbreak of war between Russia and the Ottoman Empire in 1853, followed by an Anglo-French coalition entering the war against Russia in 1854, shortsighted, inconsistent, willful, sometimes incompetent diplomacy prevailed. Hence the avoidability of this particular war if the states people and the diplomats had been more focused, less willful, less ideological, more competent, and more aware of the dangers involved. It began, really, with Napoleon III (our friend) and his concern to please Catholics internally in France, and his concern to uproot the Vienna settlement, and his concern to gain more power and legitimacy, successfully pressing the Ottomans to expand the rights of Latin, western Christians in the Holy Land—in fact, to give them control over the Church of the Nativity in Bethlehem, which the Ottoman Sultan did. Chagrined, Tsar Nicholas sought not only a reversal of this but the formal right to protect Orthodox Christians throughout the entire Ottoman Empire, a huge step forward. Now here's where it begins to get dicey. As an inducement in his discussion with the Sultan, in June 1853, Russian troops occupy the Ottoman provinces of Moldavia and Wallachia, which just happen to be the core of present-day Rumania, which at that point were part of the Balkans, were part of the Ottoman Empire. So let's have a discussion that I'm going to take a good piece of your territory to see that you discuss it the way I want to discuss it. Okay.

Receiving conflicting indications from separate British diplomats (very interesting)—a lot of Cabinet shuffles, a lot of shuffles within seats in the Cabinet posts, different British diplomats advising the Sultan in different ways—the Sultan took a hard line and finally declared war against Russia, followed by the Russian destruction of the Ottoman fleet, the so-called "Massacre of Sinope" in November 1853. The Russian fleet was no marvel to behold. It was stronger than the Ottoman fleet, but when you call something a massacre, something unfair has happened. The Russians defeated the Ottomans. The British and the French were angry at the Russians to begin with. They called it a massacre, and it was presented in the press as a massacre. And in more modernized Britain and France by the 1850s, the press already mattered; public opinion already mattered, and it even began to hamper the way diplomats would make decisions.

Widespread outrage in the west (especially in Great Britain) convinced the tsar to change course and to suggest a compromise agreement to the powers meeting at Vienna in February 1854. Here, again, we get a clear deciding point. This would have been the old Concert of Europe functioning. The tsar stepped out too far. The British and the French called him back. The tsar agreed to compromise. The British and the French ought to have agreed to compromise as well, and then they would have gotten on with their business of doing whatever they wanted to do with the outsider, the Ottoman Empire. Except that the British and the French didn't play ball. The Anglo-French refusal to consider these offers, and their subsequent declaration of war in March, represents a clear breakdown of the Concert, and a breakdown of the will for peace, and rather the desire to teach the Russians a lesson.

Especially in Great Britain, this also demonstrates the problematic nature of the role of public opinion in matters of war and peace, even in a democracy. And one can see diplomats bewail that at the end of the 19th century, especially because it used to be a good old boys' club—a small group. They knew each other. They socialized together. They intermarried. They weren't bothered by outsiders—but the public was an outsider. Napoleon III, rather, sought to undo the Vienna settlement, to consolidate his legitimacy by acting in concert with the British through military success to gain even more domestic and European-wide status.

Moving to the war itself. Although the Crimean War was relatively localized, it was a bloody mess. It was pregnant with consequences and deep implications. Between September 1854 and December 1855, Anglo-French forces besieged Sebastopol, the most important Russian Black Sea naval base. Although superior western technology allowed their forces to concentrate more effectively than the Russians, lacking adequate railroads in Russia, all of the armies performed poorly, although the French performed less poorly than the others. The Russians performed very poorly. They couldn't get their forces mobilized. There was peasant resistance to being conscripted. The British didn't do too well. The French army, comparatively, looked better than the others of three societies that don't do well at that time. They hadn't had a good war in a long time. It takes practice.

Despite the courage of Florence Nightingale, her farsightedness creating the Red Cross; despite the daring charge of the Light Brigade; all reported via incipient new "yellow journalism" (public interest accentuated journalism) this was the most costly European war between 1815 and 1914. Approximately 500,000 combatants died, including large numbers from disease and exposure.

During the course of the war, Prussia, Austria, and Piedmont—the states most affected by 1848, moreover—further jockeyed for position and advantage. Courting the favor of Britain and France, under Cavour, Piedmont joined the Allies in January 1855, wanting to get attention for itself and courting the positive gains it might have from Britain and France as a result of its actions.

Austria looked the worst. Although pressed by Britain and France to engage, Austria was unable to get Prussian acquiescence to intervene in the meetings of the Germanic Confederation. The Austrians said they would do so, to bring the Russians to heel, but only if the Prussians would do so at the Bund, in the Confederation, where the Prussians used to basically agree with the Austrian position. Now Bismarck was representing the Prussians, and they weren't going to agree to go ahead with the Austrians. And the Austrians weren't going to go ahead without the Prussians, because—guess what?—they were next to Russia, and if they went ahead alone, they might be facing the Russian army, which the Austrians did not need to do and did not want to do. Here you have the British and the French pushing the Austrians, and the Austrians really, really looking weak. Austria loses face. Austria's plight looks pathetic.

However, finally, Austria sends an ultimatum to Russia in December 1855, about the same time as the fall of Sebastopol, and this, of course (understandably), really, really angers Russia, without gaining Anglo-French good grace in response. What kind of thanks was that to the Russians, for all of the help the Russians (at no cost) had given to the Austrians at their moment of need during the revolutions of 1848?

Although the Peace of Paris (again, Paris becoming the diplomatic center), negotiated between February and April 1856, seemed to bring closure to this unfortunate situation, and to demonstrate the renewed power of collective European action or concert, this was much more apparent than real. Russia agreed to a number of demands made by the other great powers—including demilitarization of the Black Sea, and free trade in the Black Sea (no warships there), a European commission's control of the Danube River (free navigation), the complete independence of the Ottoman Empire (which now became accepted as part of the Concert), and the loss of any Russian rights over Moldavia and Wallachia, Rumania now declared virtually independent. Also, Serbia becomes autonomous at this time, and there were a number of other engagements such as "Free ships make free goods," freedom of the seas, and the like. Russian compliance was a product of *force majeur*. Russian compliance was a product of defeat, rather than acceptance of any of these positions. The Russians were going to be revisionist at the earliest moment at which it was possible and to their advantage to do so.

Count Camillo di Cavour of Piedmont was given the opportunity of bringing the plight of Italy before the assembled powers, to the discomfiture of Austria, and this would begin a pattern of Austrian discomfiture. Piedmont's being at the conference, even, was a slap at Austrian legitimacy and control of northern Italy. Both Prussia and Austria, almost not invited to Paris, were not only concerned about their great-power status, but at odds with each other, even more so.

In the case of Prussia, what this led to was the Prussian recognition that its great-power status was in question, requiring it to do something about its internal structure. And this led to the recognition that the Prussian army had better be reorganized and updated. And it was, in fact, the attempt to organize and update this Prussian army that brought the monarch into conflict with his own Parliament, which came into being directly as a result of 1848 through the constitution, which gave the Diet (the Parliament) some control over expenditures. In fact, the issue was so important that several elections were held, and the liberals continued to get more power, and the king was almost going to resign. And at that point, the minister of war convinces the kaiser to bring Bismarck into office as chancellor, because only he could save the issue. But before that, he was so dangerous, so conservative, so reactionary, they thought, that you would never want to bring him into power. That's throwing down the gauntlet to liberals, unless you absolutely needed him. The Prussians were really concerned about their great-power status. They were not particularly pleased (that's an understatement) that the Austrians tried to pressure them into a war with Russia that would have done them no good, and they would have faced Russian armies, potentially, also—because the Russian armies could have gotten to Austria and to Prussia much more easily than they could have gotten to the British and the French deep in the Crimea.

Austria faces the same situation—worse, because Austria has upset Britain and France. Austria has really upset Russia. Austria has upset Prussia. Austria economically has not kept pace with Britain, France, or Prussia. Austria does not have the wherewithal to totally modernize its military because it has not kept pace economically, and not even fully technologically. So, they have to do something, however, to reestablish their great-power legitimacy. Where will they go for that? They'll go back to that same Germanic Confederation to try to reestablish their own power there. And they will be continuously blocked there by Prussia. And it's during this time period, in the 1850s, that Bismarck—who is going to be the man of the hour (the next hour, in the 1860s)—during the 1850s, Bismarck, initially so respectful of the Austrians because of their conservatism, came to believe that Germany just wasn't big enough for both Prussia and Austria. And since he was Prussia, it would be Prussia that would predominate, and that itself was of considerable importance.

So, the Austrians will go back and try to tie up their power base internally in their own empire—try to expand their base of power in the Germanic Confederation, and be blocked there, further, by Prussia.

Our friend Napoleon III, having gotten much of what he wanted by a process of gamesmanship, was encouraged to play again. He obviously got legitimacy. Holding a major peace conference among all the great powers, the Concert of Europe, meeting in your presence when you have been denied even acceptance by your brother emperors and monarchs is quite a feat—especially since your army did pretty well at a cost that was acceptable. Napoleon III, getting away with it, had his appetite whetted—even a military action of some consequence in terms of the loss of life. And Napoleon III, unlike his uncle, was not bloodthirsty; Napoleon III was a totally different kind of individual. He didn't go to war just for the sake of going to war. If he had a choice between war and peace, all things being equal, he would have preferred peace in most cases, which is interesting, because he goes to war so many times, because all things weren't equal, and he could make gains. Napoleon III decides to play again, and again, and again—mostly because, even though there were some defeats along the way, until the mid-1860s, he was still the key player, mainly calling the shots, and France in some way seemed to be benefiting.

Most important, Great Britain and especially Russia, chastened by this experience, hurting in one way or another, entered into an era of internal stocktaking and reform. The British, with their vaunted military success, their vaunted aristocracy—the aristocracy didn't do too well, the army didn't do too well—these people did not seem to be born to rule as they liked to think of themselves as being, and England goes into a period of internal reform, including the passage of the Second Reform Bill, giving the rest of the middle class and the working class the right to vote, military reform, and a whole series of other civil rights actions, actually also spurred by the American Civil War, which brought up deep ideological issues in Europe, and especially in England, which was closer to America. So, Britain goes into a period of relative isolation. Relative.

For Russia, it's deeper. For Russia, it is reform, or begin to look like the Ottoman Empire. It is catch up with industrialization, catch up with internal stability and the capacity to mobilize your people, or really dramatically fall behind. That's what the war demonstrated. The British and the French could mobilize their power, their human potential, and then take it hundreds and hundreds and hundreds of miles away because of technical superiority. The Russians couldn't really fully mobilize their human potential. What good does it do to have the largest population if they are not willing to fight to support the regime? And if they are willing to fight and you can't get them there, that doesn't help much either. So the tsarist government, the new Tsar Alexander II, who becomes the only liberal tsar of the 19th century, between 1855 and 1881, goes into a period, from the late 1850s at least to the mid-1860s, of considerable and significant internal reform, including the emancipation of the Russian serfs, which was a process of far greater magnitude even than the freeing of the American slaves, because half the population was serfs.

But what this did was create a temporary vacuum of power in central Europe. The Russians were the main stabilizer of that vacuum of power, in addition to the Austrians. The British occasionally played a role stabilizing the continent. The British were semi-isolated. The Russians were licking their wounds and attempting to reform and to upgrade as best as they could do, and this vacuum of power allowed the new generation of *realpolitikers* (in France, Napoleon III; in Piedmont, Cavour; and very importantly, in Prussia, Bismarck) to redraw the map of Europe to their advantage. Summing up the entire experience, historian David Thompson says:

> It was a fumbling war. Probably unnecessary. Largely futile. Certainly extravagant. Yet rich in unintended consequences. It broke the spell of peace, and it removed the shadow of Russian power from central European affairs. It therefore cleared the way for the remodeling of Germany and Italy by means of war.

Thank you.

Lecture Eleven
From Napoleon to Napoleon—France, 1815–1852

Scope:

More than the American Revolution, the French Revolution left a legacy of debris-disputed claims of legitimacy, disputed rights, and grievances. Restoration monarch Louis XVIII had the sense to accept the moderate elements of the revolution, including a limited constitution, the main property changes, and the Napoleonic Code, although his reign still saw the competing claims of liberals and ultra-conservatives.

Louis XVIII's death in 1824 brought his *ultra* brother to the throne as Charles X, ushering in six years of confrontation. A divine-right monarchist, Charles X claimed to heal illnesses by the laying on of hands. A showdown was hastened by agrarian and urban economic distress from 1826–1827; Charles brought the issue to a head in July 1830, when he issued decrees that essentially reestablished an absolutist monarchy. Barricades went up in Paris, supported by liberal and republican elites and the masses, and Charles X fled abroad. Accepting the throne as "King of the French," Charles's successor, cousin Louis Philippe, was different; his regime resembled pre-1832 British rule but with less middle-class participation, more repression, and a less enlightened political elite. Louis Philippe's regime is sometimes characterized as government by the plutocracy (the upper bourgeoisie), and France experienced gradual economic modernization and stability but without national gratification.

Severe agrarian and urban distress in 1846–1847, followed by a quarrel between two factions of the governing elites, led to the outbreak of revolution in February 1848, which saw King Louis Philippe flee. But who would govern France and how would France be governed? Following nearly a year of ferment, climaxed by the violent Parisian June Days, Louis Napoleon Bonaparte, nephew of Napoleon, was elected president of the Second Republic for a non-renewable four-year term. A man of sincere humanity but with contradictions and character flaws, Louis outsmarted his opponents, courted the army and masses, named himself president for 10 years in December 1851, and declared himself Emperor Napoleon III in November 1852.

Outline

I. The restoration of Bourbon King Louis XVIII was a compromise solution, leaving considerable dissatisfaction, both on the left and the right.

   A. Although he accepted many of the moderate legacies of 1789, including a charter, the Napoleonic Code, and property changes, Louis XVIII's claim to rule by divine right concerned liberals.

   B. Among more conservative elements, known as *ultras*, there was a desire to return to an alliance between throne and altar, to compensate nobles for losses, indeed, to return to the Old Regime.

II. This situation was exacerbated when Louis XVIII's ultra brother became king in 1824, following Louis's death.

   A. Favoring landed aristocratic interests to those of the urban liberal bourgeoisie, Charles implemented a series of unpopular policies.

      1. Ultras returned to power as his advisers, and aristocrats were compensated for some of their property losses.

      2. The alliance between throne and altar became more open, as the church was given further control over education.

      3. More censorship was introduced, and the largely middle-class National Guard was abolished.

   B. Equally upsetting was the changed tone of the regime, supported by Romantic conservatives. Charles X's coronation was medieval in nature; he was the last French monarch who claimed to cure scrofula by the laying on of his hands.

III. Following a pitiable harvest in 1826, leading in 1827 to a distressed urban economy, more liberals were returned to the Chambers in successive elections, despite repression.

IV. Throwing caution to the wind, under the advice of ultra Prince Polignac, in July 1830, Charles X attempted a *coup d'état*, issuing a series of decrees. Charles abrogated the Restoration Charter of 1814, curtailed the press, reduced the number of voters, and called for elections.

V. Almost immediately, discontent on the part of a spectrum of groups and powerful individuals, including Victor Hugo and the Marquis de Lafayette, led to the overthrow of Charles X.

VI. Moderately liberal elites offered Louis Philippe, Duc d'Orléans, the throne of France on the part of the French people; although Louis Philippe wished to rule as well as to reign, he accepted this compromise, becoming the Bourgeois King, or the Citizens' King, from 1830–1848.

VII. Although the kingship of Louis Philippe was often uninspired, sometimes repressive, and even corrupt, these were generally good years, a respite between the revolutions of 1830 and 1848.

    A. Following a series of leftist revolts in the early 1830s, relative calm lasted for nearly 15 years.

    B. Though suffering an occasional setback, French diplomacy was cautious and France lived within its means.

    C. Although favoring more conservative liberals, Louis Philippe accepted constitutional constraints.

    D. His regime fostered economic development, a modernized infrastructure, and expanded secular education.

VIII. Still, discontent persisted, especially as a result of the tensions from the 1840s industrial urban expansion, exacerbated by the poor harvests of 1846–1847 and the resulting urban depression of 1847.

    A. Nationalists received little satisfaction from this moderate regime.

    B. Artisans and urban workers were often dissatisfied, while newer elements in the middle class wanted jobs and the vote.

    C. Little sensitivity could be expected from the Guizot Ministry. As Alexis de Tocqueville uttered in a parliamentary speech: "Can't you feel the breath of revolution in the air?"

IX. The outbreak of revolution in Paris, when the more liberal former prime minister Adolphe Thiers held banquets to protest Guizot's policies, was a manifestation of the law of unintended consequences.

    A. Thiers even cancelled a meeting, following Guizot's orders, only to have "guests" show up, clash with gendarmes, and repeat the known Parisian barricade scenario, putting Louis to flight.

B. This placed the questions bequeathed by 1789 on the table, complicated by the growing industrial, urban change.

   1. In play were the moderate and radical ideas of 1789, from limited-suffrage liberalism, to universal-suffrage democracy, to forms of utopian or practical socialism, making Paris the most combustible European city in 1848.

   2. However, although a "revolutionary" committee contained these three positions and proclaimed universal suffrage and a system of national workshops, most elites and most Frenchmen wanted order and stability.

   3. This became apparent when civil war erupted in Paris in the bloody June Days following the closure of the national workshops; the middle-class National Guard, with peasant military recruits, quashed the rebels, leaving thousands dead and a legacy of class hatred, popularized by Karl Marx in his 1852 essay *The 18th Brumaire of Louis Napoleon Bonaparte*.

X. Prince Louis Napoleon, nephew of Napoleon Bonaparte and a fascinating 19th-century statesman, was pleased to assume leadership, although almost all groups who voted for him in December 1848 got different results than they bargained for. Extremely enigmatic, Louis Napoleon was a composite of many of the conflicting forces of the age, refracted through his understanding of his uncle's legacy; this romantic adventurer was influenced by a mélange of prevalent monarchist, liberal, democratic, socialist, and liberal/nationalist sentiments.

XI. Following his dramatic election in December 1848 as president of the Republic, by an overwhelming majority of voters, Louis's main problem, from 1849–1851, was how to remain in power, because the constitution forbade successive terms.

A. Unable to obtain legislative remedy, although the conservative legislators, elected in May 1849, ended universal suffrage, Louis courted the urban and rural masses and the military, created a leadership cadre, and pulled off a *coup d'état* on December 1–2, 1851, imprisoning opponents and suppressing a workers' revolt .

B. He then dissolved the parliament, called for new "republican" plebiscitary elections with universal suffrage, and triumphing, established a new form of parliamentary structure and a 10-year presidency.

C. One year later, with another referendum (7.8 million versus 250,000), Louis established a hereditary empire and changed his name to Napoleon III.

Essential Reading:

Jan Goldstein and John W. Boyer, *Nineteenth-Century Europe*, pp. 215–269 (de Tocqueville, Marx, and Napoleon III).

Jeremy D. Popkin, *A History of Modern France*, pp. 78–115.

Supplementary Reading:

Jan Goldstein and John W. Boyer, *Nineteenth-Century Europe*, pp. 121–129 (Cousin), pp. 159–201 (Fourier, Saint-Simonians, Tristan).

Lloyd Kramer, *Lafayette in Two Worlds*.

Gordon Wright, *France in Modern Times*.

Questions to Consider:

1. Why did the Restoration era prove to be so conflict-ridden in France?

2. What were the major changes in French society between 1815–1850 or so?

Lecture Eleven—Transcript
From Napoleon to Napoleon—France, 1815–1852

Having just personally negotiated the Treaty of Paris with you in our previous commentary, bringing Napoleon III into center stage in all of his glory, we return to France and a set of comments entitled "From Napoleon to Napoleon—France, 1815–1852." And if you have an interest in a deeper understanding of the background of France in the 19th century, indeed, of all of French history, I would suggest tackling a mammoth, wonderful book by my friend James Collins of Georgetown University, entitled *From Tribes to Nation: France 500 to 1799*. The book is a mouthful, and that's a mouthful itself, and it's worth your effort.

Even the Second Restoration of Bourbon King Louis XVIII was a compromise solution, which left considerable dissatisfaction both among the left (the liberals and the radicals) and the right (from conservatives all the way to ultra-conservatives). Although he wisely accepted many of the moderate legacies of 1789, including a charter, the Napoleonic Code, and the major property changes that occurred during the revolution, as well as the major administrative changes, namely the centralization and the reduction of tolls that divided everyone, he claimed to rule by divine right. This still concerned liberals. This was of even greater concern during the 1820s, when, following the assassination of an apparent successor, voting rights were restricted somewhat and other forms of repression were employed—even by Louis XVIII. Among the more conservative elements, known as the *ultras*, there was a desire, in fact, to return to the alliance between throne and altar, to compensate nobles for their losses during the revolution, indeed to pretty much return to the *Ancien Regime* (and there were still people who wanted to do this almost 100 years later. Indeed, several years ago I saw a monarchist demonstration in the center of Paris at the Place de la Concorde, with 5,000 participants).

This situation was exacerbated when Louis XVIII's ultra brother became king in 1824, following Louis's death. Charles X made no secret of the fact that he favored landed, aristocratic interests to those of the urban, more liberal bourgeoisie, and he quickly implemented a series of unpopular policies. Ultras returned to power as his advisors, and aristocrats were compensated for some of their property losses during the revolution, obviously at public expense. The alliance between throne and altar became more open, and the church was given further control over education. More severe censorship was introduced, and the largely middle-class National Guard was abolished, Lafayette notwithstanding.

Equally upsetting was the changed tone of the regime, supported by a number of powerful Romantic conservatives—De Maistre, Bonald, Chateaubriand. One of them had said, "As right is of itself a force, so force can be of itself a right." Charles X's coronation was medieval in nature. He was the last French monarch who claimed to cure such diseases as scrofula (a skin disease) by the laying on of his hands. (Nicholas II of Russia still thought he could do that in 1917.)

Following a severe harvest in 1826, leading in 1827 to a distressed urban economy as well, more liberals were returned to the Chambers in two successive elections, despite the use of repression, scandalizing the ultras. In other words, even within a very restricted voting possibility, people did not want ultra control or a return to the past. Seeing this and throwing caution to the wind, under the advice of ultra Prince Polignac, in July 1830, Charles X attempted a *coup d'état*, issuing a series of draconian decrees. Charles X abrogated the Restoration Charter of 1814 by which Louis XVIII had come back into power, severely curtailed the press, further reduced the number of eligible voters, and then called for new elections, which of course he could pack. Almost immediately, Parisians (who knew how to do this well) streamed into the streets, simmering with discontent on the part of a broad spectrum of groups—from middle class, to working class, to artisan—including powerful individuals such as Victor Hugo and the Marquis de Lafayette, and returned to powers immediately in the re-formed National Guard, leading to the overthrow of the regime of Charles X, who fled to London.

Moderately liberal elites representing a goodly segment of the non-ultra establishment then offered Louis Philippe, Duc d'Orléans, the throne of France on the part of the French people. He would be King of the French, not King of France. Although Louis Philippe wished to rule, as well as to reign, to govern, he wisely accepted this compromise, becoming known pretty much as the Bourgeois King, or the Citizens' King, or, later, to his detractors, scandalized beautifully, magnificently, by Daumier's caricatures simply as "*La Poire*" ("The Pear"), which he looked like.

Although the kingship of Louis Philippe was often uninspired, sometimes repressive, and even corrupt, these were generally good years for France, and surely a kind of respite between the revolutions of 1830 and 1848. Following a series of leftist revolts in the early 1830s, including in Lyons, among the silk workers (that was the inspiration for Hugo's *Les Miserables*, a poignant masterpiece—massive, worth crying through), relative calm without severe repression lasted for nearly 15 years.

Though suffering an occasional diplomatic setback, even at the hands of Great Britain, French diplomacy was relatively cautious and, importantly, France lived within its means—always a good choice for government. Although favoring more conservative liberals, rather than expanding the franchise, Louis Philippe accepted constitutional constraints and surrounded himself with more bourgeois advisors even than aristocrats.

His regime also fostered a variety of economic developments, expanded secular education, had low taxes, and continued to grow a more modernized infrastructure. Still, discontent persisted, especially as a result of tensions attending the gradual expansion of industrial areas and, especially, in the 1840s, with poor harvests (especially in 1846 and in 1847), which, once again, then transferred to urban distress. But it has to be emphasized that, in general, this was a period of considerable stability, considerable order, and general prosperity before the late 1840s.

At the same time, nationalists received little satisfaction from this moderate, and even boring, regime. Remember, de Tocqueville had said that France is a nation that is bored. Artisans and urban workers were often dissatisfied and insecure, while many newer elements in the middle class—including students, journalists, lawyers and intellectuals—wanted jobs and the right to vote. And this kind of situation continues even today in many parts of Europe, including France; when you produce more educated people than you have decent jobs for, there is tension—especially when it is known that the people who already have those jobs may not have them because of their merit, but because of their connections.

Little inspiration or sensitivity could be expected from the Guizot Ministry, or the political elite in general. Guizot was a great historian—one of the early historians of the French Revolution—multi-volume, magnificent, large volumes. But he was a moderate liberal, or a moderate conservative. He didn't mind if you voted. He just said, "Work and grow rich, and then you will be able to vote," or "Two things are necessary to govern: common sense and cannon." Well, he didn't, in the end, have enough of either, at least the willingness to use the cannon when the time of crisis finally came.

As de Tocqueville uttered in one of his prophetic parliamentary speeches, "Can't you feel the breath of revolution in the air?" Indeed, the outbreak of revolution in Paris, when a slightly more liberal former prime minister, Adolphe Thiers, called a series of public banquets to protest Guizot's policies, was a clear manifestation of the law of unintended consequences. Thiers was just slightly more liberal than Guizot. What Thiers basically wanted on a certain level was what the British had gotten in 1832, bringing in another swathe of the middle class. What Thiers clearly wanted was to replace Guizot. In fact, Thiers would remain in government off and on in France for the next 40 years or so.

Thiers, told to cancel the meeting by Guizot, even followed Guizot's orders, but a crowd showed up anyway, and so did the gendarmes. Barricades were set up, shots were fired, and Paris repeated the scenario it had learned so very well in 1789 and repeated in 1830, and often in between. King Louis Philippe panicked, as did so many of the other monarchs in 1848, and King Louis Philippe also on some level was a moderate citizens' king. He did not want to unleash radical bloodshed, especially in those urban areas, and he fled to London. London was a great place for émigrés.

What this did, basically, however, is place back on the table directly all of the issues that had been at stake from 1789. You have a temporary vacuum of power. This means that moderate liberals will want to have their say. This means that democrats or radicals will want to have their say. This means that utopian socialists and more pragmatic socialists (again, I don't want to distinguish between the two overwhelmingly) will want to have their say. And, increasingly, it also means that the growing urban population will also very much want to have its say, especially in terms of food and work, following two years of agrarian and urban depression.

In play, therefore, were the popular representatives of everything from moderates to real radicals, wanting either limited-suffrage liberalism, to universal-suffrage democracy, to forms of social welfare in time of crisis, making Paris, perhaps, the most interesting and combustible European city in 1848. (Although, personally, I still find Paris to be the most interesting city in Europe, anyway. Even when it's combustible. My wife and I have watched powerful demonstrations file past our hotel for the better part of 8 to 12 hours, with hundreds of thousands of people carrying placards representing all kinds of things, some reasonable and some really not very reasonable.)

However, although a hastily created "revolutionary" committee contained elements from all of these different positions and proclaimed universal suffrage and a system of national workshops to create jobs, both in Paris and in Lyons, most Frenchmen wanted the restoration of order and stability, and they sought ways to achieve this. Or, should I say, "most propertied Frenchmen" wanted the restoration of order and stability? Actually, it would have been both because most Frenchmen were peasants still at that time. Only about 25 percent of them lived in cities, and the peasants overwhelmingly really were a conservative force, and they would behave conservatively during this time period in France since they already had some property and they already were emancipated by the universal suffrage.

On the other hand, liberals, moderates did not want to allow things to get out of control, so at least temporarily, they obviously proclaimed universal suffrage. And, following the ideas of some of the utopian socialists, they set up these national workshops. Now, what do you think happened? If you have workshops set up in Paris, or Lyons (kind of like the things that were set up during the 1930s in the American Depression), people from the countryside who are unemployed are going to flood into those areas, making the cities even more dangerous and combustible. But this was part of the Constitution of 1793—the right to work, the right to subsistence as a citizen of France.

However, once things calmed down, the moderates—who thought that the workshops were an excuse for laziness—and the peasants— who had had enough of Paris anyway, and also thought that the workshops were an excuse for laziness—closed the national workshops, leading to the workers revolting and setting up their barricades again, leading to the bloody June Days, from June 23 to June 26, when thousands of people were killed in another tragic mini-French civil war that would leave a legacy of increased class hatred.

The largely middle-class National Guard, combined with peasant military recruits, quashed the urban rebels, leaving thousands of dead and imprisoned and a legacy of class hatred, popularized by Karl Marx in his long essay (written in 1851 and published in 1852) *The 18th Brumaire of Louis Napoleon Bonaparte*. Thereafter, in some manner, as L. C. B. Seaman maintains in his book *From Vienna to Versailles*, and we are serializing this book as part of the supplementary readings in this course—Seaman says, "From June 1848 until the *coup d'état* of Louis Napoleon in December 1851, the Second Republic was a monarchy in search of a king."

Seaman is always cynical. He's brilliant, but cynical. In a sense, he's really right. These moderate liberals needed a monarch to restore things. They didn't want Louis Philippe necessarily to flee. They wanted him to expand the franchise. They wanted moderate change. But he was gone. He couldn't be called back. What to do?

So they formed an interim system. And of all things, in the context of this interim system, Prince Louis Napoleon, nephew of Napoleon Bonaparte and one of the most fascinating of 19th-century statesmen, was only too pleased to play this role, although almost all groups who voted for him in the universal suffrage (male suffrage) democratic elections of December 1848 got much more, or much different, than they had bargained for.

Extremely enigmatic in nature, Louis Napoleon was a strange composite of many of the conflicting forces of the age, refracted through his understanding and belief in the memoirs his uncle Napoleon had bequeathed him. Now, Napoleon wrote his memoirs to tell us what he wanted us to believe he was doing—totally different than what he actually did and what he actually knew he was doing. But Louis Napoleon believed in a lot of the liberal press that Napoleon put into his memoirs.

Believing in his star, his right to rule, his legitimate right to rule France, on behalf of the people and to improve the plight of humanity universally, this Romantic adventurer was influenced by a mélange of monarchic, liberal, democratic, socialist, and liberal/nationalist sentiments so prevalent at the time. He was a composite of so many different forces, I wonder if he ever understood himself.

Educated in exile, by a republican tutor on the myths propounded by his uncle in his memoirs, Louis twice attempted to overthrow Louis Philippe's regime. After all, he was legitimate, both in 1836 and in 1840, and he spent time in prison. The second time was wonderful because he escaped, dressed as a painter, carrying a stepladder out of the prison. And then he wrote a socialist-inspired pamphlet entitled *The Extinction of Poverty*, and then he served as a constable in London during the chartist demonstrations on the eve of 1848. No wonder the voters didn't know what they were getting. I wonder if Louis Napoleon knew what he was giving?

On a certain level, indeed he did. Conservative voters thought that he would be a moderate monarch, malleable. Liberals thought he might be liberal. Democrats thought he might really be better than the people who just put down the workers. Peasants thought he represented France. And Frenchmen, in general, still preferred the glory of Napoleon; they had forgotten the carnage and remembered the glory.

Following his dramatic election in December 1848 as president of the Republic, by an overwhelming majority of voters, against several other well-known republican candidates, Louis's main problem, between 1849 and 1851, was how to remain in power. One thing the moderates did in creating the constitution is to forbid a second term for the president. What to do? Louis tried to see if he could get that particular stricture to be changed. But it wasn't possible. And he intended to stay in power.

Unable to obtain legislative legitimate-due-process remedy, although the increasingly conservative legislators, elected in May 1849, even ended universal suffrage and placed secondary education in the hands of the church, Louis courted the urban and rural masses, courted the military, created a loyal leadership cadre, replaced some members of the military with other people who were closer to him and more loyal, and pulled off a *coup d'état* in Paris on December 1–2, 1851, imprisoning a large coterie of opponents and suppressing workers who set up those barricades in a revolt that ensued and was repressed. He believed he had no choice, but left a legacy that was very, very deep. As his wife Eugenie said, "A *coup d'état* is like a convict's ball and chain. You drag it along, and eventually it paralyzes your leg."

Everything he did at this point made him another enemy of tremendous importance in a sense. Victor Hugo went into exile and wrote a scurrilous pamphlet, a scathing pamphlet: *Napoleon Le Petit Par Victor Le Grand* (*Napoleon the Little by Victor the Great*), in which Hugo described those terrible two days:

> [The workers massed and] they cried, 'Down with Bonaparte!'...[The troops were in front of them, of course.] Suddenly, at a given signal, a musket shot being fired, no matter where, no matter by whom, the shower of bullets poured upon the crowd. A shower of bullets is also a crowd; it is death scattered, broadcast. It does not know whither it goes, nor what it does; it kills and passes on. ...

> [Later Hugo continues] I reached the boulevard; the scene was indescribable. I witnessed this crime, this butchery, this tragedy. I saw the rain of blind death; I saw the distracted victims fall around me in crowds. It is for this I have signed myself in this book an EYE-WITNESS.

And indeed, this comes from [John] Carey's book *Our Eyewitness Accounts* [sic *Eyewitness to History*]. So, this kind of primary source material that I find really helpful and indeed inspirational—if this kind of material is of interest to you, then by all means get that book. It's available in most bookstores. And enjoy the reading.

Louis Napoleon then dissolved parliament and called for new "republican" elections with universal suffrage by plebiscite, and he was overwhelmingly supported, establishing a new form of parliamentary structure, with universal suffrage and a 10-year presidency.

One year later, on December 2, 1852, following another successful referendum (nearly 8 million votes for him and only about 250,000 votes against him) Louis Napoleon established a hereditary empire, changed his name to Napoleon III, and proclaimed that the empire would stand for peace and well-being. "*L'Empire, c'est le paix.*"

But guess what? We already know that "*L'Empire c'est la guerre,*" because we've already discussed the Crimean War, so we know that Louis Napoleon didn't hold to that particular word. The word he did hold for was to try to deal justly, fairly, and kindly for the overwhelming majority of the French people, as best he could. However, this was not an easy task. Louis Napoleon had shed the blood of workers. Getting their attention was very, very difficult to do. Louis Napoleon had outraged many conservatives for his part during the revolution of 1848. Louis Napoleon had upset liberals and democrats. Even the liberals who wanted to reestablish a monarchy wanted to reestablish their own monarchy, not his monarchy. Louis Napoleon had upset some Catholics by some of his actions. Louis Napoleon had to juggle balls between so many disparate groups, because the legacy of the French Revolution continued to leave a legacy of disparate groups. It is sometimes said that France is a nation that has too much history. Many nations do not have enough. France, indeed, had too much. And the representatives of every segment of that history still believed (to this day, in many cases) that they represented the true France—the true French history—just as Louis Napoleon believed he did so himself.

Some have called him a proto-fascist, I think unwisely. Some have called him a Saint-Simonean on horseback, a utopian socialist on horseback. Some have called him a Caesarian democrat. Some have called him, in a sense, a modern totalitarian, and that's what a proto-fascist is. In our next meeting together, we'll discuss all of these various ideas; take a very, very careful look at the largely successful domestic politics that Napoleon implemented; and take an equally careful look at the very, very unsuccessful foreign policy that ultimately brought him down in 1870.

Thank you.

Lecture Twelve
Napoleon III—An Evaluation

Scope:

Fascinating and enigmatic, Napoleon III faced the daunting task of establishing legitimacy and creating a liberal, constitutional monarchy in a bitterly divided France and a Europe threatened by his name. Ruling longer than any 19th-century French monarch, Napoleon III's legacy was marred by France's defeat in the Franco-Prussian War, for which he must ultimately be blamed.

Still, on the domestic front, Napoleon III governed France creatively, attempting to improve the lives of the agrarian and urban masses, facilitate economic expansion and modernization (which would benefit the middle classes and the wealthy), and maintain the support of Catholics. During the greater part of his regime, prosperity and growth ensued.

Napoleon III's 1850s regime was dictatorial, although not capricious; it was characterized by bureaucratic manipulation and the courting of the masses. In the 1860s, Napoleon III allowed a constitutional regime to develop, including free elections. In foreign policy, the source of his demise, Napoleon III was energetic and temporarily successful, making France the center of European diplomacy from 1856–1866. However, his character flaws and risk-taking were catastrophic. Favoring moderate self-determination in Italy and Germany, as long as France gained in prestige and territory, Napoleon III facilitated events that led to the "unification" of Italy and Germany. Ill and sharing power with new political elites by the mid-1860s, Napoleon III lost control of events and was "bested" by Bismarck, a statesman of greater focus, intelligence, and ruthlessness.

Outline

I. Although somewhat artificial, given that domestic and foreign policy are interrelated, Napoleon III's regime can be analyzed in two components, a largely successful and imaginative domestic sphere and an adventurous and finally disastrous foreign policy. Even within the domestic sphere, the regime was composed, at least politically, of two eras, the moderately dictatorial 1850s and the increasingly liberal 1860s.

A. During the 1850s, Napoleon III ruled dictatorially, using prefect-dominated pseudo-elections (with universal suffrage) and moderate repression.

B. At the same time, he attempted to be all things to all people, governing on behalf of the French people.

  1. He encouraged industry, commerce, railroads, agricultural development, public works, and foreign investment.

  2. He encouraged the expansion of credit, establishing a series of semi-public banks and public bond issues (railroads up four times in the 1850s), while also expanding free trade with the Anglo-French Cobden-Chevalier Treaty in 1860.

  3. He encouraged scientific farming, urban renewal, expanded education, hospitals, and other social agencies.

  4. He encouraged the arts.

C. Napoleon III liberalized his regime in the 1860s, attempting to establish a hereditary constitutional monarchy to "crown the edifice with liberty."

  1. In 1860, the lower and upper houses of Parliament gained the right to respond to the emperor's major speeches.

  2. In 1861, the lower house obtained more control over the "budget"; in 1862, ministers were required to defend government policies before the chamber.

  3. Political prisoners were amnestied and more freedom of the press was allowed.

  4. With the legislative elections of 1863, prefectoral "rigging" of elections was called off; opposition groups formed.

  5. In 1864, workers were allowed to unionize and to strike.

  6. In the hopes of educating the new "workers" of France, during 1865–1866, widespread educational reforms were introduced by Victor Duruy.

  7. Between 1867–1869, freedom of the press and assembly were restored; Parliament obtained expanded powers, including over taxation; and a free 1869 election gave

Napoleon III a comfortable majority, but with 3.35 million votes for "opposition" candidates.

8. Accepting a ministry headed by liberal Émile Ollivier in January 1870, Napoleon III won an overwhelming victory (7.33 million versus 1.57 million votes) in a May 1870 referendum, seeming to have created a liberal empire.

II. In foreign policy, source of his demise, it must be remembered that Napoleon III seemed to be dominating the fate of Europe, at least until the Austro-Prussian War of 1866.

A. Again, Napoleon was an activist, from a combination of motives—courting patriotic and Catholic support, seeking legitimacy, supporting the cause of liberal nationalism, and seeking French gain.

B. Even when well intentioned, his policies were often poorly considered, events often got out of his control, and he did not learn from past mistakes.

C. In foreign affairs, he was also playing in a high-stakes game, with such players as Otto von Bismarck being more adept and ruthless.

D. At least until 1866, this was not apparent to contemporaries; Paris again became the diplomatic capital of Europe.

III. During his first 15 years, Napoleon's foreign policy adventures, even when leading to loss of life and expenditures, usually led to French pride and Napoleon's legitimacy.

A. In the imperialist realm, Napoleon pursued a reasonably "successful" policy, expanding in the Near East, North Africa, West Africa, and Southeast Asia.

B. He expanded the concept of free trade whenever possible, most notably with Britain.

C. Although Napoleon's support for Piedmont's anti-Austrian war in 1859–1860 got out of control, it did expand liberal national constitutionalism in Italy, substantially restricted Austrian meddling from Italy, and yielded France the provinces of Nice and Savoy.

D. Napoleon's quixotic policy of attempting to impose Prince Maximilian of Bavaria as emperor of Mexico between 1861–1867 was a dramatic failure but not fatal.

E. His support for Bismarck's policy of expanding Prussia and weakening Austria, in 1865–1866, became a disastrous defeat, because Prussia unexpectedly routed Austria, coming to dominate all of north Germany.

F. Although Napoleon must be given responsibility for the events that led to the French defeat in the Franco-Prussian War (1870–1871), ending his regime, there are mitigating circumstances.

  1. During his "liberal empire" he shared control with legislators who blocked military reforms, fearing Napoleon III would use the army against domestic opponents.

  2. After 1865, he was ill and not functioning at his best.

  3. In the final crisis, once Bismarck chose war, Napoleon III was pushed into the conflict by French nationalists and those who had blocked his proposed military reforms.

  4. Still, failure is failure; he had the decency to realize the end had come and abdicated, hoping to end bloodshed and preserve the emperorship for his son.

Essential Reading:

Ralph Menning, *The Art of the Possible: Documents on Great Power Diplomacy, 1814–1914*, pp. 111–121.

Jeremy D. Popkin, *A History of Modern France*, pp. 116–131.

L. C. B. Seaman, *From Vienna to Versailles*, pp. 55–68.

Supplementary Reading:

Otto Friedrich, *Olympia: Paris in the Age of Manet*.

James McMillan, *Napoleon III*.

Questions to Consider:

1. What makes Napoleon III such a fascinating subject for historians?

2. What were his major accomplishments, and what were his major failures?

Lecture Twelve—Transcript
Napoleon III—An Evaluation

Today I hope will be a real pleasure for you, and I know it will be a real pleasure for me, because it's the first time in our series that I'm going to have the opportunity to basically speak about the same country twice in a row, continuing the story of Napoleon III in France. Moreover, in the next series of lectures, we will be doing the same thing: two on Italy, two on Germany, and then several one-time lectures on the other great powers, giving us more concentration, more depth, more focus. The main theme should be becoming more familiar and more easily understood as we proceed in this particular manner.

Although somewhat artificial, since domestic and foreign policy are always interrelated, Napoleon III's regime can be analyzed in two components: a largely successful and imaginative domestic sphere, and an adventuresome and finally disastrous foreign policy. Even within the domestic sphere, the regime was composed, at least politically, of two eras, the moderately dictatorial 1850s and the increasingly liberal 1860s.

During the 1850s, advised by a diverse political elite not representing a single party therefore, but generally loyal to Napoleon III, Napoleon did rule dictatorially, using prefect-dominated pseudo-elections (with universal suffrage) (but you can fix elections) and moderate repression where necessary, including censorship and a police apparatus. At the same time, he attempted to be all things to all people—his hallmark: governing broadly on behalf of the French people, even on behalf of the interests of people who opposed him. Following an activist socioeconomic policy, he encouraged industry, commerce, railroads, agricultural development with special banks for that, public works, and foreign investment. He expanded credit, both industrial and agrarian, helping to found a series of semi-public banks and public bond issues. Railroads increased by four times in the 1850s. He also expanded free trade, climaxing with the Anglo-French Cobden-Chevalier Treaty in 1860. Even that is a peculiar combination. Free trade, which is liberal, laissez-faire, Adam Smith economics, combined with public expenditure, government intervention in the economy, showing how imaginative he was. Others might say how confused he was. I think it was imaginative.

He encouraged work on scientific farming, widespread urban renewal, expanded education, and he constructed hospitals and worked on other social agencies. In fact, he even confiscated the property of the Orleanist monarchy and used the money for social welfare. For those of you who love to walk the streets of Paris, I'm sure that many of you realize that those broad boulevards come from the work of Baron Haussmann, who architected that work under the inspiration and support of Napoleon III. Even there, multiple purposes. Those boulevards are magnificent. It is much harder to set up barricades across them if you want to rebel, and it's much easier to have cannon and troops go down them if you want to put down rebellions—so, multiple-purposed, reconstituing the city of Paris, to make it ever more beautiful.

He encouraged the arts, employing mild censorship there, but still encouraging the arts, which did flourish.

Maintaining the thrust of these domestic policies, Napoleon proceeded to liberalize his regime in the 1860s, attempting to establish a type of hereditary constitutional monarchy and, as he said he would do, to "crown the edifice with liberty." Now, again, this was very, very difficult. What he is trying to do is to bridge the gap between someone who took power by a *coup d'état*, even with a majority of the people supporting him, and someone who wanted to establish a legitimate hereditary monarchy somewhat like what existed in England, except with more power in the hands of the monarch, but clearly with shared governance, the rule of law (fair law; equal law). And scholars debate whether these liberal changes in the 1860s came out of political necessity or whether they came because he wanted them to occur. Political necessity may have accelerated the pace from time to time, but at no time until the Franco-Prussian War did he ever lose the support of the army, did he ever lose the support of the bureaucracy, did he ever lose the support of the overwhelming majority of the French people. He could have ruled by force and by decree if that's what he chose to do. He chose otherwise.

In 1860, both the lower and upper houses of Parliament, in published form, gained the right to respond to the emperor's major speeches, leading to wider public debate. In 1861, the lower house obtained more control over the "budget," while in 1862, ministers were required to defend government policies before the chamber—budget and ministers before the chamber. Control over the budget in any society is always a main perk. If you can control the budget, you can alter the policy. Having your ministers stand before the Parliament to explain their policies puts them on notice that they better know what they're doing.

During the early 1860s, political prisoners were amnestied and more freedom of the press was allowed. Beginning with the legislative elections of 1863, the "rigging" of elections by prefects was called off, and opposition groups formed in the chamber. If you want to read in detail the history of how all of this happened, read Theodore Zeldin's wonderful little book *The Political System of Napoleon III*. Zeldin is one of the great scholars of modern French history and modern French culture.

Significantly, in 1864, workers were allowed to unionize and to strike. More clearly (actually, in some ways, even in England this happened at the same time) a worker's delegation is sent to the first International Working Men's Conference, held in London at that year. So, he attempted to do everything he could to bring the workers back into his bosom.

In the hopes of educating the new "workers" of France, during 1865–1866, widespread educational reforms were introduced by Victor Duruy with full Napoleonic support, expanding primary education, expanding vocational education, even expanding education for women and improving secondary education, all with less clerical control. In virtually every one of the countries in Europe, control over education was to be a main bone of contention between church and state, because the belief was that if you could control the mind of a young person you could control that person's future. Many of the most powerful revolutionaries, in fact, went to Catholic schools. So, the belief is not the reality. Those of us in education for our entire lives know that, but it's nice to believe anyway.

Between 1867–1869, freedom of the press and assembly were restored. Both houses of Parliament obtained expanded powers, including overtaxation, and including over unpopular ministers. A free election in 1869 still gave Napoleon III a comfortable majority, but with more than 3 million votes for "opposition" candidates who now sat in the legislature. Accepting a ministry headed by a former opposition liberal, Émile Ollivier, in January 1870, Napoleon III won an overwhelming victory in a referendum (more than 7 million votes to a million and a half votes)—a May 1870 referendum concerning the previous collective reforms, seeming to have successfully created a liberal empire just on the eve of the Franco-Prussian War. In other words, he seemed to have really, really done it—achieved a ministry of more liberal people willing to work with him, still with the overwhelming support of the majority of French people on his side in a country that was very prosperous at that time, beautiful, booming culturally, doing well economically, and in a process in which virtually every group in French society had benefited from those changes, except, of course, those people who died in those riots, who never got to achieve the benefits.

In the realm of foreign policy, the source of his eventual demise, it has to be remembered that Napoleon III seemed to be dominating the fate of Europe, at least until the Austro-Prussian War of 1866. In other words, in an area in which he found his ultimate demise, contemporaries thought he was still in the saddle, as did he. As in the case of domestic politics, Napoleon was an activist—an activist from a combination of motives: courting patriotic and Catholic interests, seeking legitimacy, supporting the cause of liberal nationalism, while simultaneously seeking moderate French aggrandizement, as well—again, another tension. Napoleon seemed to believe in the liberal nationalism of the first half of the 19th century—that every people had its own karma, and every meaningful people (relatively large, at least) should have some form of national self-determination, some ability to express its political sensibility, some ability to express its culture. He was willing to support that, taking risks—but he would only do so if France could gain something, as well. So, his heart and his mind were sometimes (in fact, usually) in conflict.

However, as distinct from domestic policies, even when well intentioned, his politics were often quixotic, insufficiently considered, events often got out of control, and he didn't seem to learn from past mistakes. In domestic policies he adjusted well. In domestic policy he took risks. In domestic policy he knew how to support people of quality who carried out programs of magnitude. He stayed with them.

His learning curve in foreign policy truly was pathetic, because what he didn't recognize was that foreign policy is another element of war. And war gets out of control. And he didn't understand it. And he should have, because it happened to him enough that he should have learned. In foreign affairs, he was playing a high-stakes game, with players such as Otto von Bismarck and Camillo di Cavour who were more adept and (in terms of Bismarck, let us also remember) much more ruthless than Napoleon III. He was out of his league in foreign policy. At least until 1866, however, this was not apparent to contemporaries, and Paris seems to have once again become the diplomatic capital of Europe—the place from which initiative and action occurred. In terms of the first 15 years of his reign, Napoleon's foreign policy adventures, even when leading to loss of life and unnecessary expenditures, usually redounded to French national pride and did strengthen Napoleon's legitimacy.

In the imperialist realm (not one of my favorites, but liked by contemporaries), Napoleon pursued a reasonably "successful" policy, expanding French interests in the Near East, Algeria, Syria, North Africa, West Africa, Southeast Asia, and Vietnam. Whenever possible, he did these things in cooperation with Great Britain. Cooperating with Great Britain economically and imperially was one of his designs, and he knew Britain. He had lived there. And he was comfortable with their form of government—very comfortable with their form of government. He expanded the concept of free trade whenever possible, most notably with Britain, but with other states as well. This period of 1850 to 1870 was, in fact, the peak of free trade in Europe, which is an important thing to remember, because free trade has a psychology of its own. If you have free trade with other states, it leads to other forms of pacification. It leads to other forms of communication. Whereas, when you have tariffs, it leads to competition. Competition leads to bad feelings. Napoleon III was good on this issue with respect to his policy of tariffs.

Although Napoleon's support for Piedmont's anti-Austrian war in 1859–1860 got out of control (and we'll spend a good bit of time on this when we talk about the "unification" of Italy)—angering French Catholics because the pope was against this, and leading to greater Piedmontese expansion than was anticipated, because the plan was really hopefully to form some kind of Italian confederation with the pope nominally being in charge and the Piedmontese really being in charge—this adventure did expand liberal national constitutionalism in Italy. It substantially restricted Austrian meddling from the affairs of northern Italy and southern Italy, which was very poorly governed, and it provided France with the provinces of Nice and Savoy. If you visit Nice while you are in France, it used to be part of

Italy. Earlier it had been part of France. It was Franco-Italian in culture.

It even yielded Napoleon a show princess for his son, and the document in which that was negotiated between Cavour and Napoleon III, and Cavour and his emperor, is quite a document—the meeting at Plombiere. And Cavour afterward said to his emperor, "Listen. This is a good deal. We have to go along with his wishes."

Napoleon's quixotic policy of attempting to impose Prince Maximilian of Bavaria as emperor of Mexico between 1861–1867, which again would have pleased Catholics and would have brought France further national kudos, was a dramatic and even silly failure—but not a fatal one. Indeed, it was fatal for Maximilian, because even after the French troops left Mexico when, following the American Civil War, we advised them (not too politely) to leave Mexico, Maximilian believed in his star, too; he was finally captured and put to death by the Mexicans who took over their own country.

His support for Bismarck's policy of expanding Prussia and further weakening Austria, in 1865–1866, was a disastrous defeat, since Prussia unexpectedly routed Austria and her German allies, coming to dominate all of north Germany. Again, that was not expected. Prussia and Austria were relatively equal in strength, although Prussia clearly had the nod by that time, although not everybody realized it. Remember, Austria was the historic dominator. But Prussia had expanded its military more powerfully, and Prussia's economy had expanded, and its focus was much stronger than the Austrian focus, and its generals were much stronger than the Austrian generals, and Bismarck was in charge. However, bets were that there would have been a longer war, and France would have intervened to settle and moderate the war and gain compensation on France's eastern border—maybe taking the border a little bit back to what it was in 1792, during the early part of the French Revolution. But in any case, France would, once again, have been the arbiter of the fate of central Europe. This is what more people thought was going to happen.

After Napoleon had gone through the experience of Italy, in 1859–1861, he simply should have known better. He should have known better. That war got out of control. He could not control it, and he should not have played. That was a dramatic and continuous character flaw. That was part of the very nature of the individual. He had a retarded learning curve. He always seemed to need to be on the move. He also was ill by that point, suffering in pain. But for that kind of decision, it's not a good excuse.

Although Napoleon has to be given overall responsibility for the events that led to the dramatic French defeat in the Franco-Prussian War in 1870–1871, ending his regime, there are mitigating circumstances to consider. During the era of his "liberal empire," he shared control with legislators who blocked needed military reforms and who blocked needed expenditures. Remember, they had gotten more control over taxation and the purse, but they feared Napoleon III would use the strengthened army to put them down and reestablish a dictatorship. In other words, they didn't believe his liberal intentions. He had done so many various things along the course of his career that when he said he would crown his edifice with liberty, and, therefore, he was behaving exactly as he had promised, they didn't believe it. And, therefore, they would not accord him the expenditures.

After 1865, Napoleon III was seriously ill, and he was not functioning at his best. And that is clear.

In the final crisis, once Bismarck had decided for war, Napoleon III was pushed into the conflict by French nationalists and by the very legislators who had blocked his proposed military reform. Bismarck did this very skillfully. He edited the "Ems Dispatch" telegram, making it appear as though the Kaiser had willingly, openly, and directly insulted French honor. That was like putting a flag in front of a bull, and France was the bull, and they bit. And Bismarck had the war that apparently even he had not decided upon until just a year or two before at the earliest. It was a late-minute decision for Bismarck, but he knew how to do those things. He did them brilliantly, and he made it work.

Still, failure is failure. The French army was not up to the task. The Germans mobilized more quickly. The French were defeated at a series of decisive battles at the beginning of the war. What Napoleon III did at that time, realizing that the war was lost, was to abdicate and to surrender directly to the Prussians in the hope of ending further bloodshed and, perhaps, in the hope of preserving the emperorship for his son. Neither of those things would happen. Further bloodshed there would be. The French people would resist for another half a year or so. Paris would be besieged for months.

Most of the wealthy would leave. The poor would be happy occasionally to eat rats. Then, the French followed that up in the spring of 1871 with a wonderful little civil war called the Commune. More on that when we talk about late-19th-century France.

Some final thoughts are in order. As Theodore Zeldin has commented, Napoleon seems to have been "an innovator in politics as others were in diplomacy"—strengthening France in many ways, and leaving her wealthier and also freer than he had found her. Indeed, our friend L.C.B. Seaman is one of the great criticizers of Napoleon III. He doesn't give Napoleon III credit for a great deal of intelligence. He doesn't give Napoleon III credit for a great deal of power. He says that conspiracy was the only game he knew. And yet, even Seaman concludes, saying:

> Unique among dictators in ending his career with a government that provided his country with more freedom than the government he started with.

Even with the significant loss of Alsace and part of Lorraine, if you've traveled to Alsace and Lorraine, you know how beautiful it is, and it was going to be a bone of contention between Germany and France for the next 45 years until World War I began. Even with the loss and the bloody French civil war known as the Commune in the spring of 1871, France paid back the 5-billion-franc German indemnity far more quickly than expected, and France began a process of normal recovery. In other words, Napoleon III had left France far wealthier than he found her. Again, some people argue over how much of that was situational, how much of that was periodic. There was a general European expansion during that time period. But it's very, very evident (rethinking about the comments of today) that he pursued an activist economic policy, broadly based, that furthered the interests of industry, that furthered the interests of agriculture, that furthered the interests of science and technology, that furthered the interests of education, that furthered the interests of banking, that provided a level of security, that provided a level of order and domestic tranquillity, and that also provided a level of room for people to breathe, even during the first decade of his years in power.

It is notable that except for the Vichy regime, the fall of France to Nazi Germany in June 1940, Marshal Petain's Vichy regime from 1940 to 1944, it is notable that after Napoleon III's regime, universal suffrage was the norm, at least for men, for French history until the present time, with women having gained the right to vote in France after World War II. Remember, again, there were lots of people, particularly among the elites, who were against universal male suffrage and who thought that even the lower middle class, people without lots of property, people without lots of education, should not have the right to vote. Napoleon III believed in universal male suffrage, and then he went about trying to gain the support of most people in France.

Although often well intentioned, foreign affairs revealed Napoleon III's most serious character flaws. And he was finally "bested" by two of the brightest and most successful statesmen of the century: Camillo di Cavour and Otto von Bismarck. In fact, there is a book by Jules Cambon, a French diplomat at the end of the 19th century, on precisely the question of who was greater, Cavour or Bismarck, and Cambon actually said that Cavour was greater because he had a smaller deck of cards. Bismarck had a big deck of cards. I don't know if I accept that judgment anyway, but it's nice in any case to have a goodly sized deck of cards, meaning industry and a good army and good generals, if you're going to play foreign policy.

Since neither the French, nor most people for that matter, suffer those responsible for military defeat easily, most French people still revered his uncle, for whom I have not a great deal of respect, responsible for several million unnecessary deaths in war. And most Frenchmen still underestimate the contribution Napoleon III made to the development of French civilization.

Under his regime, France experienced more positive social legislation for a wider variety of its citizens than any other regime until the post-World War II era. He was an innovator in domestic politics. He was, in the end, a tragic failure in foreign policy—and, ultimately, the toughest area of foreign policy, the area of war.

Our next lecture will be on Italy, its history prior to the era of unification, its unification. We'll follow that up with two commentaries on Germany, following the same procedure: going back into the past, setting a foundation, giving you a context, and watching that context develop.

Thank you.

Timeline

1774	Louis XVI takes the throne in France.
1775	Beginning of the American Revolution (through 1783).
1776	Adam Smith writes *Wealth of Nations*.
1777	General Lafayette and his volunteers assist in the American Revolution.
1778	Deaths of Voltaire and Rousseau.
1781	Kant writes *Critique of Pure Reason*.
1783	Peace of Versailles ends the American Revolution; Great Britain recognizes the independence of the United States.
1784	Treaty of Constantinople: Russia annexes the Crimea with Turkish agreement.
1787	The Austrian Netherlands is declared a province of the Habsburg monarchy; assembly of Notables in France.
1788	The Parlement of Paris presents a list of grievances, and Louis XVI decides to call the Estates-General for May 1789; Austria declares war on Turkey.
1789	The French Revolution: The Estates-General convenes at Versailles, and the Third Estate declares itself the National Assembly. The Bastille is stormed on July 14. The feudal system is abolished, and the Declaration of the

Rights of Man is drawn up. The king and court move from Versailles to Paris during the October Days (October 5–6); the Austrian Netherlands declares independence as Belgium.

1791 ....France: Louis XVI flees Paris but is caught and returned; the Constitution is promulgated; the National Assembly dissolves.

1792 ....Denmark becomes the first nation to abolish the slave trade; the Peace of Jassy ends the war between Russia and Turkey; France: The Girondists form a ministry in France; the Tuileries is mobbed; a revolutionary Commune is established in Paris; the Legislative Assembly is suspended; and the royal family is imprisoned. The French Republic is proclaimed on September 22. The Jacobins seize power, and Louis XVI is put on trial. France declares war on Austria, Prussia, and Sardinia; France takes Brussels and conquers the Austrian Netherlands.

1793 ....France: Louis XVI, Queen Marie Antoinette, and the Duke of Orleans are executed. The Constitution of 1793 is promulgated. The Reign of Terror begins with Robespierre as a member of the Committee for Public Safety. Roman Catholicism is banned, and the Holy Roman Empire declares war on France. Napoleon takes Toulon. War is declared on Britain, Spain, and the Dutch Republic. The Austrians reconquer Belgium. The Louvre becomes a national art gallery.

1794 ....France again regains Belgium from Austria; Robespierre is executed. The Thermidorian Reaction occurs.

1795 ....France: Third Constitution enacted; the Directory receives power. The bread riots and White Terror take place in Paris. Austria signs an armistice with the French, while the French occupy Mannheim and Belgium. Freedom of worship is granted; Napoleon is appointed the commander-in-chief in Italy; The Third Partition of Poland is made by Russia, Austria, and Prussia.

1796 ....Napoleon takes power in Italy, defeating the Austrians and the Piedmontese.

1797 ....A preliminary peace treaty is signed between France and Austria at Léoben, as well as the Peace of Campo Formio.

1798 ....Napoleon leads an army to conquer Egypt (and does so at the Battle of the Pyramids); the French capture Rome, Malta, and Alexandria; the British navy defeats Napoleon's fleet.

1799 ....Napoleon advances to Syria. Later, he overthrows the French Directory and appoints himself First Consul; the French are defeated in a number of battles with Austria and Russia. The French are chased out of Italy.

1800 ....Napoleon wins some battles for France against the Turks and

Austrians. France regains Italy; the British capture Malta.

1801 .... The Act of Union comes into force between Britain and Ireland; Napoleon signs a concordat with the papacy.

1802 .... Napoleon becomes the president of the Italian Republic, names himself First Consul for life, and annexes Piedmont, Parma, and Piacenza; the Peace of Amiens is signed between Britain and France.

1803 .... War resumes between Britain and France.

1804 .... Napoleon is proclaimed emperor by the Senate and Tribunate in Paris.

1805 .... The Treaty of St. Petersburg is signed by Britain, Russia, and Austria against France; Napoleon is crowned king of Italy; Napoleon's victory at the Battle of Austerlitz against Austro-Russian forces results in the Peace of Pressburg between Austria and France.

1806 .... Prussia declares war on France; Napoleon names his brothers as kings of Holland and Naples; the Confederation of the Rhine is founded by Napoleon, marking the official end of the Holy Roman Empire.

1807 .... The Treaty of Tilsit ends war on the continent between France, Russia, and Prussia; the slave trade is abolished in Britain.

1808 .... The French army occupies Rome and invades Spain, taking Madrid and Barcelona. Later in the year, Madrid rebels against the French, and they are forced to flee.

1809 .... War resumes between France and Austria, but after a few battles, Austria is defeated and the Treaty of Schönbrunn is signed; Napoleon annexes the Papal States, and Pope Pius VII is taken prisoner; Seeking an heir, Napoleon divorces his wife, Josephine de Beauharnais.

1810 .... Napoleon annexes the Netherlands and the northwestern coast of Germany, issues the Decree of Fontainebleau requiring the confiscation of British goods, and marries the archduchess of Austria, Marie Louise, producing an heir.

1811 .... The Luddites riot in northern Britain, against industrial change; Austria is bankrupt.

1812 .... Napoleon enters Russia with his army of 600,000 but is later forced to retreat; only 40,000 of his troops return; the United States declares war on Britain.

1813 .... Napoleon is defeated. Prussia declares war on France but is defeated. Austria declares war on France, and in the Battle of the Nations at Leipzig, Napoleon is defeated and forced to give up Germany. The Prussian army begins invasion of France in December.

1814 .... The Allied armies defeat the French and enter Paris. In response, Napoleon abdicates the throne and is exiled to Elba. Louis XVIII takes the throne as his hereditary right. The First Treaty of Paris is signed and France is given its 1792 frontiers; the Congress of Vienna opens; the Treaty of Ghent ends the British-American war.

1815 ....Napoleon returns from Elba and the "Hundred Days" begin. Napoleon is defeated at Waterloo by British and Prussian forces. The Second Treaty of Paris leaves France with its 1789 frontiers. Napoleon abdicates again and is banished to St. Helena; the Congress of Vienna closes.

1816 ....Prince Metternich opens the Diet of the German Confederation at Frankfurt.

1817 ....At Wartburg, the German Student Organization organizes a nationalist festival to commemorate the Reformation.

1818 ....The Allies evacuate their troops from France; Prussia abolishes its internal customs barriers.

1819 ....The "Peterloo" Massacre occurs in Manchester, Britain; freedom of the press is declared in France; in Germany, the Carlsbad decrees introduce strict censorship and political repression.

1820 ....The Final Act of the Vienna Congress is passed.

1821 ....Revolts break out in Greece and Naples but are put down by Austrian troops; revolution in Piedmont causes Victor Emmanuel to abdicate; Napoleon dies.

1822 ....The Turks invade Greece; the Congress of Verona is opened to discuss problems in Europe.

1823 ....Europeans are no longer welcome to form colonial settlements in America, decreed by the Monroe Doctrine; the Catholic Association of Ireland is formed by Daniel O'Connell.

1824 ....The Combination Acts are repealed, allowing British workers to form unions.

1825 ....Following the death of Alexander I, the Decembrist Revolt in Russia is crushed.

1826 ....Russia declares war on Persia, defeating her in 1827.

1827 ....Russia, France, and Britain recognize Greek independence and agree to force an end to hostilities between Greece and Turkey under the Treaty of London.

1828 ....War is declared on Turkey by Russia.

1829 ....Russo-Turkish war is ended by the Peace of Adrianople, and Turkey finally recognizes Greek independence; the Catholic Emancipation Act is passed in Britain, allowing Catholics to hold office.

1830 ....Revolution and revolts run rampant throughout Europe: The revolution in France results in Charles X's abdication of his throne; Louis Philippe is crowned. In Belgium, revolts against Dutch rule eventually end in Belgian independence. Revolts take place in some German principalities, such as Saxony and Hannover. Poles revolt against Russian rule.

1831 ....War is fought between Egypt and Turkey; rebellions continue around Europe in Modena, Parma, and the Papal States, along with uprisings in France caused by abominable working conditions; the great cholera pandemic spreads throughout Asia and Europe, from India in 1826, reaching Scotland in 1832.

1832 ....National and Liberal demonstrations held in Hambach, Germany; the First Reform Act in Britain doubles enfranchised voters; Giuseppe Mazzini forms "Young Italy."

1833 ....Educational reform takes place in France under Guizot.

1834 ....All German states join the Zollverein; Austria is excluded; slavery is abolished in Britain and all her territories.

1835 ....The first German railroad line opens between Nuremburg and Furth.

1836 ....The Chartist movement begins in Britain, marking the first national working-class movement there.

1837 ....Victoria becomes queen of Britain; Mazzini is exiled to Britain.

1839 ....The First Opium War breaks out between China and Britain.

1840 ....King Frederick William III of Prussia dies and is replaced by his son Frederick William IV; French crisis: Louis Napoleon Bonaparte begins a new conspiracy and is arrested; the London Conference leads to the London Straits Convention, under which the Bosphorous and Dardanelles are closed to warships of all powers and the Black Sea is closed to Russian warships; the Afghan War ends with the surrender of Afghan troops to the British.

1841 ....Turkey's sovereignty is guaranteed by the great powers.

1842 ....The end of the Opium War between China and Britain is marked by the Treaty of Nanking, under which Hong Kong is ceded to Britain; riots and strikes occur throughout the industrial areas of northern Britain.

1844 ....French war in Morocco is ended by the Treaty of Tangier.

1845 ....The Great Famine begins in Ireland.

1846 ....The Corn Laws are repealed in Britain, lowering food costs; revolts break out in Poland; Louis Napoleon escapes prison and goes to London.

1847 ....The British Factory Act restricts the working day for women and children to 10 hours.

1848 ....Revolts and revolutions break out all over Europe: A revolt in Paris results in the abdication of Louis Philippe, uprisings of workers, the

June Days, and Louis Napoleon's election as president of the new French Republic. Revolution takes place in Vienna, resulting in the resignation of Metternich and Franz Joseph I's ascension as emperor. Revolutions also occur in Venice, Milan, Berlin, and Parma. Czech revolts are put down by Austrian troops. Revolt occurs in Rome. The Prussian revolution is defeated; Sardinia declares war on Austria but is eventually defeated and forced to leave Venice, where a republic is proclaimed; Switzerland adopts a new constitution, under which it becomes a federal union; Serfdom is abolished in Austria and Prussia.

1849 .... A republic is proclaimed in Rome, but later, the French enter Rome and restore Pope Pius IX; Hungary is reconquered by Austrian and Russian forces; Venice surrenders to Austria.

1850 .... Prussian war with the Danish ends, and a constitution is decreed in Prussia; Cavour becomes minister in Piedmont; a limited constitution is adopted in Prussia; the "humiliation of Olmütz" is signed, under which Prussia agrees not to form a Germanic union.

1851 .... Louis Napoleon executes a coup d'état; the German Confederation is restored; Austria's centralist constitution is abolished.

1852 .... Under the new French constitution, the president is given monarchical powers; two weeks after this grant,

Louis Napoleon proclaims himself Emperor Napoleon III, and the reign of the Second Empire begins.

1853 ....The Crimean War begins after the Turks reject the Russian ultimatum.

1854 ....Britain and France enter into an alliance with Turkey and declare war against Russia, entering the Black Sea and beginning the siege of Sebastopol.

1855 ....The Russians surrender, and Allied troops take over Sebastopol.

1856 ....The Crimean War ends with the Peace of Paris; war begins between Britain and China.

1857 ....France aids Britain in its war against China; relatively new to the throne, Tsar Alexander II calls the Assembly of Nobles in Moscow to consider the emancipation of the serfs.

1858 ....The Anglo-Chinese War ends with the Treaty of Tientsin; France comes to an agreement with Piedmont to act against Austria after Cavour and Napoleon meet at Plombières.

1859 ....War is declared on Austria by France, and the Franco-Austrian War begins, ending later that year with Austria defeated under the Peace Treaty of Zurich. Austria cedes Lombardy, and Piedmont cedes Nice and Savoy (in return, getting Lombardy); the German National Association is formed.

1860 ....Garibaldi and his 1,000 troops of red shirts sail for Sicily and take Sicily and Naples; the king of Piedmont-Sardinia, Victor Emmanuel II, takes the Papal States, and Garibaldi gives Sicily and Naples to him; Victor Emmanuel is declared the king of Italy.

1861 ....The Italian Parliament proclaims Italy to be a kingdom; the Warsaw Massacre takes place in Russian Poland, when demonstrators speak out against Russian rule; Russian serfs are finally emancipated, and other major reforms are enacted.

1862 ....Bismarck becomes prime minister of Prussia.

1863 ....Revolts take place in Poland, protesting Russian rule.

1864 ....Prussia and Austria attack Denmark; Denmark cedes Schleswig and Holstein to Prussia and Austria.

1866 ....The Austro-Prussian War begins and lasts seven weeks (Italy fights alongside Prussia). Prussia defeats Austria at the Battle of Sadowa. The Treaty of Prague excludes Austria from Germany; Austria cedes Venetia to Italy under the Treaty of Vienna; Prussia annexes Schelswig-Holstein, Hannover, and Frankfurt; the Northern German Confederation is established.

1867 ....The Second British Reform Bill is passed; the Dual Monarchy begins in Austria-Hungary (the *Ausgleich*); Russia sells Alaska to the United States; Garibaldi is taken prisoner during his march on Rome by French and papal troops.

1868 ....Revolution takes place in Spain, causing Queen Isabella to be deposed and flee; the first Gladstone ministry takes power and rules until 1874.

1869 ....The Ollivier ministry rules the French government.

1870 ....Bismarck sends his Ems Telegram; France declares war on Prussia and is defeated in multiple battles; Napoleon III is taken prisoner; Paris is besieged, and the Third Republic is proclaimed; Italian forces enter Rome and declare it their capital.

1871 ....Wilhelm I, king of Prussia, is proclaimed the emperor of Germany at Versailles; Paris capitulates, and the Revolutionary Commune rules Paris for two months; the Peace of Frankfurt ends the war between Germany and France; the French cede Alsace and Lorraine to Germany; Thiers is elected president of France; the British Parliament legalizes labor unions; the *Kulturkampf* begins in Germany.

1872 ....Civil war erupts in Spain; the Three Emperors' League is formed by Austria-Hungary, Germany, and Russia; the Ballot Act in Britain introduces voting by secret ballot.

1873 ....A republic is proclaimed in Spain.

1874 ....Disraeli becomes prime minister of Britain; civil marriage is made compulsory in Germany.

1875	The Public Health Act is passed in Britain.
1876	Turkish troops massacre Bulgarians; Serbia declares war on Turkey, with Montenegro.
1877	Russia declares war on Turkey, finally defeating Turkey at the Battle of Plevna.
1878	In June, the Congress of Berlin addresses the "eastern question," and Russia loses most gains; a small Bulgaria is created, which is fully autonomous; and Serbia, Rumania, and Montenegro become independent; the Anti-Socialist Law is enacted in Germany.
1879	Austria and Germany form an alliance after the end of the liberal era in both countries; the French government returns to Paris.
1880	A split in the German National Liberal Party ends the parliamentary dominance of liberalism.
1881	Tsar Alexander II is assassinated; the French occupy Tunis; the Three Emperors' League is renewed.
1882	The Triple Alliance among Germany, Austria, and Italy is formed.
1883	Bismarck introduces sickness insurance in Germany.
1884	In November, a conference is held in Berlin addressing African affairs and colonial conquests.
1885	Germany annexes more land in Africa.

1886 ....W. E. Gladstone introduces a bill for Irish Home Rule; the Bonaparte and Orléans families are banished from France; Georges Boulanger becomes French war minister; the Bulgarian crisis occurs.

1887 ....In June, the Russo-German Reinsurance Treaty is formed.

1888 ....Boulanger is retired from the French army and elected to the Chamber of Deputies; Wilhelm II becomes Kaiser after the deaths of Wilhelm I and Frederick III.

1889 ....Accused of conspiracy, Boulanger flees France; Hitler is born.

1890 ....Bismarck is forced to resign by Wilhelm II; the Reinsurance Treaty lapses; Charles de Gaulle is born.

1891 ....The Triple Alliance is renewed among Germany, Austria, and Italy; Russia turns from Germany and enters into the Russo-French Entente.

1892 ....Gladstone becomes prime minister of Britain.

1893 ....The Independent Labour Party is formed in Britain by Hardie; an alliance is signed between France and Russia.

1894 ....The Dreyfus Affair occurs in France: French army Captain Alfred Dreyfus is arrested and convicted for treason and sent to Devil's Island.

1896	Kaiser Wilhelm II sends the Kruger telegram; the first modern Olympics is held in Athens.
1897	The real spy in the Dreyfus Affair is discovered to be Major M. C. Esterhazy; Germany begins to build a battle fleet.
1898	Esterhazy is acquitted in the Dreyfus forgery trial, and later, Colonel Henry admits to the forgery of a document in the case. Emile Zola publishes his "*J'accuse*" letter to the French president, flees, and is consequently imprisoned; the Paris Métro is opened; the Fashoda incident: France and Britain confront each other in the Sudan.
1899	After being reconvicted by the military, Dreyfus is pardoned by presidential decree; the First Peace Conference occurs in The Hague.
1900	The Boxer Risings occur in China against Europeans; Bernhard von Bülow is named German chancellor.
1901	Queen Victoria dies.
1902	The Anglo-Japanese Alliance is signed; the Triple Alliance is renewed again for another six years.
1903	The Russian Social Democratic Party splits into Bolsheviks and Mensheviks; the Austro-Serb crisis takes place.
1904	War breaks out between Russia and Japan; Russia experiences multiple defeats; an *entente cordiale* is reached between France and Britain.

1905	Russia surrenders to Japan: A demonstration in St. Petersburg against the war is crushed by police and comes to be known as *Bloody Sunday*. The tsar's October Manifesto establishes reforms, and the Imperial Duma (parliament) is created; the Anglo-Japanese Alliance is renewed; Germany provokes the first Moroccan crisis.
1906	Algeciras Conference gives France and Spain control of Morocco and ends the first Moroccan crisis; the Russian Duma is dissolved for the first time.
1907	The second Russian Duma is created and soon dissolved, followed by a third; universal direct suffrage is instituted in Austria but not in Hungary; a peace conference takes place in The Hague, Netherlands.
1908	After German threats, Russia agrees to the Austrian annexation of Bosnia and Herzegovina; *The Daily Telegraph* publishes its famous interview with Kaiser Wilhelm II.
1909	Bülow resigns as chancellor.
1910	Japan annexes Korea; revolution in Portugal results in the formation of the Portuguese Republic.
1911	The second Moroccan crisis takes place; war is declared between Turkey and Italy and ends with a decisive Italian victory.
1912	Workers strike throughout Britain; the Social Democratic Party

becomes the strongest party in the German Parliament; the first Balkan War occurs.

1913 .... The second and third Balkan Wars occur, and Albania is created; the second Russo-Serb humiliation occurs.

1914 .... World War I begins: Archduke Franz Ferdinand and his wife are assassinated on June 28; Austria declares war on Serbia on July 28. Germany declares war on Russia and France, then invades Belgium. In response, Britain declares war on Germany; Austria declares war on Russia; France, Britain, and Serbia declare war on Austria. The Germans invade France; Russians invades East Prussia. The Germans are pushed back by the French at the Battle of the Marne. The Russians are defeated at the Battle of Tannenberg. The Russians invade Hungary.

1915 .... World War I: The first German submarine attack occurs at Le Havre; Germans blockade Britain; Italy joins with Allies; zeppelins attack London for the first time; many battles are fought near the Isonzo River in Italy; the Russians are defeated at the Battle of the Masurian Lakes; British and French troops land in Gallipoli.

1916 .... World War I: The first zeppelin raids occur in Paris; the Battle of Verdun begins; Germany declares war on Portugal; the Easter Rebellion occurs in Ireland; the

Battle of Jutland; the Allied Somme offensive is launched; there are strikes and mutinies in Russia; Germany sends a peace note to the Allies; gas masks are introduced.

1917 .... World War I: Nicholas II abdicates after the February Revolution in Russia; many Germans withdraw from the eastern front; the United States enters the war on the side of the Allies against Germany, and troops arrive in France in June; China declares war on Germany and Austria; the October Revolution takes place in Russia; a German-Russian armistice is signed at Brest.

1918 .... World War I: Woodrow Wilson's Fourteen Points on peace; peace treaty of Brest-Litovsk is signed between Russia and the central powers; the German Luftwaffe is assembled; German offensive on the western front; Germans bomb Paris; Second Battle of the Marne pushes Germans back again; in July, the Allied forces, including American troops, make advances; Germany and Austria agree to retreat to their territories before the armistice is signed; Germans suspend submarine warfare; the armistice ending World War I is signed on November 11 between the Allies and Germany; Nicholas II and his family are executed by the Bolsheviks; German Communist Workers' Party is founded in Berlin; Austria becomes a republic; civil war breaks out in Russia and lasts until 1921.

1919	Irish Home Rule is proclaimed; League of Nations meeting run by President Wilson in Paris; the Habsburgs are exiled from Austria; the Treaty of Versailles officially ends World War I after the Versailles conference (January through June) sets the terms of peace; the first woman is elected to the British Parliament.
1922	Mussolini comes to power.
1923	The Beer Hall Putsch, Hitler's famous attempted coup, takes place.
1924	Lenin dies.
1928	Stalin obtains full power.
1929	The stock market crashes.
1933	Adolf Hitler comes to power; Dachau is opened.
1937	Japan attacks China.
1938	The Munich Conference meets.
1939	The beginning of World War II is marked by the attack on Poland by Germany.
1940	France falls in June; Hitler gives up the Battle of Britain.
1941	Hitler attacks Russia; the Japanese bomb Pearl Harbor.
1942	The Wannsee Conference takes place; Auschwitz is opened; the Battle of Stalingrad begins and ends in 1943.
1944	The beaches of Normandy are stormed.

1945 ....Hitler commits suicide, and Germany surrenders; the United States drops the atomic bombs on Hiroshima and Nagasaki; the United Nations is created.

Glossary

absolutism: The principle or practice of a political system in which unrestricted power is vested in a monarch, dictator, or another with absolute power (also known as *despotism*).

Ancien Régime: The political and social system of France before the Revolution of 1789.

bête noir: A person or thing that someone particularly dislikes or dreads.

coup d'état: The sudden violent seizure of a government in which power changes hands illegally.

détente: A relaxation of tensions between nations.

dialectic: An interpretive method in which the contradiction between a proposition (thesis) and its antithesis is resolved at a higher level of truth (synthesis).

dialectical idealism: The system put forth by Hegel, under which he states that ideas are the generators of historical progress and that the clash of ideas is the motivating force.

dialectical materialism: The economic, political, and philosophical system of Karl Marx and Friedrich Engels that combines traditional materialism and Hegelian dialectics, producing a system in which historical progress develops, largely as a result of material forces, in a dialectical fashion.

émigré: One forced to leave his or her native country for political reasons.

entente/entente cordiale: A friendly agreement or understanding between political powers; less formal than an alliance.

faux pas: A social blunder or indiscretion.

fin de siècle: Literally, the end of the century. Refers especially to the sensibility at the end of the 19th century, when the phrase first came into use as a concept.

Gemeinschaft: A social group united by common beliefs, family ties, and similar bonds.

Gesellschaft: A social group held together by practical concerns, formal and impersonal relationships, and so on.

hegemon: Ascendancy or domination of one power or state within a league, confederation, or similar group or of one social class over others, leading to hegemony.

humanism: The rejection of religion in favor of a belief in the advancement of humanity by its own efforts. Also a movement during the Renaissance that focused on classical studies, human improvement, and the well-balanced individual.

left: Refers to a political group with radical beliefs. The term was first used at the time of the French Revolution, when the radical party sat on the left in the Assembly.

modernization: The adoption of ways more akin to those of modern society, in particular the process that began in late-18th–century western Europe and has spread (and continues to spread) to the present day.

persona non grata: A diplomatic or consular officer who is not acceptable to the government or sovereign to whom he or she is accredited.

Porte: Government of the Ottoman Empire.

positivism: A strong form of empiricism, especially as established in the philosophical system of Auguste Comte, that rejects metaphysics and theology as seeking knowledge beyond the scope of experience and holds that experimental investigation and observation are the only sources of substantial knowledge.

raison d'état: An action undertaken by the state, therefore legitimizing it. The action can be immoral or even illegal.

realpolitik/realpolitikers: A ruthlessly realistic and opportunist approach to statesmanship, rather than a moralistic one; exemplified by Bismarck.

right: Refers to a political group with conservative beliefs.

sans: Without.

sine qua non: An essential condition or requirement.

Social Darwinism: The adaptation of Darwin's concept of "survival of the fittest" (phrase first coined by Herbert Spencer) to explain the struggle between nations for superiority. It was used to explain the differences between races and to justify the conquest of "backward" peoples in Africa and Asia.

terra incognita: Unknown territory.

trasformismo: The situation of "political musical chairs" that occurred in late-19th–century Italian politics.

utilitarianism: The belief that the morally correct course of action consists in the greatest good for the greatest number, that is, in maximizing the total benefit resulting, without undue regard to the distribution of benefits and burdens.

volkish: The form of nationalism that emphasizes ethnicity, race, blood, and soil, mainly in 19th-century Germany and Austria.

zero sum: The case in which the gains to one side are equal to the losses of the other.

Biographical Notes

Charles Albert (1798–1849): King of Piedmont-Sardinia from 1831–1849. In a rather undistinguished political career, he modified the army and the state's fiscal system and tried to stave off revolution in the 1840s by implementing a number of moderate reforms, including a constitution in 1848. Desiring to rid northern Italy of Austrian domination, he twice supported unsuccessful revolutions against Habsburg positions in Lombardy and was forced to abdicate in favor of his son, Victor Emmanuel II.

Alexander I (1777–1825): Tsar of Russia from 1801–1825. Cosmopolitan in his vision, he implemented liberal reforms in the police department and educational system while abating restrictions on travel. He allied against Napoleon in 1805 but signed a treaty with the emperor in 1807 at Tilsit after humbling defeats at Austerlitz and Friedland that all but decimated Russian resistance. Alexander added to the size of the empire by obtaining lands in the Caucasus region, as a result of a war with the Persians (1804–1813), and Besserabia, after a war with the Turks (1806–1812). After helping to defeat Napoleon's fateful expeditions into Russia's interior, he became more conservative and reactionary, rescinding many of his more progressive measures.

Alexander II (1818–1881): Successor to his father, Nicholas I, as tsar of Russia from 1855–1881. He emancipated the serfs in 1861, reformed the judiciary, granted more local autonomy to the *zemstvos* (local assemblies), and relieved press censorship and educational restrictions—all of which contrasted sharply with the violent repression imposed on the Polish insurrections of 1863. Alexander worked quickly to achieve a peace with Britain and France after the Crimean War but pursued an aggressive policy of conquest and expansion in central and east Asia. He sold Alaska to the United States in 1867 and committed Russia to the Three Emperors' League alliance with Austria-Hungary and Germany, a tenuous situation because of the conflicting Balkan interests of Russia and the Dual Monarchy. Alexander was assassinated in 1881 by members of a radical terrorist organization.

Alexander III (1845–1894): Succeeded his father, Alexander II, as tsar of Russia from 1881–1894. He did much to rescind many of the progressive achievements of the previous regime. Police powers were augmented, education was made increasingly conservative, the autonomy of local *zemstvos* and judicial bodies was curbed, and religious freedom was curtailed. Despite efforts for peace in European relations, his rule saw Russian expansionary endeavors in Asia and chronic disputes with Austria-Hungary over the explosive Balkans region.

Marie Antoinette (1755–1793): Wife of King Louis XVI of France and daughter of Austrian Archduchess Maria Theresa and Francis I, Holy Roman Emperor. Her marriage was arranged to strengthen the ties between long-time rivals France and Austria. Unhappy in her relationship, she turned to a life of debauchery and material excesses. Her queenship was embroiled in scandal and rumor, most notably the Diamond Necklace Affair. Her hostility to the revolution and her hatred of the popular minister of finance, Jacques Necker, brought public scorn. She was tried in front of a revolutionary tribunal on October 14–15, 1793; found guilty; and guillotined.

Herbert Asquith (1852-1928): British politician. Entered Parliament as a liberal in 1886, served as junior counsel to Charles Parnell, advocated free-trade and imperialist policies (particularly toward Africa), and served as Chancellor of the Exchequer before replacing Sir Henry Campbell-Bannerman as prime minister in 1908. Asquith instituted social welfare reforms and led a push for Irish Home Rule. His wartime cooperation with the conservatives dissolved amidst military failures, compelling him to resign in 1916 in favor of David Lloyd George.

Alexander Bach (1813–1893): Austrian statesmen. Initially a liberal revolutionary in 1848, Bach turned conservative, beginning his political career as minister of justice later that year. He served as minister of the interior before becoming prime minister in 1852. Best known for implementing his infamous Bach System, a program of rigid bureaucratic centralization characterized by a powerful secret police organization bent on suppressing liberal opposition. The program also saw the elimination of the domestic tariff system, the emancipation of the serfs, and the return of Catholic influence throughout the kingdom.

Mikhail Bakunin (1814–1876): Russian revolutionary and anarchist. Bakunin participated in the 1848–1849 revolutions in Paris and Dresden and spent time in exile in Siberia. He was a leading figure of the First International and was an advocate of militant revolutionary measures for the procurement of natural human liberty.

Ludwig van Beethoven (1770–1827): Widely regarded as one of the greatest composers of all time. Beethoven spent much of his life in Vienna, where he learned from some of the most renowned composers of the age, including Mozart. Profiting greatly from the patronage of Vienna's elite, he produced some of music's most breathtaking achievements, including his Third (1803–1804), Fifth (1809), and Ninth (1817–1823) Symphonies.

Jeremy Bentham (1748–1832): English philosopher and political author. Founded the philosophy of utilitarianism as a synthesis of his studies on morality and legislation. His beliefs were predicated on the notion that all life consists in the pursuit of pleasures and the avoidance of pains and that government should operate to maximize these parameters to the greatest possible extent. His works were instrumental in the reformation of British suffrage and labor legislation in the early and mid-19th century.

Leopold Berchtold (1863–1942): Foreign minister of Austria-Hungary from 1912–1915. At the conclusion of the Balkan Wars of 1912–1913, Berchtold played a crucial role in the creation of a sovereign Albanian state, effectively blocking Serbian aspirations for access to the Adriatic. His caustic ultimatum to Belgrade following Archduke Franz Ferdinand's assassination in the summer of 1914 made armed conflict with Serbia all but a foregone conclusion and set all of Europe on a path toward war.

Henri Bergson (1859–1941): French philosopher. Bergson argued that human experience owes its path and substance to individual intuition rather than reason. He posited that scientific explanations were inadequate in human analyses and invoked the notion of a collective *élan vital*, or "life force," that consisted of mankind's creative capacities. His rejection of science as deterministic and incapable of explaining everything brought widespread popularity among the religious and those disillusioned with the positivism of Comte.

Eduard Bernstein (1850–1932): German socialist and leader of the moderate, revisionist socialist movement. In his *Evolutionary Socialism* (1898), he argued that capitalism was far from doomed and that social reform and progress could be achieved within the parliamentary process; thus, he rejected those, like Kautsky, who espoused militant Marxist agendas.

Theobald von Bethmann-Hollweg (1856–1921): German chancellor from 1909–1917. More concerned with the maintenance of Austria-Hungary's great-power status and with making Russia appear the aggressor in a great-power conflict, his support of the Dual Monarchy's ultimatum to Serbia contributed to war between the great powers of Europe in the summer of 1914.

Otto von Bismarck (1815–1898): German statesman and architect of unification. A Prussian nationalist, his background in law, the Prussian Landtag, and ambassadorships to St. Petersburg and Paris developed the sagacity that characterized his reign as Prussian prime minister under Wilhelm I after 1862. In foreign politics, he proved to be both aggressive and shrewd, greatly expanding Prussian borders and prestige in successive wars against Denmark (1864), Austria (1866), and France (1870–1871), while remaining adverse to large-scale conflict thereafter. Domestically, Bismarck was just as cunning, dissolving Parliament to obtain funds for the army, allying with the liberals against the Catholic Church and Catholic Center Party in the *Kulturkampf* of the early 1870s, alternatively passing repressive legislation to stem the tide of socialist sympathy throughout the empire during the late 1870s, and finally, implementing modern social legislation in the form of accident, sickness, and old age insurance and widespread labor reform in the late 1880s. Initially averse to overseas exploits, he oversaw the establishment of German colonies in west, southwest, and east Africa before being dismissed by Wilhelm II, in 1890.

Louis Blanc (1811-1882): French politician, historian, and social theorist. A member of the provisional government of 1848 and exiled after the June Days to England, Blanc returned to France as a liberal in 1871 and a member of the national assembly. His socialist beliefs were combined with a desire to see society, within which each individual got what he or she needed and provided what he or she could, transformed into a web of national workshops facilitated by the state.

Louis Napoleon Bonaparte (1808–1873): Emperor of the French (1852–1870). After spending time in exile and prison for participating in two insurrections in 1836 and 1840, Louis returned to France after the February Revolution, was elected to the national assembly, and was soon elected president of the Second Republic (1848). He dissolved the legislative assembly in the coup of December 1851, ended a subsequent insurrection, and was elected Emperor of the French by plebiscite in 1852. Louis oversaw victory in the Crimean War (1854–1856) and patronized Piedmontese wars against Austrian positions in Italy (1859–1860). His reign saw the completion of the Suez Canal, imperial conquests in Southeast Asia and China, the death of Maximilien in Mexico (1867), and the end of the Second Empire at the humiliating conclusion of the Franco-Prussian War. Domestically, many of France's cities were refurbished, construction and investment were encouraged, and civil liberties and legislative authorities were augmented, creating a liberal and social empire.

Napoleon Bonaparte (1769–1821): Born to Corsican parents and educated in French military schools, Napoleon was a member of the Jacobins during the revolution and rose to prominence by defeating the British at Toulon in 1793 and putting down a royalist uprising in Paris in 1795. The Convention promoted him to commander of the army of Italy, where his successes led to the treaty of Campo Formio. On November 9–10 of 1799, he overthrew the Directory in the coup of 18 Brumaire with the help of Talleyrand and Sieyès. A concordat with the Catholic Church was signed in 1801, while the Napoleonic Code of 1804 made French laws uniform and declared freedom of religion and equality before the law. His armies fought and conquered the counterrevolutionary forces of monarchical Europe from the Iberian Peninsula to the outskirts of Moscow until 1814–1815. He lived in captivity for the rest of his life after a defeat at Waterloo in 1815.

Bernhard von Bülow (1849–1929): German foreign secretary and chancellor of Germany from 1900–1909. As an extension of Wilhelm II's temerity in colonial and diplomatic affairs, von Bülow exacerbated Germany's political isolation. His hard-line stance during the Moroccan Affair in 1905 and his consent to the Dual Monarchy's diplomatic endeavors in the Balkans soured relations with France, Britain, and Russia.

Edmund Burke (1729–1797): British writer and politician. Burke became a member of Parliament in 1765 and clamored for a more socially prudent policy toward the American colonies and relations with the Indian peoples. Despite some leftist leanings and reform proposals, his *Reflections on the Revolution in France* (1790) made him a beacon of the conservative and anti-revolutionary ideology. His dual liberal and conservative tendencies illustrate that, above all else, he held political stability as vital to the nation-state. Burke viewed reform as valuable and desirable so long as it did not interfere with political and religious tranquility.

Lord George Byron (1788–1824): English poet of the Romantic period and friend of fellow Romantic poet Percy Bysshe Shelley. Byron attended Trinity College and began writing extensively thereafter. Unique in his flamboyance and satirical inclinations, he personified the Romantic period in life and death, succumbing to a fever in 1824 while devoting himself to the cause of Greek independence from the Ottomans. Some of his more notable works include *Don Juan* (1819–1824), *English Bards and Scotch Reviewers* (1809), and *Childe Harold* (1812, 1816, and 1818).

George Canning (1770–1827): British politician. Canning was undersecretary for foreign affairs under William Pitt, treasurer of the Navy (1804–1806), and foreign minister from 1807–1809 and again in 1822, after Castlereagh's suicide. He reversed his predecessor's policy of cooperation with autocratic powers in the repression of European insurrections, supporting leftists in Portugal, recognizing Latin American independence gains, and organizing a British, French, and Russian alliance that eventually secured the independence of Greece. He was prime minister briefly before his death.

Viscount Robert Castlereagh (1769–1822): English politician who served in the Irish Parliament before becoming a member of the British Parliament in 1794 and a proponent of Catholic emancipation. President of the India Board of Control (1802–1806) and secretary of war on two occasions from 1805 to 1809. As foreign secretary from 1812–1822, he was instrumental in the formation of the Quadruple Alliance and the Congress system, established at the Congress of Vienna to maintain stability in Europe. He lacked the charisma and sagacity of Metternich and was criticized for his dealings with the autocratic powers of the Holy Alliance and for his support of some of the repressive measures used in cases of domestic disturbance. Castlereagh committed suicide in 1822.

Louis Cavaignac (1802–1857): French army general. Cavaignac was appointed to general in 1844 after his service in the conquest of

Algeria and was made governor-general of Algeria in 1848 but returned to Paris as minister of war and quashed the June Days insurrection. He lost in the presidential elections of 1848 to Louis Napoleon.

Camillo di Cavour (1810–1861): Prime minister of Piedmont-Sardinia and a key orchestrator of Italian unification under the monarchy of Victor Emmanuel II. Long before war against Austria, he had set about modernizing the kingdom, reforming the bureaucratic, military, commercial, and fiscal sectors of the state. He obtained the assistance of Napoleon III in the expulsion of the Austrians from northern Italy in return for the cessation of Nice and Savoy. His leadership brought the annexation of much of northern Italy, the end of Garibaldi's insurrections in the Papal States, and the inclusion of the Kingdom of the Two Sicilies under Victor Emmanuel II.

Joseph Chamberlain (1836–1914): British politician. Chamberlain was mayor of Birmingham from 1873–1876, where he was hailed for his municipal reforms and became a liberal member of Parliament at the conclusion of his term. A proponent of social reform, he split with his one-time mentor, William Gladstone, over the issue of Irish Home Rule, siding with the Liberal Unionists. As a conservative colonial secretary in 1895, he advocated imperial expansion and sought to integrate the empire. Chamberlain is perhaps best known for his proposal of a preferential imperial tariff program that ran counter to England's liberal free-trade tradition. He resigned amidst controversy and spent the next few years pushing for tariff reform, an issue that split the Liberal Unionist-Conservative coalition before the 1906 election.

Charles X (1757–1836): Successor to Louis XVIII as king of France (1824–1830). Charles augmented the influence of the clergy throughout the state and oversaw preliminary military operations in Algeria. His censorship of the press, dissolution of the Chamber of Deputies, and abatement of suffrage rights amongst the bourgeois class led to the July Revolution of 1830 that resulted in his abdication in favor of Louis-Philippe of the Orléans house.

Karl von Clausewitz (1780–1831): Prussian army general and writer. Von Clausewitz fought in the coalition against Napoleon in Russia and at Waterloo. He is best known for his 1832 masterpiece *On War*, in which he muses on the vagaries of battle while anticipating the possible outbreak of total warfare that pits the sum total of a nation's resources against an equally strong enemy.

Georges Clemenceau (1841–1929): French radical and Dreyfusard. Clemenceau was a mainstay in the Chamber of Deputies from 1876 to 1893. Made prime minister in 1906, he helped forge amiable relations with Britain in the face of what he perceived to be a growing German naval and imperial menace. Faltering French morale on the front during World War I prompted his replacement of Paul Painlevé as prime minister in 1917; the result was a unification of Allied forces and reaffirmation of French commitment to the war, personifying French determination. Representing French interests at the Paris Peace Conference, Clemenceau stood opposed to the leniency proffered by Woodrow Wilson, pushing instead for severe German penalties that he believed necessary for French security.

Auguste Comte (1798–1857): French philosopher and founder of positivist philosophy. Deeply influenced by his relations with Saint-Simon, he was an idealist who saw the potential for a more comfortable, enjoyable society in the application of science and technology and a rejection of theological or metaphysical systems.

Marquis de Condorcet (1743–1794): A tragedy of the French Revolution, Condorcet was a mathematician and philosopher and was appointed to the Academy of Sciences in 1769 and to the French Academy in 1782. He foresaw the perfection of man at the conclusion of the French Revolution in his *Sketch for a Historical Picture of the Progress of the Human Mind* (1795). He advocated universal suffrage and equality under the law and fought against the death penalty, slavery, and the subordination of women.

Francesco Crispi (1819–1901): Twice Italian prime minister (1887–1891, 1893–1896). A revolutionary in 1848 and again in cooperation with Garibaldi, Crispi was initially a liberal member of the Italian Parliament in 1861 but became increasingly conservative, harboring the belief that only monarchy could unite northern and southern Italy. He was minister of the interior before succeeding Agostino Depretis as prime minister in 1887, at which time he reaffirmed the Triple Alliance with Austria-Hungary and Germany and encouraged Italian ventures into North Africa. His reactionary domestic policies included the repression of labor movements, police intimidation, and mass disenfranchisement, which coupled with the humiliating defeat at Adwa in 1896, led to his forced resignation.

Georges Jacques Danton (1759–1794): French statesman who became the figurehead of the *Cordeliers* club early in the revolution, as well as a member of the Paris Commune of August 1792. Danton was a member of the Constitutional Convention and a leading figure in the Committee of Public Safety in its early stages. He urged restraint in foreign policy and within the Committee of Public Safety, denouncing the atrocities of the Terror. He and some of his associates in the *Cordeliers* club were charged with conspiracy in March 1794 and were guillotined.

Charles Darwin (1809–1882): English natural scientist. Darwin was the author of the famed *On the Origin of Species* (1859), an account of his travels and findings during his five-year hiatus aboard the H.M.S. *Beagle* and a comprehensive outline of his theory of evolution. He later penned the supplementary *Descent of Man* (1871), which further explained natural selection as the key mechanism operating throughout nature, whereby those species that are best suited to their environments survive and multiply. His theories met with great skepticism and animosity for proposing that all life had, through a series of countless and minuscule adaptations, evolved from a single ancestor and, by implication, for denying a divine hand in the human predicament.

Theophile Delcassé (1852–1905): Chief French architect of amiable and fruitful diplomatic cooperation with Britain that saw colonial disputes in Morocco, the Sudan, and Egypt reconciled—achievements manifested in the *entente cordiale* of 1904. He was largely responsible for strengthening France's alliance with Russia and improving relations with Italy as well.

Charles Dickens (1812–1870): English novelist and most popular English writer of his time. His works, often written in installments, include *Oliver Twist* (1838), *A Christmas Carol* (1843), *A Tale of Two Cities* (1859), *Great Expectations* (1861), and *David Copperfield* (1850). He often wrote from personal experience and used his imagination to extrapolate from there. His books pulsed with the rhythms, misfortunes, and political evils of London, all endured by his unforgettable characters. Because of his enormous popularity, his works helped foment social reforms in England's crowded cities.

Benjamin Disraeli (1804–1881): British politician and writer, originally of Jewish origin. Disraeli wrote extensively and achieved moderate fame before being elected to Parliament in 1837, where he became a strong opponent of Peel and his reformist leanings. He became a prominent Tory leader after the party split, precipitated by the repeal of the Corn Laws in 1846. He was made prime minister in 1874 and aided the lot of the poor by improving housing, public health services, and labor conditions throughout the country. Disraeli oversaw war against the Boers in South Africa and the subsequent annexation of the Transvaal, the conquest of the Fiji Islands, and the purchase of majority shares in the Suez Canal operation.

Emile Durkheim (1858–1917): French sociologist. Influenced by the nascent sociology of Weber and positivism of Comte, Durkheim believed in the applicability of scientific observation and analysis to the study of contemporary society. He posited that urban growth, scientific progress, and a steady abatement of religious influence had disrupted social order and propriety, which in turn, was causing individual angst and anomie throughout urban Europe.

Edward VII (1841–1910): Successor to his mother, Queen Victoria, as king of England (1901–1910). Edward was well known for generosity toward the arts and sciences and for debauchery. As king, he was interested in the diplomatic maneuverings of the time and took it upon himself to act as an emissary while abroad. He was instrumental in improving relations with France and the subsequent Anglo-French entente of 1904.

Victor Emmanuel II (1820–1878): Succeeded his father, Charles Albert, as king of Piedmont-Sardinia from 1849–1861. Popular with his people for social reforms and general tolerance, Victor Emmanuel, with Prime Minister Camillo di Cavour, obtained France's assistance in a war with Austria in 1859. He benefited from the rebellions in southern Italy when Garibaldi liberated the Kingdom of the Two Sicilies and, after a plebiscite, surrendered them to annexation by Piedmont-Sardinia. Victor Emmanuel was declared king of a united Italy in 1861. Venetia was added to the kingdom after Austria's defeat at the hands of Prussia in 1866 and Rome in 1870, when French troops were recalled during the Franco-Prussian War.

Friedrich Engels (1820–1895): German socialist, social agitator, and friend of Karl Marx. Engels published *The Condition of the Working Class in England* in 1844 while working as a manager in a factory in Manchester. He organized revolutionary movements throughout western Europe in the late 1840s and collaborated with Marx in the famous 1848 *Communist Manifesto*. Engels was a key figure in both the First and Second Internationals and spent much of his life after Marx's death editing his friend's works in *Das Kapital* while himself elaborating on the theory of historical materialism.

Erich von Falkenhayn (1861–1922): German minister of war from 1906 to 1915 and head of the German general staff from 1914 to 1916. His tenure saw early German victories in the east balanced by stalemate in the west, concluding in 1916, when he was removed from duty following the terrifying consequences of his Verdun campaign.

Franz Ferdinand (1863–1914): Archduke of Austria and heir to the Austro-Hungarian throne. His suggestion for the incorporation of a proposed Slavic kingdom into the Dual Monarchy enraged Serbian nationalists, and his assassination in Sarajevo in June 1914 set Austria-Hungary and Serbia at odds, eventually precipitating the First World War.

Jules Ferry (1832–1893): French politician. As minister of public instruction (1879–1880 and 1882), Ferry made primary education free, compulsory, and open to all, while lessening religious influence in France's public school system. As prime minister (1880–1881 and 1883–1885), he oversaw French imperialist pursuits in Tunis, Madagascar, Indochina, and the Congo and Niger River basins.

Johann Gottlieb Fichte (1762–1814): German philosopher. Educated in theology and a student of Kant, Fichte posited the existence of a universal ethical volition emanating from a single, omniscient entity and, though antisemitic, became increasingly identified with liberal and nationalist struggles. His 1808 *Addresses to the German Nation* called on all German people to discover their special spiritual unity, as opposed to French cultural domination.

Charles Fourier (1772–1837): French philosopher. A utopian and believer in the intrinsic goodness of man, Fourier propounded the idea of the *phalanstery*, a contrived community of 1,500 to 2,000 people that could be self-sufficient, with work divided into specialized fields, and allow for a harmonious environment denied by contemporary society immersed in cutthroat capitalism.

Frederick the Great (II) (1712–1786): King of Prussia (1740–1786). A close friend of Voltaire and admirer of the arts and music,

Frederick was one of Europe's eminent figures of the 18th century. He obtained Silesia in the war of Austrian Succession (1740–1748) but saw Berlin occupied by Austrian and Russian forces in 1760 when Silesian suzerainty prompted war again. The Peace of Hubertusberg (1763) with Russia permitted him to expand Prussian frontiers into Austria and Poland. Frederick was recognized for his military brilliance while commanding possibly the world's greatest army during his reign. His domestic reforms were equally worthy: He strengthened sectors of the army, the educational and legal systems, and the transportation network, while remaining relatively tolerant in matters of religion.

Frederick William II (1744–1797): Nephew of Frederick the Great and king of Prussia from 1786–1797. Lacking the sagacity of some of his predecessors, he allied against French revolutionary forces in a coalition of conservative, counterrevolutionary European monarchies but acquiesced to the treaty of Basel (1795) with France as a result of fiscal shortcomings and insurrectionary movements in Prussian-held Poland. His personal indulgences exacerbated the kingdom's financial difficulties and made him the object of resentment.

Sigmund Freud (1856–1939): Austrian psychiatrist and founder of psychoanalysis. Freud became famous for his collaboration with Josef Breuer and their practice of the cathartic method, a hypnotic state in which one is able to recall a previous psychological trauma that has been repressed and is responsible for present hysteria. He later abandoned this method in favor of free association, a technique that identifies a causal nexus between sensitive material stored in the unconscious and similar elements in the conscious. His insistence on the prevailing influence of childhood sexuality or a correlative Oedipus complex isolated him from eminent psychologists of his time. He nonetheless revolutionized his field of study and continues to do so today. Some of his works include *The Interpretation of Dreams* (1900), *Three Essays on the Theory of Sexuality* (1905), and *The Ego and the Id* (1923).

Heinrich von Gagern (1799–1880): German statesman. As a member of the Hessian Parliament, he was an outspoken proponent of German unification and was later made president of the Frankfurt Parliament, a body formed by political liberals throughout the German Confederation to pave the way for unification. He preached the importance of Prussian and Austrian cooperation within a unified

German entity and warned of dire consequences if such cooperation was not forthcoming.

Léon Gambetta (1838–1882): French politician. Elected to the Chamber of Deputies in 1869 and renowned for his anticlericalism, he became an outspoken figure in the provisional government that succeeded the fall of the empire in 1870. As interior minister, Gambetta organized a government of national defense against the Prussian siege, but his platform of continued struggle was not accepted by the rural population, which sided with Thiers and acquiesced to Prussian demands. The rest of Gambetta's career was devoted to the establishment of the Third Republic and its constitution, as well as attempts to reconcile warring parliamentary factions.

Mohandas Gandhi (1869–1948): Eminent Indian activist and politician. Harboring an ascetic commitment to nonviolent expressions of civil disobedience as a righteous weapon against tyranny, Gandhi led an organized protest against persistent injustices toward the Indian minority in South Africa, bringing him broad fame in his home country. After a 22-year hiatus there, he returned home to spearhead the Indian nationalist movement, directing the Indian National Congress for much of the rest of his life. Along with Mohammad Ali Jinnah, he was instrumental in the granting of Indian independence in 1947 by the British. He remains a martyred paragon for reasoned and responsible resistance long after his assassination in 1948.

Giuseppe Garibaldi (1807–1882): Italian revolutionary leader. Garibaldi participated in the failed Piedmontese rebellion against Austria in 1848 and the unsuccessful Roman uprising of 1849. He broke with Mazzini and his dream of a unified Italian republic in favor of the more feasible option of a united Italy under Victor Emmanuel II. He led the conquest of the Kingdom of the Two Sicilies in 1860 with a thousand followers and delivered the kingdom to the rule of Victor Emmanuel II.

David Lloyd George (1863–1945): British politician. A liberal and anti-imperialist in Parliament after 1890, Lloyd George won fame from the left for his welfare reform proposals. He was minister of war in 1916 before becoming prime minister later that year; he pursued an aggressive war policy and helped unify allied forces under Marshal Ferdinand Foch. Lloyd George represented British interests at the Paris Peace Conference amidst the more assertive proposals of Clemenceau and Wilson. He was responsible for the treaty that established an independent Irish Free State in 1922.

Giovanni Giolitti (1842–1928): Italian statesman and prime minister on five separate occasions from 1892 to 1921. Giolitti introduced social and agrarian reforms after the turn of the century and brought universal male suffrage to Italy in 1912. He sponsored the Libyan conquest, helped bring about an accord with Yugoslavia after World War I, and bears the stigma of having aided the fascists in their rise to power in the early 1920s.

William Gladstone (1809–1898): British politician and leading figure of the liberal party in England during much of the second half of the 19th century. Gladstone became a member of Parliament in 1833 and was made undersecretary of war and colonies in 1835 by Sir Robert Peel. He split with the Tory party after the repeal of the Corn Laws in 1846 and served four separate terms as prime minister, during which time, he improved relations with Catholic Ireland; revamped parts of the army, educational system, and judiciary; and expanded male suffrage with the Reform Bills of 1884 and 1885.

Johan Wolfgang von Goethe (1749–1832): German poet, writer, and scientist. Goethe's genius knew no bounds. A student of both law and biology, he was the leading figure of the German *Sturm und Drang* movement in the late 18th century and chief minister of the state of Weimar during the 1770s and 1780s. He is best known for his groundbreaking epic poem *Faust* (1808), his unique take on the 16th-century legend.

Olympe de Gouges (1748–1793): French revolutionary feminist and author of *The Rights of Women* (1791). In this treatise, she argued that the law must represent the general will of the people, of which women were an indispensable part. She fought for educational opportunities, property rights, and equal divorce rights.

Sir Edward Grey (1862–1933): British foreign secretary from 1905 to 1916. In the face of a mounting German threat, he consistently backed France diplomatically and aligned Britain with Russia in the Entente of 1907, clearly positioning the English in opposition to the aggressiveness of Wilhelm II.

Jules Guesde (1845–1922): French Marxist and leader of the *Parti Ouvrier Français* (French Workers' Party). He firmly rejected political compromise in his pursuit of socialist reforms, maintaining the necessity of a proletarian revolution to end exploitative capitalism.

Francois Guizot (1787–1874): French politician and historian. Guizot was a history professor before participating in the July Revolution, which served as his springboard into a political career. He implemented reforms in the French educational system and served as prime minister several times, including from 1847–1848. He firmly embraced France's bourgeois character during the July Monarchy but did not favor expanding the franchise.

Douglas Haig (1861–1928): British general. Haig directed the disastrously ineffective British offensives at the Battles of the Somme in 1916 and Ypres in 1917, despite horrifying results in previous offensive efforts and intelligence reports portending the same.

Keir Hardie (1856–1915): Scottish labor spokesman and politician. A background in coal mining introduced Hardie to union politics. He formed the Scottish Labor party in 1888 and was made a member of Parliament in 1892. A year later, he established the Independent Labor Party, which with the nascent Fabian Society, was a precursor in the formation of the Labor Representation Committee in 1900, later renamed the Labor Party in 1906.

Baron Georges Hausmann (1809–1891): French architect and municipal designer. Responsible for the renovation of Paris under Napoleon III. He widened city streets to mitigate traffic congestion; rerouted city and public transportation; and constructed parks, monuments, and countless other amenities.

Georg Wilhelm Friedrich Hegel (1770–1831): Eminent German philosopher. Schooled in theology, Hegel spent time as a professor at Jena, Heidelberg, and Berlin, writing on history, religion, and ethics. He is known as the father of *dialectics*, whereby opposing ideas are rationalized and synthesized into a logical conclusion. He held that history could be described as a spirit, or *Geist*, in perpetual flux (with human progress as manifestation of a spiritual self-realization), becoming increasingly less alienated from itself. Hegel had a profound influence on future generations of students, among them Marx and Sartre.

Heinrich Heine (1797–1856): Eminent German poet who immersed himself in history and literature, Heine was a member of the Romantic, Saint-Simonian, and Young Germany movements. Inspired by the folk and Romantic German traditions, as well as by his Jewish and Christian backgrounds (he had converted from Judaism to Christianity), his colorful prose is illustrated in such works as *Die Harzreise* (1826), *Buch der Lieder* (1827), and *Reisebilder* (1827–1831).

Johann Gottfried von Herder (1744–1803): German philosopher and clergyman. A student of theology and Kantian philosophy, he was best known for his work in comparative religion, mythology, philology, and nationalist thought, while also propounding the theory of a distinctly epochal nature of historical development in his *Outlines of the Philosophy of Man* (1784–1791).

Aleksandr Herzen (1812–1870): Russian writer and revolutionary agitator. A socialist, Herzen initially believed that Russia should follow western paths to political reform. He spent much of his life abroad, where he endorsed liberal revolutionary causes in 1848–1849 and wrote extensively about his homeland. His most famous work, *From the Other Shore* (1855), explored the failed revolutions of 1848–1849 and expressed his belief that socialism could take hold in Russia because it was an outgrowth of the communal village lifestyle entrenched throughout her provinces.

Theodor Herzl (1860–1904): Father of the modern Zionist movement. Following the Dreyfus Affair, Herzl argued that Jews could never ingratiate themselves with European society successfully because of the pernicious anti-Semitism they would always encounter. He advocated the establishment of a national Jewish state that would provide a haven for the Jews dispersed about the world, in his book, *Das Judenstaat* (*The Jewish State*), and at early Zionist congresses he called.

Paul von Hindenburg (1847–1934): German field general and president of Germany from 1925–1934. Impressive victories on the eastern front in the First World War against Russian forces led to his appointment as commander of the German war machine in 1916, an authority he wielded with General Erich Ludendorff. His directives brought Russia to its knees in 1917 before superior Allied forces, strengthened by American intervention, overwhelmed the German lines. His tenure as president was relatively uneventful, executive

©2005 The Teaching Company.

authority being rather circumscribed in the new Weimar Republic, until a burgeoning national socialist movement and the prodding of close advisors convinced him to appoint Adolf Hitler chancellor in January 1933.

Victor Hugo (1802–1885): French novelist and poet. One of the great Romantics of his era, Hugo was best known for authoring *Notre Dame de Paris* (1831) and *Les Miserables* (1862), which like many of his works, combine the themes of love, despair, heroism, and tragedy. He supported liberal and democratic causes on behalf of the poor.

Thomas Huxley (1825–1895): Biologist and scientific apologist. The foremost proponent of Darwinian evolutionary theory, Huxley saw civilization as mankind's triumph over evolution and believed that human ethics and reason set man apart from the rest of nature in the evolutionary process; at the same time, he went to great lengths to prove the human anthropological proximity to apes.

Aleksandr Izvolsky (1856–1919): Russian foreign minister from 1906–1910. In the wake of Russia's humiliating defeat in the Russo-Japanese war of 1905, Izvolsky cultivated an accord with the British that settled disputes in Persia and Afghanistan—an agreement that fostered the creation of the Triple Entente of 1907 among France, Britain, and Russia. An attempt to gain Russian warship access to the Dardanelles in return for his conciliation in Austro-Hungarian annexation of Bosnia-Herzegovina backfired when the Dual Monarchy refused to keep its end of the bargain.

Jean Jaurès (1859–1914): French socialist leader. Known for his public-speaking prowess and ability to cooperate effectively with friends and opponents, he saw socialism as a counter to virulent nationalism, economic exploitation, and immorality. His socialist programs were intended to co-opt many different classes beside the industrial proletariat. He championed the separation of church and state and individual civil liberties, allied himself with the Dreyfusard cause, and led an antiwar movement before being assassinated by a radical nationalist on the eve of war.

Joseph Joffre (1852–1931): Commander-in-Chief of the French army from 1911–1916. Joffre's aggressive assaults at Ypres, the Champagne, and the Somme produced horrifying casualties. His inability to appreciate the futility of offensive operations in trench warfare and initial French setbacks at the Battle of Verdun in 1916 resulted in his dismissal by Prime Minister Aristide Briand in 1916.

Franz Joseph (1830–1916): Succeeded his uncle Ferdinand, upon his abdication in 1848, as emperor of Austria (1848–1916). His reign saw the loss of Austrian influence in Italy in 1859, and a defeat by the Prussians in 1866 relegated Austria to a subordinate position in central Europe. He yielded to Hungarian nationalist demands in 1867 with the creation of the Dual Monarchy and saw his country threatened for the next 40 years by Russian interests in the Balkans. Despite the fractious nature of his multinational empire, he was able to maintain order by repressing nationalist uprisings, making rare compromises (that is, Hungary in 1867), and keeping the loyalty of his army.

Joseph II (1741–1790): Holy Roman Emperor (1765–1790), son of Maria Theresa and Emperor Francis I. A champion of the common folk and a nuisance to the Roman Catholic Church, he abolished serfdom and feudal dues in 1781; built hospitals, poorhouses, parks, and gardens; and even funded programs to provide food to the needy. He ended the practice of torture and the death penalty. His *Patent of Tolerance* (1781) allowed for broad freedom of worship throughout the Holy Roman Empire, but it was abandoned after his death.

Karl Kautsky (1854–1938): German socialist and a leading adherent of Marxist doctrine in the Second International and German Social Democratic Party (SPD). Kautsky consistently opposed those, like Eduard Bernstein, who sought socialist reform by political means and insisted that capitalism would soon crumble under the weight of a united, revolutionary proletariat.

Aleksandr Kerensky (1881–1970): A socialist and labor party representative in the pre-war Russian parliament (Duma), Kerensky became head of a provisional government that assumed power after Tsar Nicholas II was forced to abdicate in February of 1917 amidst desertions in the army and food shortages in the cities. His determination to continue in the war and an inability to ameliorate the economic and food emergencies led to his overthrow by the Bolsheviks and their leader, Vladimir Lenin.

Rudyard Kipling (1865–1936): English writer and poet. Born in India and educated in England, Kipling's works reflect a lifelong fascination with both extremes of the British Empire. He aggrandized the Brit as cunning, daring, and righteous in his attempts to tame the mysteries and energies of the Indian subcontinent. His most acclaimed works include *The Jungle Book* (1894), *If* (1910), *Gunga Din* (1892), and *The White Man's Burden* (1899). He was England's first Nobel Prize recipient for literature in 1907.

Horatio Kitchener (1850–1916): English soldier, politician, and colonial official. Kitchener was made governor of the Sudan after extended service as commander of the Egyptian army that saw the annihilation of Mahdist forces in the region, culminating in the famous Battle of Omdurman in 1898. He served in South Africa, where he was instrumental in the suppression of the Boers, before a troubled tenure as secretary of state for war during World War I.

Lajos Kossuth (1802–1894): Hungarian revolutionary. As a member of the Hungarian diet, Kossuth's nationalist and liberal policies brought him popularity, but his opposition to Slavic and German nationalistic ambitions within Hungary brought resentment. A leader of the Hungarian revolution of 1848, he was named president of the breakaway Republic of Hungary (1849) before Austrian and Russian forces put down the uprising. He lived in exile for the rest of his life, hailed for his national and liberal ambitions.

Alfred Krupp (1854–1902): Son of Friedrich Krupp (1787–1826). Inherited his father's steel plant and greatly increased its productive capacity by incorporating modern technology. The company flourished in the arms and mining industries and was largely responsible for Prussian and German military might from the time of unification to the Second World War.

Marquis de Lafayette (1757–1834): French general and politician. Despite his country's neutrality, Lafayette espoused the colonist cause in the American Revolution in 1777, earning the position of major general in the Continental Army. In France, he was a member of the Assembly of Notables in 1787 and the Estates General in 1789. He was made commander of the National Guard after the fall of the Bastille and tried to mediate between radicals and conservatives. Lafayette was set to fight the Austrians but, after attempting to defend the monarchy in Paris in 1792, fled and was captured by the Habsburg armies. He was liberated by Napoleon in 1797 and lived in retirement during the empire, reentering politics as a liberal member of the Chamber of Deputies during the Restoration.

He helped facilitate an orderly transition during the Revolution of 1830.

Ferdinand Lasalle (1825–1864): German socialist and founder of the first Independent Workers Party in the German Confederation. His party had little clout but was a precursor of the German Social Democratic Party (SPD), formed in 1875, which would come to wield influence in German politics.

Leo XIII (1810–1903): Succeeded Pius IX as pope from 1878–1903. Leo was more amenable than his predecessor, making it a goal of his to reconcile the Catholic Church with modern science and thought. He brought about an end to the *Kulturkampf* in 1887; encouraged Catholic participation in secular, republican states; exalted the teachings of St. Thomas Aquinas; opened the Vatican archives to all; and encouraged scientific and intellectual exploration. His famous encyclical, *Rerum Novarum* (1891), refuted socialism, castigated the evils of capitalist exploitation, and reaffirmed the importance of the church in all aspects of life.

Leopold II (1835–1909): Succeeded Leopold I as king of the Belgians from 1865–1909. He backed Henry Morton Stanley's explorations of Africa's Congo River basin, presided over the Berlin Congress of 1884–1885 (which outlined basic regulations for the colonization of the African continent), and proclaimed the establishment of the Congo Free State under his personal dominion. Operations in the Congo brought him wealth, until allegations of extortion, exploitation, and scandal forced him to cede control to the Belgian government in 1908.

Ferdinand de Lesseps (1805–1894): French statesmen and engineer. He oversaw the construction and financing of the Suez Canal (1859–1869) and was president of the company constructing the Panama Canal before its dissolution due to lack of funding amidst widespread corruption charges.

Friedrich List (1789–1846): German economist. A professor of economics at Tübingen and a politician in Württemberg, List advocated a system of close trading partnerships among the numerous German states and, as such, was instrumental in the formation of the *Zollverein*, the German customs union. He also pressed for the implementation of protective tariffs for nascent industries.

David Livingstone (1813–1873): As the first European to extensively explore the African interior, Livingstone sought to eradicate native slaving operations by creating missionary outposts along the continent's major waterways. His adventures familiarized him with such natural marvels as Lake Tanganyika and Victoria Falls in his ongoing pursuit of the Nile's origins.

Louis XIV (1638–1715): King of France (1643–1715), with his mother, Anne of Austria, serving as regent and advised by Cardinals Richelieu and Mazarin until 1661. Absolute monarchy, justified by divine right, was at its zenith during his reign, which was identified by a centralized bureaucracy to facilitate tax collection and an aggressive foreign policy bent on expansion. He sought religious uniformity for France, actively rooting out non-Catholic influences and persecuting the Huguenots, going so far as to rescind the Edict of Nantes in 1685. His Palace at Versailles and patronage of the arts and literature added to his unique renown and influence.

Louis XV (1710–1774): King of France (1715–1774) with Phillip II, the duke of Orléans, serving as regent until 1723. He married Marie Leszcynska of Poland, prompting France's involvement in the War of Polish Succession. He presided over France's involvement in the Seven Years War (1756–1763), which with the Treaty of Paris, resulted in the loss of much of France's empire. His domestic extravagance, iniquitous tax system, and war spending played a part in setting the table for the French Revolution of 1789.

Louis XVI (1754–1793): Grandson and successor to Louis XV as king of France (1774–1792). He married Austrian Archduchess Marie Antoinette in 1770. Reserved and demure, he relied on ministers for advice. His rule was plagued by financial difficulty that had many of its root causes in the Seven Years War and the American Revolution. His unwillingness to change the format and function of the Estates General in 1789 led to the proclamation of the National Assembly by the Third Estate. He was caught trying to flee France and forced to sign the Constitution of 1791 that substantially curbed his powers. He was later tried by the Convention and guillotined in January of 1793.

Louis XVIII (1755–1824): Brother of Louis XVI and king of France (1814–24). Restored to the throne in 1814 by the powers after the fall of Paris and again in 1815 after Napoleon's defeat at Waterloo, his reign was moderate at first, including a tolerant policy toward revolutionaries and the granting of a constitution. Under the direction of royalist ministers, he became more reactionary as new legislation increased the privilege of the aristocracy while abridging civil liberties.

Louis-Philippe (1773–1850): King of the French (1830–1848). Louis-Philippe fled France during the revolution and lived in exile until the Bourbon Restoration, when he returned as a liberal opponent to the monarchy. With the help of the Marquis de Lafayette, he was appointed king of the French after the July Revolution of 1830. His regime was characterized by bourgeois prominence and apathy toward the poor. He oversaw the conquest of Algeria and patronized Belgian independence. Bourbon legitimists and suffrage movements made his tenure precarious throughout the 1840s, until his abdication in 1848 following the February Revolution.

Erich Ludendorff (1865–1937): German general. Instrumental in the decisive German offensives on the eastern front, Ludendorff saw his authority greatly enhanced after fellow General Paul von Hindenburg's appointment as commander-in-chief of German forces in 1916 and used the authority to direct subsequent operations against Allied positions in the west. A participant alongside Adolf Hitler in the Beer Hall Putsch of 1923, he adopted virulent anti-Semitic and Aryan supremacist sentiments in the post-war years, becoming an exponent of national socialist rhetoric during the 1920s.

Rosa Luxemburg (1871–1919): European social revolutionary. Luxemburg was a key figure in the Polish and German social democratic parties and in the Second International, where she opposed the reformist socialism of Bernstein and insisted on the revolutionary toppling of bourgeois capitalism. She founded, with Karl Liebknecht, the Spartacus Party in 1916, which would become the German Communist Party after December 1918. She was killed after her arrest for participating in the Spartacist revolt of January 1919 in Berlin.

Thomas Macaulay (1800–1859): English historian and political writer. A regular contributor to the *Edinburgh Review*, Macaulay was elected member of Parliament in 1830 as a Whig and became known for his speaking prowess. He was a member of the supreme council of the East India Company (1834–1838) and improved the educational system and instituted a legal code in India. He was secretary of war (1839–1841) and member of Parliament again from 1839–1847 and 1852–1856. A progressive, Macaulay preached the necessity of parliamentary reform, especially in 1832, to avoid the revolutionary unrest that had shaken continental Europe.

Thomas Malthus (1766–1834): English economist. Malthus is known for his 1798 *Essay on the Principle of Population*, in which he portends the plight of mankind caused by population growth that human means of subsistence cannot accommodate. Only such inhibitors as famine, warfare, disease, and sexual abstinence, he argued, keep population and subsistence levels in accord.

Fillippo Marinetti (1876–1944): Italian poet and founder of futurism, an artistic movement that exalted speed, youth, war, the synthesis of man and machine, and recklessness, while vilifying women, the aged, and various establishment intellectual entities, all the while sharing theoretical ties to fascism.

Karl Marx (1818–1883): German socialist. Marx obtained his Ph.D. from the University of Jena (1841) and almost instantly concerned himself with the welfare of the poor and the need for radical political and social reform. He coauthored, with his lifelong friend and fellow socialist Friedrich Engels, such classic works as *The German Ideology* (1846), *The Communist Manifesto* (1848), and *Das Kapital* (1867), and was a salient factor in the founding of the First International in 1864. His economic studies convinced him of the inevitable swelling of the proletarian class as a result of exploitation by the propertied class and called for worker solidarity for the eventual overthrow of bourgeois society. His theory of historical materialism argued that any epoch, and all of history, could be described by the particular economic relationships and needs existing at a given time so that any aspect of society was merely a manifestation of its economic character.

Ferdinand Maximilien (1832–1867): Emperor of Mexico (1864–1867) and brother of Austrian Emperor Franz Joseph. Maximilien served in the Austrian navy and was governor general of Lombardy-Venetia (1857–1859) before acquiescing to Napoleon III and conservative Mexican aspirations for an imperial order in Central America. His liberal leanings and the execution of loyal Benito Juarez followers alienated him from conservatives and liberals alike. When Napoleon III recalled French forces aiding the beleaguered emperor in 1866, he was captured by Mexican revolutionaries and executed.

Giuseppe Mazzini (1805–1872): Inspirational Italian nationalist, political writer, and revolutionary. Mazzini founded the Young Italy movement, which sought a united, representative government for the Italian peninsula. He participated in several revolutionary uprisings throughout Italy that supported a sovereign national identity, stemming from the democratic participation of the people.

Klemens von Metternich (1773–1859): Austrian diplomat. Widely referred to as the "Coachman of Europe" for his shrewd political mind, Metternich was named Austrian foreign minister in 1809 and spent much of his career working to mediate between French and Russian interests, while employing all means to improve Austria's standing in Europe. He fought to keep Austrian influence in Italy paramount, while remaining opposed to German unification, preferring Austrian preeminence in the German Confederation. He was the mouthpiece of conservative, monarchical Europe from 1815–1848.

John Stuart Mill (1806–1873): British philosopher, economist, and political writer. Educated by his well-known and demanding father, James Mill, John Stuart Mill served as a clerk in the East India Company while contributing to journals on political theory and economics. He married prominent feminist Harriet Taylor in 1851 and published his most famous work, *On Liberty*, in 1859. Mill followed this with pieces on utilitarianism and positivism in the tradition of his father and Jeremy Bentham. He exalted empiricism and inductive rationalism and took up the causes of broader suffrage, female rights, and labor rights. He served as member of Parliament from 1865–1868.

Alexandre Millerand (1859–1943): French politician. As a socialist in the Chamber of Deputies, Millerand was censured and eventually expelled from the Socialist Party for his relatively rightist stance on labor. He served as minister of war twice (1912–1913 and 1914–1915) and was made prime minister in 1920, all the while becoming increasingly conservative and nationalistic. He was elected president in 1920 but because of a hostile leftist majority in the Chamber, was forced to resign in 1924.

Helmuth von Moltke (1848–1916): Chief of the German general staff from 1906–1914. Ignoring the advice of his predecessor, Alfred von Schlieffen, Moltke weakened the right flank of the initial German offensive on Paris and, thus, left the German forces inadequate for a conclusive push at the Battle of the Marne, just 35 miles outside the French capital.

Nicholas I (1796–1855): Brother of and successor to Alexander I as tsar of Russia (1825–1855). Nicholas crushed the Decembrist uprising of 1825 upon his ascent to power and helped improve the lot of the peasants slightly through modest legislation. His regime was identified with the suppression of the press; rigid control of education; a strong, centralized police force; and close association with the Orthodox Church. He snuffed out the Polish insurrection of 1830–1831 and aided the Austrian repression of Hungarian rebels in 1849. A victory over the Turks at Navarino (1827) brought territories along the Black Sea, but a defeat in the Crimean War (1853–1856) ended Russian hopes for a broad influence in the Balkans.

Nicholas II (1868–1918): Tsar from 1894–1917, he was an autocratic ruler who opposed the liberal aspirations of his subjects, rejecting political reforms petitioned by the *zemstvos*. As a result of industrial unrest, bad harvests, and the disastrous Russo-Japanese war, Nicholas II was a prime cause of the Revolution of 1905. Despite being forced to summon a Duma, he tried to rule absolutely, eventually naming himself supreme commander of the Russian Armies. In 1917, he was forced to abdicate, and in 1918, he and his family were murdered by Bolshevik forces.

Friedrich Nietzsche (1844–1900): Influential German philosopher. Nietzsche rejected western bourgeois rationalism and Christian influence as enervating and decadent. He venerated the ideological *superman* for his strength, social-Darwinist aspirations, and apathy toward those who fettered his "will to power." Nietzsche saw morality as subjective, amenable to the instincts of competing persons.

Florence Nightingale (1820–1910): English nurse and social activist. Nightingale achieved fame for her brave service during the Crimean War. She set up schools for the training of nurses in Britain and agitated for more quality hospitals, while helping to make nursing a more respected profession. She became the first woman to be awarded the British Order of Merit in 1907.

Robert Owen (1771–1858): British socialist. After early success in the cotton and textile industries, Owen achieved fame for the establishment of the New Lanarck community in Scotland, a utopian experiment that also provided homes, schools, and good working environments with the aim of social unity and economic efficiency. He was revered by the working class for encouraging trade unions and cooperatives.

Thomas Paine (1737–1809): A writer and political theorist, Paine spent much of his life in England and America and penned *Common Sense* (1776), arguing that the American colonies no longer needed England. His *Rights of Man* (1791–1792) was a rejection of Burke's *Reflections on the Revolution in France* (1790) and a defense of democracy. Paine was a member of the National Convention in France in 1792 but was imprisoned by the Jacobins during the Terror. His anticlericalism and castigation of George Washington later alienated him from the public.

Viscount Henry John Palmerston (1784–1865). English Statesman. A Tory and secretary of war (1809–1828), Palmerston split with his party over parliamentary reform and became foreign minister under Earl Grey. He helped obtain Belgian independence and preserve Ottoman presence in the Balkans by forming a coalition against Egypt's Muhammed Ali. He was home secretary from 1852–1855, when he succeeded George Aberdeen as prime minister. Palmerston oversaw British operations in the Crimean War and put down the Sepoy Rebellion of 1857–1858 in India.

Emmeline Pankhurst (1858–1928). British feminist and a leader of the women's suffrage movement of the late 19th and early 20th centuries. Pankhurst founded the women's Social and Political Union, whose members prosecuted a militant political and social campaign for women's rights that consisted of property destruction and hunger strikes.

Charles Stewart Parnell (1846–1891): Irish nationalist and exponent of Home Rule and land reform. Parnell's unwavering championship of the Irish cause in Parliament brought the admiration of his countrymen, notably the belligerent Fenian Society, devoted to the independence of Ireland. As president of the National Land League, he endorsed the boycott to induce reform in Irish land legislation. Though influential in Parliament, Gladstone's proposed Home Rule Bill in 1886 was rejected amidst a divided liberal vote.

Sir Robert Peel (1788–1850): British politician. Chief secretary for Ireland (1812–1818), where he opposed Catholic emancipation, and home secretary twice from 1822 to 1830, where he reformed the penal system and reorganized the London police force. Peel opposed parliamentary reform but warmed to the idea in his Tamworth Manifesto, in which he accepted the Reform Acts, signaling a split in the conservative right. As a Tory prime minister (1841–1846), he was instrumental in the repeal of the Corn Laws in 1846, which catered to landed interests at the expense of the urban poor; he then resigned amidst discord within the party.

Phillipe Pétain (1856–1951): French general in World War I and chief of state of unoccupied Vichy France during World War II. Renowned for his defense during the Verdun campaign, Pétain was rewarded with a promotion to commander-in-chief in 1917. He succeeded Paul Reynaud as prime minister in May of 1940 and quickly moved to sign an armistice with Germany, weeks after the commencement of armed combat. As head of Vichy France, he collaborated with the Nazi regime, introducing a largely reactionary "national revolution." After the war, he was tried and convicted of treason and spent the rest of his life behind bars.

Pablo Picasso (1881–1973): Spanish painter and sculptor, widely regarded as one of the 20th century's greatest artists. Some of Picasso's most famous contributions include his work during the morose Blue Period (1901–1904), which focused on the poor; the more sanguine Rose Period (1905–1906); and his abstract Cubist pieces, a product of his post-impressionistic and African influences. His *Les Demoiselles d'Avignon* (1907) and *Female Nude* (1910) are some of his most recognizable Cubist illustrations. His highly symbolic *Guernica* (1937) is a lasting memory of the Spanish Civil War.

William Pitt the Younger (1759–1806): A lawyer, member of Parliament, and Chancellor of the Exchequer, Pitt became prime minister of Great Britain in 1874. He instituted new taxes and reduced expenditures to reduce public debt. He brought Parliament authority in India and tried to avoid the French revolutionary wars until France declared war on Britain in 1793. His tenure saw British victories at sea (Trafalgar, the Nile), continental failures, and the burden of counterrevolutionary financing.

Pius IX (1792–1878): Pope from 1846–1878. Despite granting the Papal States a constitution, Pius was forced to flee Rome during the 1848 revolutions and returned under French protection in 1850. He refused to recognize Victor Emmanuel II's annexations of the Papal States (1860) and Rome itself in 1870. He is known for his 1864 encyclical *Syllabus of Errors*, a rejection of secularization, a denunciation of liberalism and progress, and an affirmation of the church's preeminent position.

Raymond Poincaré (1860–1934): French statesman. Elected to the Chamber of Deputies in 1887, he served as prime minister and foreign minister before succeeding Armand Fallières as president of France from 1913–1920. Poincaré increased the length of military service and bound France to more concrete diplomatic alliances with Russia and Britain before World War I. He appointed Georges Clemenceau prime minister in 1917 to resuscitate the French war effort and pushed for a draconian peace settlement after German surrender. He was appointed prime minister in 1922 and, upon German failure to meet its reparations payments, ordered the occupation of the Ruhr a year later. When a fiscal crisis compelled his return to the premiership from 1926–1929, Poincaré boldly devalued the franc to 20 percent of its 1914 value, raised taxes, and reduced government expenditures to make the franc reflect its diminished value in the post-war economy.

Pierre-Joseph Proudhon (1809–1865): French writer, one of the fathers of European anarchist thought. Advocated a society centered on *mutualism*, whereby economic, political, and other issues would be discussed and resolved amongst small associations, thus relieving the need for strong, centralized government. Like some of the utopians, he believed in the moral potential of the human race and foresaw the day when government would be unnecessary.

Joseph Radetzky (1766–1858): Austrian army commander and a fixture of the counterrevolution in the Austrian empire. Despite desertions and low morale, his armies won key victories at Custozza (1848) and Novara (1849) that stabilized the Austrian hold on northern Italy and forced the abdication of Charles Albert of Piedmont-Sardinia. He was made governor of upper Italy from 1849 to 1857.

⋯t Renan (1823–1892): French historian. His theological and ⋯⋯l backgrounds converged to produce profound explorations of theological doctrines in unique historical contexts. Renan argued that the Bible should be read and criticized like any other document and questioned the divinity of Jesus, preferring to view him as a unique historical figure in a particular epoch.

Cecil Rhodes (1853–1902): Colonial British official and businessman. Rhodes established the De Beers Mining Company in South Africa in 1880 and, after being made a member of Parliament in Cape Colony in 1881, was the chief exponent of British conquest in the region. As prime minister of Cape Colony after 1890, he ensured the disenfranchisement of local Africans and supported the Jamison raid of 1895 in his pursuit of a unified South Africa under British sovereignty.

David Ricardo (1772–1823): British economist. Ricardo is best known for his 1817 *The Principles of Political Economy and Taxation*, in which he presented his theory of the iron law of wages, arguing that they tend to fix themselves at or near subsistence level. Also credited with the theory of comparative advantage, he spent a good deal of time musing on the apparent correlation between a good's value and price level.

Maximilien Robespierre (1758–1794): An admirer of Rousseau, Robespierre was a member of the Estates General of 1789, a leading figure of the Jacobin club, and an elected member of the Paris Commune of August 1792. He was an important player in the power jockeying that took place between the Girondins and Jacobins and was elected to the Committee of Public Safety, where he played a paramount role during the Reign of Terror. Amidst further threats of purges and disillusionment with the committee during the Terror, he and his Jacobin followers were ousted from power during the Thermidor uprising that was backed by the majority in the convention and guillotined on July 27, 1794.

Jean-Jacques Rousseau (1712–1778): Swiss-French philosopher, political theorist, and writer. A fixture of the Enlightenment tradition, Rousseau argued that men were intrinsically good but were corrupted by the vices of modern civilization. He was concerned with the moral righteousness of man and a believer in the sanctity of individual freedom and self-sacrifice toward the common good. Freedom, he proffered, was found in self-denial, made manifest in a social contract that gives sanction to the community or state.

Count Henri Saint-Simon (1760–1825): French philosopher. Greatly inspired by Adam Smith and the onset of the Industrial Revolution, he believed that society should be run by scientists and businessmen to achieve efficiency and progress. Father of the Saint-Simonian movements, a philosophy well ahead of its time, portending the socialist and feminist movements of the latter part of the 19th century.

Siegfried Sassoon (1886–1967): English poet and writer. His poetry recounts the horror of war in lurid depictions of trench warfare on the western front.

Sergei Sazanov (1861–1927): Russian foreign minister from 1910 to 1916. Fearing a loss of Russian prestige should the nation acquiesce to bullying again and lacking in the sagacity required of his position, Sazanov advocated a hard-line stance toward Austro-Hungarian pursuits in the Balkans. He eventually convinced Nicholas II to respond firmly to the Dual Monarchy's declaration of war on Serbia by a mass mobilization that all but precluded any chance for reconciliation.

Friedrich von Schiller (1759–1805): Great German poet, historian, and writer of the Romantic era and contributor to the German *Sturm und Drang* movement. Along with Goethe, Schiller is considered one of the fathers of the German literary outpourings of the 19th century. Schooled in medicine, he spent time in theater at Manheim (1783–1784) and as a history professor at Jena (1789). His works embrace the magnanimous and sublime in the human experience, the dreamer at odds with depravity and impediments to spiritual liberty.

Sir Walter Scott (1771–1832): Scottish writer and poet. One of the great storytellers of the Romantic period, his most famous works include *The Waverly Novels* (1814–1819) and *Ivanhoe* (1820). Known for his colorful heroes and lyric prowess, he brought historical events to life in his works.

Percy Bysshe Shelley (1792–1822): Revered English poet of the Romantic era, he attended Oxford, eloped at 19, and spent many years agitating for social reform. His poetry exalted love, beauty, and the Enlightenment principles of progress and reason. *Prometheus Unbound* (1820), *Adonais* (1821), and *Epipsychidion* (1821) are some of his more famous achievements.

Abbé Emmanuel Sieyès (1748–1836): A clergyman before the revolution, Sieyès turned statesman during it and was popular for attacking noble and clerical privileges. He was elected deputy from the Third Estate to the Estates General in 1789 and was involved in the penning of the Declaration of the Rights of Man and Citizen and the Constitution of 1791. After isolating himself from the political spotlight during the Terror, Sieyès joined the Directory in 1799 and assisted Napoleon in his coup of 18 Brumaire. He became a senator in the subsequent empire.

Adam Smith (1723–1790): Scottish economist. Attended Glasgow and Oxford and authored the famed *Wealth of Nations* (1776) that extolled the practice of specialization in production and laissez-faire economic policies as in the best interests of the population as a whole.

Georges Sorel (1847–1922): French philosopher and writer. A Marxist, Sorel was one of the leading exponents of revolutionary syndicalism, whereby industrial production is inhibited by strikes, walkouts, sabotages, and so on in the hope of elevating the trade union to economic and social predominance. His most famous piece, *Reflections on Violence* (1908), is an exaltation of physical force to topple the bourgeois order. Even the myth of an imminent general strike, he argued, could unite the proletariat and foment revolution.

Charles Maurice de Talleyrand (1754–1838): Initially a clergyman, Talleyrand became an eminent French statesmen and diplomat. He represented the clergy at the States-General in 1789 but was excommunicated by the pope in 1791. Following the fall of the monarchy in 1792, he spent time in England and America before returning to France to become foreign minister in 1797; he aided Napoleon's coup of 18 Brumaire and helped bring about the Concordat with the Vatican (1801). A constitutional monarchist at heart, Talleyrand was often at odds with Napoleon, preaching restraint. He represented France at the Congress of Vienna and resigned after the second Bourbon restoration.

Harriet Taylor (1807–1858): English feminist. Taylor preached the desirability of the equality of the sexes and sought the elimination of female oppression before the law and through greater educational opportunities. She married John Stuart Mill in 1851, after her first husband's death.

Adolphe Thiers (1797–1877): French politician and historian. Thiers was prime minister under the July Monarchy but was dismissed for aggressive foreign policies that were inconsistent with those of his boss. An opponent of Napoleon III's emperorship, he criticized French policies leading up to the Franco-Prussian War. After the defeat, he was made head of the provisional government and negotiated a peace with Bismarck and put down the Paris Commune uprising of 1871. Thiers was made president of the French Third Republic in 1871 but resigned two years later when he lost parliamentary support.

Heinrich von Treitschke (1834–1896): German historian and fervent nationalist. A liberal member of the Reichstag during his early political career, he became increasingly conservative and nationalistic in the latter stages of his life. Deeply anti-Semitic, he advocated a militant German foreign policy that would elevate the nation to world preeminence, befitting inherent German greatness.

Flora Tristan (1803–1844): French feminist, socialist. Agitated for feminist and worker rights and fought for the cooperation of men and women in socialist pursuits, arguing that their fate was linked.

Ivan Turgenev (1818–1883): One of the great Russian writers of the 19th century and proponent of Russian westernization. He attacked the evils of serfdom and concerned himself with the social and political problems plaguing Russia at the time.

Queen Victoria (1819–1901): Queen of England from 1837 to 1901. Was a fervent imperialist and popular for the concern she maintained for her imperial subjects. Her relationships with various prime ministers ran hot and cold, with Benjamin Disraeli being her favorite. The Victorian Era, as the 19th century in Britain has been dubbed, was characterized by a heightened morality and prevailing male and female roles within society, endorsed by the queen.

Richard Wagner (1813–1883): German composer, nationalist, and virulent anti-Semite. As musical director at the Dresden theatre, Wagner was influenced by Beethoven and the German and Italian Romantic traditions. He was involved in the revolutions of 1848 in Dresden and spent much of the remainder of his life working on his five-part masterpiece, *Der Ring Des Nibelungen*, based in part on a series of medieval European legends.

Max Weber (1864–1920): German sociologist, writer, and economist. One of history's first sociologists, he was concerned with German social and economic issues. He explored such variables as religion, culture, wealth, and nationality and how they shaped their societies. His systematic approach to the social sciences let to the formulation of archetypes, which he used with economic data to compare different communities and predict their composition and development.

Arthur Wellesley Wellington (1769–1852): English soldier and politician. Served as both division commander and major general in India before being elected member of Parliament in 1806. Wellington assumed command of British, Portuguese, and Spanish forces during the Peninsular War (1808–1814) and helped defeat Napoleon at Waterloo. A Tory in Parliament, he was made prime minister in 1828 and served as foreign secretary in the Peel government from 1834–1835.

Wilhelm I (1797-1888): King of Prussia from 1861–1888 and emperor of the German state from 1871–1888. A military traditionalist in the Prussian mold, Wilhelm I appointed Otto von Bismarck prime minister to strengthen the army and bypass legislative opposition. His reign saw victories against Denmark (1864), Austria (1866), and France (1870–1871). His coronation in the Hall of Mirrors at Versailles made him emperor of unified Germany. Because Wilhelm was known for his warmongering, conservative domestic pursuits, most Prussian and, ultimately, German policy was dictated by Bismarck during his reign.

Wilhelm II (1859–1941): King of Prussia and German emperor from 1888 to 1918. A traditional conservative, Wilhelm II claimed that liberalism weakened the state. He dismissed his chancellor, Otto von Bismarck, whose own visions for Germany were inconsistent with the emperor's imperial and naval aspirations, which threatened Britain and France and led to their *entente cordiale* of 1904. Wilhelm II isolated Germany by patronizing Austro-Hungarian hegemony in the Balkans at the expense of Russia and further soured hopes of reconciliation with France when the Moroccan crises were precipitated. German military failures in 1918 led to his forced abdication in November of that year.

Woodrow Wilson (1856–1934): President of the United States from 1913 to 1921. Wilson was initially averse to U.S. involvement in

World War I, but unbridled German submarine operations prompted a declaration of war in April 1917. His 14-point peace proposal at the Paris Peace Conference proclaimed the importance of national self-determination and proffered a League of Nations that would regulate international conflicts. He opposed the harsh proposals of Clemenceau, advocating a more lenient reparations policy. Severely ill, Wilson failed to gain Senate approval either for Versailles or for the League.

Alfred Windischgratz (1787–1862): Austrian army commander. He put down the insurrections of 1848 in Vienna and Prague. To placate revolutionaries, he helped usher out Emperor Ferdinand in favor of Franz Joseph but was later demoted for his military failures during the Hungarian uprisings of 1849.

Mary Wollstonecraft (1759–1797): Leading feminist and author. She is best known for her groundbreaking *A Vindication of the Rights of Women* (1792), in which she argued that women should have the right to vote, hold office, and have equality in marriage. Wollstonecraft spent much of the French Revolution in Paris and died in 1797 after giving birth to Mary Shelley, future wife of Percy Bysshe Shelley and author of *Frankenstein* (1818).

Emile Zola (1840–1902): Prolific French writer. Zola's novels revealed an inclination toward a scientific social criticism, in which French life was probed. Many of his works followed the predicament of the poor and screamed for reform. He is best remembered for his article *J'accuse*, a biting indictment of the army and government during the Dreyfus Affair, earning him praise and rebuke.

Bibliography

Anderson, M. S. *The Ascendancy of Europe, 1815–1914.* Edinburgh Gate, Great Britain: Pearson Education Ltd. (Longman), 1972. Rev. 3rd ed., 2003. Still an excellent analysis of the major themes in European history but with less attention paid to cultural developments.

Audoin-Rouzeau, Stéphane, and Anette Becker. *14–18: Understanding the Great War.* New York: Hill and Wang, 2002. Excellent treatment of the nature and impact of World War I.

Bartlett, C. J. *Peace, War, and the European Powers, 1814–1914.* New York: St. Martin's Press, 1996. Thoughtful and clear overview of European diplomacy between 1814–1914.

Bayly, C. A. *The Birth of the Modern World, 1780–1914.* Malden, MA: Blackwell Publishing Ltd., 2004. Brilliant analysis, placing European history in the context of worldwide developments; excellent response to the Eurocentric view of the world.

Bell, P. M. H. *The Origins of the Second World War in Europe.* New York: Longman, Inc., 1986. Thoughtful introduction to this topic, organized around the pros and cons of the Thirty Years' War thesis.

Berlin, Isaiah. *Russian Thinkers.* New York: The Viking Press, 1978. An excellent selection of essays on Russian intellectuals and revolutionaries by one of Britain's great 20th-century intellectuals.

Birnbaum, P., and I. Katzuelson, eds. *Paths of Emancipation: Jews, States, and Citizenship.* Princeton, NJ: Princeton University Press, 1995. Excellent anthology of various routes to Jewish emancipation and its impact in 19th-century Europe.

Blackbourn, David. *The Long Nineteenth Century: A History of Germany, 1780–1918.* Great Britain: Fontana Press, 1997. Published in the United States, New York: Oxford University Press, 1998. Thorough and detailed treatment of Germany during this entire era.

Blanning, T. C. B., ed. *The Oxford History of Modern Europe.* Oxford: Oxford University Press, 1996. Published in the United States in 2000. Thoughtful topical essays by major scholars, with a useful introduction by Blanning and an excellent timeline and selection of maps.

Breuilly, John. *Austria, Prussia, and Germany, 1806–1871.* Essex, England: Pearson Education Ltd., 2002. Well-balanced, accessible analysis of the relationships and struggle between Austria and Prussia in the context of growing German nationalism.

Breunig, Charles, and Matthew Levinger. *The Revolutionary Era, 1789–1850*. New York: W.W. Norton and Co., 1970. A substantially revised third edition (published in 2002 by Levinger, with a new title) of a classic text by Charles Breunig, *The Age of Revolution and Reaction* (1970). Excellent overview.

Briggs, Asa. *Victorian Cities*. London: Odham Books, 1963. A classic comprehensive analysis of Victorian cities.

Burrow, J. W. *The Crisis of Reason: European Thought, 1848–1914*. New Haven, CT: Yale University Press, 2000. Brilliant in-depth analysis of European thought, combining beautiful synthesis and rich detail; difficult material but well worth the effort.

Caine, Barbara, and Glenda Sluga. *Gendering European History, 1780–1920*. London and New York: Leicester University Press, 2000. Brief but well-developed analysis of changes in women's status during this era.

Camus, Albert. *The Plague*. New York: Vintage, 1991. Classic liberal existentialist statement of confronting evil (plague) in Oran, a metaphor for France and Europe under Nazi occupation.

Carey, John, ed. *Eyewitness to History*. New York: Avon Books, 1990. Excellent selection of eyewitness accounts, covering every facet of society.

Carr, E. H. *What Is History?* New York: Vintage Books, 1961. Classic but still relevant approach to the nature and study of history.

Collins, James B. *The Ancien Régime and the French Revolution*. Toronto, Canada: Wadsworth Publishing, 2002. The last section of Collins's mega-study of France, with a good introduction and several useful documents from 1789–1793.

———. *From Tribes to Nations: The Making of France, 500–1799*. Toronto, Canada: Wadsworth Publishing, 2002. State-of-the-art analysis of the development of French civilization and nationhood.

Craig, Gordon. *Europe, 1815–1914*. New York: Holt, Rinehart and Winston, Inc., 1966. Still an excellent source, especially for country-by-country narrative history.

Dangerfield, George. *The Strange Death of Liberal England*. New York: Capricorn Books, 1961. Classis critical analysis of the pre-

©2005 The Teaching Company.

WWI liberal era in Great Britain; well written and worth encountering.

Davidson, Basil. *The Black Man's Burden: Africa and the Curse of the Nation-State*. New York: Three Rivers Press, 1992. Moving account of the impact of European imperialism in Africa, from the 1880s to the near present.

Dickens, Charles. *Hard Times*. New York: Fine Communications, 2004. Powerful novel analyzing the complicated nature of class relationships in mid-19th–century industrializing Britain; a must read.

Eksteins, Modris. *Rights of Spring: The Great War and the Birth of the Modern Age*. New York: Houghton Mifflin, 1989. Doubleday Anchor paperback, 1990. Brilliant analysis of the cultural, social, and psychological aspects of World War I and its impact, especially on Germany and Britain.

Eley, Geoff. *Forging Democracy: The History of the Left in Europe, 1850–2000*. New York: Oxford University Press, Inc., 2002. Excellent comprehensive analysis of the left in Europe between 1850–2000.

Elon, Amos. *The Pity of It All: A Portrait of the German-Jewish Epoch, 1743–1933*. New York: Henry Holt and Co., 2002. A very readable account of the emancipation and acculturation of German Jews, leading to their powerful contribution to modern civilization, in the context of the growth of modern political and racial anti-Semitism.

Ferguson, Niall. *The Pity of War*. London: Allen Lane, 1998. Basic Books paperback, 1999. Powerful analysis of World War I, asking many different questions, especially with respect to economics.

✓ Friedrich, Otto. *Olympia: Paris in the Age of Manet*. New York: Simon and Schuster, 1992. Touchstone paperback, 1993. Wonderful treatment of Parisian society and culture from the 1850s to the 1880s.

Fritzsche, Peter. *Reading Berlin, 1900*. Cambridge, MA: Harvard University Press, 1996. Excellent analysis of the nature of burgeoning Berlin at the turn of the century.

Fromkin, David. *Europe's Last Summer: Who Started the Great War in 1914?* New York: Alfred A. Knopf, 2004. Recent analysis of the origins of World War I, placing greatest blame on Wilhelmenian Germany.

Gay, Peter. *Schnitzler's Century: The Making of Middle-Class Culture, 1815–1914*. New York: W.W. Norton & Co., Inc., 2002. Brilliant analysis of European society and culture; a must read.

Gilbert, Martin. *The First World War: A Complete History*. New York: Henry Holt & Co., 1994. Large, well-written tome on all aspects of World War I.

Gildea, Robert. *Barricades and Borders: Europe, 1800–1914*. New York: Oxford University Press, 1987. Rev. 2nd ed., 1996. Thoughtful analysis of this era, organized topically and chronologically.

————. *The Third Republic from 1870 to 1914*. New York: Longman, Inc., 1988. A brief overview of this era, with a useful selection of documents as well.

Goldfrank, David. *The Origins of the Crimean War*. White Plains, NY: Longman Publishing Group, 1994. Useful and fair-minded analysis of the causes of the Crimean War.

Goldstein, Jan, and John W. Boyer, eds. *University of Chicago Readings in Western Civilization*. Vol. 8: *Nineteenth-Century Europe: Liberalism and Its Critics*. Chicago: University of Chicago Press, 1988. An excellent and well-edited selection of essential documents covering most of this era. See also Vol 9: *Twentieth-Century Europe*.

Hearder, Harry. *Italy in the Age of the Risorgimento, 1790–1870*. New York: Longman, Inc., 1983. Clear, well-organized analysis of the process of Italian unification from the French Revolution to the annexation of Rome in 1870.

Hobsbawm, E. J. *The Age of Capital, 1848–1875*. New York: Weidenfeld and Nicholson Ltd., 2004. A second brilliant analysis, emphasizing the impact of industrial capitalism on European and world civilization.

————. *The Age of Empire, 1875–1914*. New York: Random House, 1987. First Vintage Books edition, 1989. Last volume of Hobsbawm's excellent trilogy on the long 19th century; very broad in focus.

————. *The Age of Revolution, 1789–1848*. California: Textbook Publishers, 1999. A brilliant, sophisticated Marxist analysis of the era, emphasizing the dual impact of the French and Industrial Revolutions.

Horne, Alistair. *The Age of Napoleon*. New York: Modern Library, 2004. Brief, fair-minded analysis of Napoleon's rule and wider impact, both on France and Europe.

———. *The Price of Glory: Verdun, 1916*. New York: Penguin Books, 1964, reprinted 1978. A powerfully written overview of World War I's most ghastly battle.

Hugo, Victor. *Les Miserables*. New York: Fine Communications, 2003. Classic novel on the conditions of the urban poor in Louis Philippe's France, by the great liberal Romantic; wonderful read, with Kleenex.

Johnson, Paul. *Napoleon*. New York: The Penguin Group, 2002. Well-written but unfriendly analysis of Napoleon, by a major British conservative scholar.

Joll, James. *The Origins of the First World War*. New York: Longman, Inc., 1984. Rev. 2nd ed. Thoughtful, clear, and fair-minded analysis of the major causes of the First World War, organized around a series of major topics.

Jones, Peter. *The 1848 Revolutions*. Essex, England: Pearson Education Ltd., 1991. Brief, useful overview of the 1848 revolutions, with several appended documents.

Kramer, Lloyd. *Lafayette in Two Worlds: Public Cultures and Personal Identities in an Age of Revolutions*. Chapel Hill: University of North Carolina Press, 1996. Wonderful treatment of Lafayette's role in American and French history and politics, through the 1830 revolution.

Kramnick, Isaac, ed. *The Portable Enlightenment Reader*. New York: Penguin Books, 1995. Excellent selection of documents, with a useful, brief introduction.

Lafore, Laurence. *The Long Fuse: An Interpretation of the Origins of WWI*. New York: Harp College, 1990. Still a useful analysis of the origins of World War I, emphasizing the multinational structure of the Austro-Hungarian Empire as the primary cause of the war.

Levinger, Matthew. *Enlightened Nationalism: The Transformation of Prussian Political Culture, 1806–1848*. New York: Oxford University Press, 2000. In-depth analysis of Prussian political culture from the Enlightenment and French Revolution through the Revolution of 1848.

Lewis, Bernard. *What Went Wrong? The Clash between Islam and Modernity in the Middle East.* New York: Oxford University Press, 2002. Perennial paperback, 2003. Brief, clear treatment of Islam's difficult confrontation with modernity, both in the Ottoman Empire and the greater Middle East.

Lewis, David Levering. *The Race to Fashoda: European Colonialism and African Resistance in the Scramble for Africa.* New York: Weidenfeld and Nicolson, 1987. Does much to demonstrate that many Africans resisted European imperialism with whatever limited means they had.

Lichtheim, George. *A Short History of Socialism.* New York: Praeger Publishers, Inc., 1970. Still a lucid treatment of European socialism.

Lincoln, W. Bruce. *The Great Reforms: Autocracy, Bureaucracy, and the Politics of Change in Imperial Russia.* Dekalb, Illinois: Northern Illinois Press, 1990. In-depth analysis of Alexander II's reform era and its impact.

Lukacs, John. *At the End of an Age.* New Haven, CT: Yale University Press, 2002. Interesting and often unconventional musings with respect to thinking about history.

Marx, Karl. *The Communist Manifesto.* New York: Broadview Press, 2004. Essential reading; still a brilliant historical polemic.

Mazower, Mark. *The Balkans: A Short History.* New York: Modern Library, 2000. Paperback edition, 2002. An excellent, fair-minded overview of the history of this turbulent region.

McMillan, James F. *Napoleon III.* New York: Longman, Inc., 1991. Well-balanced, thoughtful analysis of the enigmatic Napoleon III, covering major aspects of his regime, as well as historiographical controversies that surround his policies and legacy.

Menning, Ralph R., ed. *The Art of the Possible: Documents on Great Power Diplomacy, 1814–1914.* New York: McGraw-Hill Companies, Inc., 1996. An excellent selection of essential documents, with substantial introductions.

Merriman, John. *A History of Modern Europe.* Vol. II: *From the French Revolution to the Present.* New York: W.W. Norton and Co., 1996. Rev. 2nd ed., 2004. A thoughtful, well-balanced, and well-written overview of modern Europe; best available primary text for this course.

Mosse, George. *Toward the Final Solution: A History of European Racism*. New York: Howard Fertig, 1978. Well-developed, accessible history of the sources and development of European racism.

Perkin, Joan. *Victorian Women*. United Kingdom: John Murray Publishers, 1993. Published by New York University Press in 1995. Excellent analysis of women's history in Great Britain from the early 19th century until World War I.

Perry M., and F. Schweitzer. *Anti-Semitism: Myth and Hate from Antiquity to the Present*. New York: Palgrave Macmillan, 2002. New, useful study of the history of anti-Semitism, especially strong in letting sources speak for themselves.

Popkin, Jeremy D. *A History of Modern France*. Upper Saddle River, NJ: Prentice-Hall, Inc., 1994. Rev. 2nd ed., 2001. Well-written, well-balanced overview of modern France, from the 18th century to the present.

———. *A Short History of the French Revolution*. Englewood Cliffs, NJ: Prentice-Hall, Inc., 1995. Excellent brief overview of the French Revolution and Napoleonic era, with several useful appended documents.

Pulzer, Peter. *Germany, 1870–1945: Politics, State Formation, and War*. New York: Oxford University Press, 1997. An excellent brief treatment of this era, with a useful timeline.

Remarque, Erich Maria. *All Quiet on the Western Front*. New York: Random House, Inc., 1996. The classic (anti-) war novel of the western front, which however, omits the stories of those who still thirsted for more.

Rich, Norman. *Great Power Diplomacy, 1814–1914*. New York: McGraw-Hill, Inc., 1992. Well-developed treatment of European diplomacy between 1814–1914.

Sanborn, Joshua A. *Drafting the Russian Nation: Military Conscription, Total War, and Mass Politics, 1905–1925*. DeKalb, IL: Northern Illinois University Press, 2003. An excellent, creative study that analyzes the impact of military service and World War I on the process of nation building and national integration in tsarist and Soviet Russia during the pivotal years between 1905 and 1925.

Schechter, Ronald, ed. *The French Revolution: The Essential Readings*. Malden, MA: Blackwell Publishers Ltd., 2001. Excellent selection of recent essays on the French Revolution, with a thoughtful introduction by Schechter.

Seaman, L. C. B. *From Vienna to Versailles*. New York: Routledge, 1991. Wonderful series of essays on 19th-century European diplomacy and politics and its main gurus. Opinionated but very thoughtful.

Shevin-Coetzee, Marilyn, and Frans Coetzee, eds. *World War I and European Society: A Sourcebook*. Lexington, MA: D.C. Heath and Co., 1995. Excellent selection of documents, covering every aspect of World War I.

Sked, Alan. *The Decline and Fall of the Habsburg Empire, 1815–1918*. New York: Longman, Inc., 2001. Excellent discussion looking at how the Habsburg Empire survived the revolutions of 1848 and the factors that led to its ultimate demise.

Smith, Denis Mack. *Cavour*. New York: Routledge, 1985. Excellent study of the central figure in Italy's "unification" process.

———. *The Making of Italy: 1796–1870*. New York: Harper and Row, 1968. Excellent collection of primary sources, covering most aspects of the "unification" process.

———. *Mazzini*. New Haven, Connecticut: Yale University Press, 1994. Wonderful biography of one of the 19th century's unique characters.

———. *Modern Italy: A Political History*. Ann Arbor, Michigan: University of Michigan Press, 1997. Impressive study by the leading historian of modern Italy.

Sperber, Jonathan. *The European Revolutions, 1848–1851*. New York: Cambridge University Press, 1994. Excellent brief overview of the revolutions of 1848–1851; a good first read on the topic.

Strachan, Hew. *The Oxford Illustrated History of the First World War*. Oxford: Oxford University Press, 1998. Paperback edition, 2000. An excellent selection of essays, by leading scholars, covering many aspects of World War I.

Taylor, A. J. P. *The Struggle for Mastery in Europe, 1848–1918*. London: Oxford University Press, 1954. In-depth analysis of European diplomacy in the period 1848–1914 by one of Britain's great scholars and authors.

Tuchman, Barbara. *The Guns of August*. New York: Bantam, 1982. Powerful account of the first months of World War I, leading especially to a stalemate in the west.

———. *Practicing History*. New York: Ballantine Books, 1982. Although dated, still a charming and thoughtful series of essays.

———. *The Proud Tower: A Portrait of the World before the War, 1890–1914*. New York: Bantam, 1983. Wonderful series of vignettes describing the nature of many of the great powers and some Europe-wide political movements in the generation before 1914.

Von Laue, Theodor. *Why Lenin? Why Stalin? A Reappraisal of the Russian Revolution, 1900–1930*. New York: J.B. Lippincott Co., 1964. Still a fascinating analysis of the origins of the Russian Revolution, emphasizing the discrepancy between Russia's great-power pretensions and status and its increasing comparative backwardness as a result of the more effective modernization of Germany, Britain, and France.

Waller, Bruce, ed. *Themes in Modern European History, 1830–1890*. London: Unwin Hyman, Inc., 1990. Excellent anthology of essays covering a number of major developments between 1830–1890; organized both topically and nationally.

Winders, James A. *European Culture Since 1848: From Modern to Postmodern and Beyond*. New York: Palgrave, 2001. Clear and thoughtful overview of the major themes in European culture from 1848 until the present; a well-balanced introduction.

Winks, Robin W., and Thomas E. Kaiser. *Europe, 1648–1815: From the Old Regime to the Age of Revolution*. New York: Oxford University Press, 2004. Excellent brief overview of this era, with several useful documents and a first-rate timeline.

Wistrich, Robert. *Anti-Semitism: The Longest Hatred*. New York: Pantheon Books, 1992. Useful chronological survey of the development of varieties of anti-Semitism from the ancient world to the near present.

Wohl, Robert. *The Generation of 1914*. Cambridge, MA: Harvard University Press, 1979. Excellent in-depth analysis of a host of young European intellectuals on the eve of World War I and immediately thereafter.

Wright, Gordon. *France in Modern Times: From the Enlightenment to the Present*. New York: W.W. Norton and Co., Inc., 1981. Rev. 5th ed., 1995. Classic interpretive text; still thought-provoking and wise.

Zola, Emile. *Germinal*. New York: Penguin Group, Inc., 2004. Powerful naturalist novel of industrial (mining) strife in mid- to late-19th–century France, emphasizing the development of socialist visions and the complex relationships between capital and labor; Kleenex suggested.

Zweig, Stefan. *The World of Yesterday: An Autobiography of Stefan Zweig*. Omaha: University of Nebraska Press, 1964. Wonderful memoir of European life, especially in central Europe from 1900 to World War II, presenting the fate of Jewish and liberal Europe in the approach of World War II.

Notes

Notes